RELATIONAL PREACHING

Langham

PREACHING RESOURCES

RELATIONAL PREACHING

Knowing God, His Word, and Your Hearers

Revised and Updated

Greg R. Scharf

PREACHING RESOURCES

CONTENTS

Foreword to the Revised Edition

I love this book!

I think it is unique in the homiletical literature as a kind of "scriptural theology of preaching" (as Greg describes it) – and also as spiritual theology. I strongly recommend it to pastors worldwide, both for individual devotions and as a resource to be used wherever pastors gather, whether in fraternals in the West or in Langham preaching clubs in the Majority World. Reading, discussing and praying through one of these meditations at the start of each meeting will add so much to the time together.

Valuable as the first edition of this book was, the second has even more to offer in terms of Scripture-saturated thinking and praying. Each meditation is now anchored in a specific passage of Scripture, which is cited at the start of the text, and each meditation is now followed by a sample prayer that will no doubt prompt further prayers and soul-searching on the part of all who read. The scriptural passages concerned are now all cited in an index of references, should you wish to return to or preach on a particular passage.

Eight entirely new meditations have been added, several of which are devoted to the important issue of what John Stott called "double listening" – that is, listening to both God's word and the world in which we proclaim it.

May meditating on this book bless you as a preacher proclaiming the Living Word to the world through the spoken word on the basis of the written word, in dependence upon the inspiring, illuminating, authenticating, and anointing work of the Spirit of God who leads people to Jesus.

Paul Windsor
Director of Langham Preaching
July 2016

Foreword to the First Edition

In many parts of the world, pastors and lay preachers proclaim God's word without the help of resources that Christians in the West tend to take for granted. These pastors faithfully serve their congregations by preaching the Bible week by week, but often with relatively little training, very few books, and only limited support.

Greg Scharf, although teaching in a resource-rich environment in the USA, has seen these pastors and lay preachers at work as he has travelled on behalf of Langham Preaching to Africa, Asia and Europe. He knows something of the challenge they face in teaching the Bible with little else to hand. That is why his book is so timely. Yet it is not simply for those with limited resources; it is for all preachers in all cultures.

In a series of accessible and thought-provoking meditations, Dr Scharf helps us see that God has provided what we need for the task of preaching. He introduces us to the reciprocal relationships between preacher, God, the Scriptures and our listeners, and demonstrates how the dynamics of these relationships can transform our preaching. Although homiletical techniques have their place, what really matters for preachers is our relationship with the God who spoke his word in Scripture – and through that word still speaks to his people – along with our relationship with our fellow believers in the church.

If we take each of these meditations to heart, our preaching will be transformed as we trust God's word, depend on God's Spirit, proclaim God's Son, and build up God's people. Then, like Martin Luther, we will be able to say: "I just threw the Bible into the congregation and the word did the work."

I warmly commend this book, the first to be published by Langham Preaching Resources. We pray it will strengthen the cause of preaching the world over.

Jonathan Lamb
CEO of Keswick Ministries

Preface

We who preach need all the help we can get, and we know it! We look for ideas, illustrations, even sermon outlines. We read books, we scour the World Wide Web and draw on our formal and informal networks. This book is yet another resource that will help you. It will not tell you what to say or exactly how to say it. But it will help you discover, or rediscover, the underlying relationships that we must attend to if our preaching is to be faithful to God and his word and sensitive to our listeners. As you read, I hope you will work on each relationship and grow in them. Then by God's grace, your listeners will hear his voice through yours week by week and be moved to faith and obedience.

I have been a preacher for over forty years. For the last several years I have discipled and equipped preachers in various countries. This has given me the opportunity to learn alongside people of different ages, backgrounds, levels of education, and theological emphases. I have coached some who were breathtakingly gifted in ministry, and others who found that their gifts lay elsewhere and wisely sought to use those other gifts. Some have been plodders, some quick thinkers, some natural storytellers and some logical, sequential thinkers, to the extreme! I have heard sermons by quiet people and shouters, winsome people and those who are less attractive.

When I began receiving invitations to help my brothers and sisters in other countries, I took up the challenge, eagerly trying to learn about, from and with these new friends. Yet I have a nagging concern that has propelled me to write this book. My concern is that when I serve the church in other cultures, and even in my classes and preaching laboratories at Trinity Evangelical Divinity School, am I guilty of foisting my subculture's system of preaching on other people? All training involves learning some methods, and all methods are culturally conditioned, if not culturally bound. I have found this to be true in my own experience as I have served with John Stott in London, in a historic Presbyterian church in Canada, and in a new Evangelical Free Church in North Dakota in the USA. On a global scale, the cultures found in these three places are very similar. However, even they have subcultures. I have found that not even the people within my own subculture agree with the way I preach or the way I teach my basic methodology course![1] So I ask myself, "Is it possible for a person from one culture to teach someone from another culture how to preach?" Or, to put the question differently, "Are there universals in homiletics (the study of preaching) that an African or Asian brother or sister could point out to me and that I could – or should – happily submit to?"

I think that there are such universals. But I am unwilling to call them "principles" because too often what we label as principles are really ideas that we learned from our culture and projected onto Scripture. I do not imagine that I can shed my cultural skin and act as a neutral observer of the world. But I do want to submit to Scripture and to invite the Holy Spirit to use it to challenge my assumptions – cultural and otherwise – and reshape my thinking and preaching. I want God, whose word I preach, to use his word to further conform me to the image of his Son. I have written my thoughts as meditations because I am increasingly convinced that merely intellectual knowledge is not enough to change behaviour. What is needed is a believing, transformed mind with a renewed perspective that enables God-pleasing obedience. Often, the Holy Spirit renews our perspectives through Scripture. So as you work through these pages, think about what I have written, but more importantly, carefully and deliberately read the biblical passages themselves.

I have quoted many passages in this book because I know how easy it is not to look up biblical texts referred to by authors. It is even tempting to skip over them even when they are right there on the page. I have done this in the past – but I hope you won't! I even dare to hope that you will open your Bible and read these passages in context.

Each day's reading begins with a short passage of Scripture that was selected to function as a sort of appetizer for what follows. It usually addresses the same truth as the following texts. Read all the passages prayerfully and invite the Holy Spirit to use them to search your heart and give you the faith that leads to obedience. Feel free to dig deeper into a passage than I do. Take your time. Write notes to clarify your thinking. Pursue the key relationships explored and illuminated by these texts. Confess the sins that impair these relationships. Learn all that you can about the parties to them. Humbly expect God to do more through his word and Spirit in this process than this book could ever promise.

---

1. You can examine my methodology in my book *Let the Earth Hear His Voice: Strategies for Overcoming Bottlenecks in Preaching God's Word* (Phillipsburg, NJ: P&R, 2015).

All these explanatory comments put the spotlight precisely where I don't want it to shine – on you. This book is not really about you. It is about putting yourself in the background by attending to three key relationships that you as a preacher are involved in: your relationships with God, Scripture, and your hearers. If working through the meditations makes you more self-conscious – or worse – more self-assured, I will have failed.

You are a party to each relationship we will work on. My goal is to help all of us (including myself) look away from ourselves and concentrate on the other parties to these relationships. I hope to do this by clarifying what the relationships should be like biblically, and will then go on to show you how to attend to them in a way that supplies an ongoing corrective to faulty preaching.

My aim is not to criticize anyone's preaching. But I do hope that as you and I grow in our relationships with God, his word, and the people to whom we speak, some of the weaknesses in our preaching will be replaced with new strengths.

Now, let me add one small detail to the little you know about me. I read books – including learned tomes on preaching – the way I eat the tasty flesh from artichoke leaves! I scrape off and swallow the vegetable's flesh and discard the prickly, fibrous leaves. I rediscovered some of the ideas in this book from Scripture myself, but I learned some of them by reading other people's books in the same way that I eat artichokes. I assimilated the good parts and long ago forgot where all the ideas came from. I am indebted to each of those authors, even if I cannot name them. But Scripture is intentionally my primary source. I believe in its sufficiency and therefore point you back to it as the basis for building (or rebuilding) a solid relational foundation for preaching.

My prayer is that these meditations will help you embrace a scriptural theology of preaching. More than that, I hope that they will move you to examine the health of three key relationships and to amend, maintain and nourish them. That will enable you to pursue the other tasks related to preaching!

To God be the glory, now and forever.

Greg Scharf

Acknowledgements

I am grateful to the regents of Trinity Evangelical Divinity School for sabbatical leave that gave me time to work on this project and to my prayer partners, including Dee Brestin, who freely shared when I sought her counsel as a writer. Debbie Head and Isobel Stevenson performed expert, necessary and successful surgeries on multiple drafts. William Hong cleaned up my edits and additions to the first edition and Kristen Brown expertly created the Scripture index. Jonathan Lamb, series editor, made useful comments. My wife, Ruth, as always, cheerfully supported this undertaking in ways too numerous to count. I am thankful to those who support Langham Preaching, and I trust that their investment in this publication will assist my fellow preachers around the world to think more biblically about our calling to preach the word. To God be the glory.

What Is Relational Preaching?

What can you and I do to make lasting improvements in our preaching? What steps can we take now that we could commend without embarrassment to other preachers from any country or culture, and, if it were possible, from any time between the ascension of Christ and the Parousia?

All of us could probably eliminate some distracting mannerisms. We could probably enunciate more clearly and project our voices better. But these are not the improvements I am thinking about. I am not even thinking about polishing our basic homiletic skills. What I am interested in knowing is what we can attend to at the most basic level that will put the art and craft of biblical preaching in its rightful place. What will make our preaching the overflow of spiritual reality, theological depth and cultural awareness?

If we want to preach as we ought to, at a minimum, we need to pay close attention to three relationships: our relationship with the triune God, our relationship with Scripture and our relationship with our listeners. Each relationship is reciprocal. That is, we not only relate to the others, but *they* relate to *us*. In fact, God initiated our relationship with him. Scripture speaks to us because it is living and active. Our listeners relate to us before, during and after we preach to them. They are not merely an audience.

Like us, Scripture has reciprocal relationships with people and God, and our listeners have reciprocal relationships with God and Scripture. This is because God relates to his word and to his creatures, some of whom are also his children.

I find that it is helpful to picture these relationships in the shape of a pyramid:

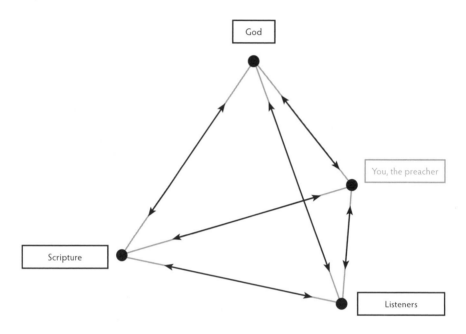

Reciprocal relationships between the preacher, God, Scripture and listeners

Notice that the diagram places you, the preacher, somewhat behind the scene, not at centre stage. God, Scripture and our listeners are more prominent.

The importance of attending to all three relationships becomes clear when we think about the results of neglecting or exaggerating one or other of them. If we over-exalt our listeners, they dictate our sermon content and displace Scripture. If we do not consider them adequately, or at all, our sermon is doomed to miss its mark, ignore their needs, pander to them or even insult them! If we exalt Scripture and neglect God, its author, the sermon can become a history or geography lesson. We can reduce it to a list of rules, desiccated life principles or a story with a moral. Although it is probably impossible to exalt God too highly, some preachers can and do refuse to let his own word speak on his behalf. And whenever we think too lowly of God, all sorts of substitutes rush in to take his rightful place.

Clearly, we cannot explore these rich relationships and the dynamic interplay between them exhaustively. So here we will focus solely on how these three relationships affect our preaching. We will do this by reviewing some of what the Bible says about these relationships.

Your goal in reading this book should not be to finish it or to be able to say that you have completed an assignment. The goal should be to come before God and meditate on the God-breathed word of Scripture so that the Holy Spirit can use it to speak to you, reform you and conform you to his image. So if as you read you recall other matters that need attention, I urge you to seriously consider whether these thoughts are the promptings of the Holy Spirit that should be acted on.

It is important always to remember that we are believers first and preachers second. Like the Apostle Paul, you may have been called to preach at the moment you came to Christ. You may even find it difficult to think of yourself as anything but a preacher. Yet, when our identity becomes inseparable from our role in the church, we put our relationships with God, Scripture and our listeners at risk. We can too easily use God, use Scripture, use people as tools or resources, as means to producing better sermons. But sacred relationships should never be used.

If we work on these relationships merely to improve our preaching, we are abusing them. Instead, let us recognize ourselves as recipients of God's grace and as members of his family so that we are in a position to love and value God supremely, treat Scripture appropriately, and see ourselves as fellow recipients of God's grace with our listeners.

Take a moment now to ask the Holy Spirit to show you whether a utilitarian mind-set is motivating you to read this book. Growth is a good and biblical thing. But growth is to be growth in Christ and in grace, wisdom and knowledge. Better preaching is only the by-product of a life of repentance in which key relationships have been amended.

Gracious Father, search my heart with your Holy Spirit for whatever may abuse or distort my relationship with you, with Scripture and with my listeners. Grant me repentance for seeking, however vainly, to make a name for myself. Help me to value you for yourself, hear your voice in your word, and love those for whom my Saviour died. Forgive my self-absorption. Soften my heart. Help me to serve you, instead of foolishly trying to commandeer you or your gifts for my own purposes. In the name of Jesus I pray, Amen.

Part One

Our Relationship with God

For us as created beings to speak of having a relationship with God – not to mention a *right* relationship with God – would be the height of arrogance had not God revealed himself to us in terms of a relationship. In Scripture, God always reveals himself as personal. The Bible may describe him as a wind, a rock and a fortress, but it uses these images to describe his personal qualities of freedom, stability and sovereignty.

The biblical writers are not guilty of anthropomorphism. They don't just describe God in personal terms so that we can imagine him. This is the way he is. He has always existed as three persons in communion and fellowship with one another. He loves, he wills, he chooses, he speaks, he feels and he listens. We can relate to him because we are made in his image. We too are personal.

God's relationship to us as preachers began before we ever thought of him. Although we cannot get our minds entirely around how this infinite, holy and transcendent God could relate to us, a brief review will help us at least arouse a sense of awe at what is involved.

So over the next thirty-four days, we will prayerfully ponder a few of the works God has done and is doing, works that directly impact our relationship with him, even though he undertakes them ultimately for his own glory. Meditate on them, asking God to use the texts cited to transform your thinking.

Then for the fifteen following days we will prayerfully consider our response to God's love. What he has done and is doing for us completely overshadows anything we could presume to do in response, but his work for us and in us not only enables our response, it requires it.

In setting out the key elements of our response to God, I am aware of the danger of simply creating a checklist, like a daily "to do list." That would reduce the relationship to an exercise, a task, or worse, an assignment. Yet, there is also danger in talking only in terms of generalizations. I wrote these meditations to draw you into Scripture, to encourage you to put yourself in a position where God could speak to you. That doesn't happen adequately when we think only in vague abstractions.

It may help you to understand what I mean if I use the example of the marriage relationship. Married couples who genuinely love each other profess that love and express it in their actions. Yet even the best of marriages can benefit from the tune-up afforded by a well-planned marriage-enrichment course. Such courses can unearth parts of the relationship that have been neglected or have become distorted. They also provide encouragement to build on current strengths of the marriage and supply resources for further growth. That is what I aim to provide in the pages that follow.

In the meditations on our response to God, I consider four overlapping and intertwined responses to God's initiatives: faith, love, obedience and service. You may not think about your relationship with God developing in this sequence. For instance, you may consider love to be the entry point, with faith, obedience and service following. That way of thinking is fine, and indeed, the Bible warrants it. As 1 John 4:19 says, "We love because he first loved us." Or you may recall John 14:21a ("Whoever has my commands and keeps them is the one who loves me") and reckon that obedience comes first. Nevertheless, I begin this summary of our response to God's love with faith, for reasons that I hope you will see.

My prayer is that as you ponder these texts, God himself will search your heart and strengthen your faith in him and love for him, and that these will overflow in the kind of obedient service he desires.

God the Creator

Come, let us sing for joy to the LORD; let us shout aloud to the
Rock of our salvation. Let us come before him with thanksgiving
and extol him with music and song. For the LORD is the great God,
the great King above all gods. In his hand are the depths of the
earth, and the mountain peaks belong to him. The sea is his, for
he made it, and his hands formed the dry land. Come, let us bow
down in worship, let us kneel before the LORD our Maker; for he is
our God and we are the people of his pasture, the flock under his
care. (Ps 95:1–7a)

God Rules

All preaching takes place in a context; it never happens in a vacuum. We
usually think of that context as the local setting, the time and place where
we actually preach. But to put our preaching in its true place, we need to put
it – and ourselves as preachers – in its largest context. We preach in the sphere
over which God rules by virtue of being creator of all. Wherever we speak in
God's name, we do so in settings of his making, and to people who are his
creatures. This is true whether those creatures recognize their Creator or not.

Slowly and thoughtfully read and reread the breath-taking words in
Isaiah 40:12–31:

Who has measured the waters in the hollow of his hand,
or with the breadth of his hand marked off the heavens?
Who has held the dust of the earth in a basket,
or weighed the mountains on the scales
and the hills in a balance?
Who can fathom the Spirit of the LORD,
or instruct the LORD as his counsellor?
Whom did the LORD consult to enlighten him,
and who taught him the right way?

Who was it that taught him knowledge,
>   or showed him the path of understanding?

Surely the nations are like a drop in a bucket;
>   they are regarded as dust on the scales;
>   he weighs the islands as though they were fine dust.
Lebanon is not sufficient for altar fires,
>   nor its animals enough for burnt offerings.
Before him all the nations are as nothing;
>   they are regarded by him as worthless
>   and less than nothing.

With whom, then, will you compare God?
>   To what image will you liken him?
As for an idol, a metalworker casts it,
>   and a goldsmith overlays it with gold
>   and fashions silver chains for it.
A person too poor to present such an offering
>   selects wood that will not rot;
they look for a skilled worker
>   to set up an idol that will not topple.

Do you not know?
>   Have you not heard?
Has it not been told you from the beginning?
>   Have you not understood since the earth was founded?
He sits enthroned above the circle of the earth,
>   and its people are like grasshoppers.
He stretches out the heavens like a canopy,
>   and spreads them out like a tent to live in.
He brings princes to naught
>   and reduces the rulers of this world to nothing.
No sooner are they planted,
>   no sooner are they sown,
>   no sooner do they take root in the ground,
than he blows on them and they wither,
>   and a whirlwind sweeps them away like chaff.

"To whom will you compare me?
　　Or who is my equal?" says the Holy One.
Lift up your eyes and look to the heavens:
　　Who created all these?
He who brings out the starry host one by one
　　and calls forth each of them by name.
Because of his great power and mighty strength,
　　not one of them is missing.

Why do you complain, Jacob?
　　Why do you say, Israel,
"My way is hidden from the LORD;
　　my cause is disregarded by my God"?
Do you not know?
　　Have you not heard?
The LORD is the everlasting God,
　　the Creator of the ends of the earth.
He will not grow tired or weary,
　　and his understanding no one can fathom.
He gives strength to the weary
　　and increases the power of the weak.
Even youths grow tired and weary,
　　and young men stumble and fall;
but those who hope in the LORD
　　will renew their strength.
They will soar on wings like eagles;
　　they will run and not grow weary,
　　they will walk and not be faint.

No one is God's equal. The greatest tangible evidence of this fact is creation itself. Its scale dwarfs us, yet he holds it in the hollow of his hand. We are caught up in history; but while nations rise and fall, God does not. He sees all that takes place. He does not grow weary. Yet he does not neglect or disregard us. Rather, he gives strength to those who hope in him.

Think about the times when you have been tempted to give God advice. We sometimes think that we know better than God what people really need to hear, even when no text of Scripture teaches it. Such thinking reflects humanity's besetting sin of pride.

Preachers are not immune to pride. Indeed, we are probably unusually susceptible to it. The antidote to self-exaltation is not merely humbling ourselves; it is exalting God in our thinking, enthroning him in his true and rightful place, "above the circle of the earth."

God is our creator. He is Lord over all he has made, and because he made us all, his good news is for *all* people and *all* nations for *all* generations (Ps 33). All of our hopes apart from him are vain, empty and misleading.

When we are clear about who God is, we are less likely to try to usurp his place or place our trust in something other than the living God: our reputations as preachers, our training, our "anointing," our knowledge of the Bible, our imagined holiness or even someone else's outline or sermon. We must repent of all misplaced trust. Take a few moments to read Psalm 33 and to worship God the Creator and affirm his rightful place as almighty sovereign.

Gracious Lord of heaven and earth, I bow my knees and heart before you. I admit that you alone are God and that I am not. Grant me a fresh vision of your matchless glory and of my utter dependence upon you that my faith in you may grow and any misplaced trust would be dispelled. Amen.

Day 2

The Son is the image of the invisible God, the firstborn over all creation. For in him all things were created: things in heaven and on earth, visible and invisible, whether thrones or powers or rulers or authorities; all things have been created through him and for him. (Col 1:15–16)

Christ Created

Even a partial review of God's work of creation must include a reminder of the Lord Jesus' role in creation. The prologue to John's gospel captures Christ's role:

In the beginning was the Word, and the Word was with God, and the Word was God. He was with God in the beginning. Through him all things were made; without him nothing was made that has been made. In him was life, and that life was the light of all mankind. The light shines in the darkness, and the darkness has not overcome it.

There was a man sent from God whose name was John. He came as a witness to testify concerning that light, so that through him all might believe. He himself was not the light; he came only as a witness to the light.

The true light that gives light to everyone was coming into the world. He was in the world, and though the world was made through him, the world did not recognize him. He came to that which was his own, but his own did not receive him. Yet to all who did receive him, to those who believed in his name, he gave the right to become children of God – children born not of natural descent, nor of human decision or a husband's will, but born of God.

The Word became flesh and made his dwelling among us. We have seen his glory, the glory of the one and only Son, who came from the Father, full of grace and truth.

(John testified concerning him. He cried out, saying, "This is the one I spoke about when I said, 'He who comes after me has surpassed me because he was before me.'") Out of his fullness we have all received grace in place of grace already given. For the law was given through Moses; grace and truth came through Jesus Christ. No one has ever seen God, but the one and only Son, who is himself God and is in closest relationship with the Father, has made him known. (John 1:1–18)

We can describe Jesus, the Word, as the agent of creation since everything was made *through* him (1:3, 10). God spoke and his Word created everything out of nothing. The comprehensiveness of this creative act (v. 3) leaves nothing and no person beyond accountability to him. Since Christ created everything, Christ gives light to every person (v. 9) so that everyone may believe (v. 7).

Christ's pre-existence (vv. 1–3, 15, 18) testifies to the timelessness, and therefore the perpetual timeliness, of the message that he came to proclaim. When Christ came to "his own" (v. 11) he came to his own people, the Jews. But he also came to the whole human race, people who are his own because he created them. He came to proclaim his message to those to whom he as their creator could already lay claim. He thus both preached and embodied a message of grace and truth. He came to "exegete" the Father (v. 18), to make the invisible God visible (John 1:1; Col 1:15; Heb 1:3).

Jesus' role in the history of redemption is unique. As verse 18 says, he is "the one and only." Yet, after his resurrection, the Saviour said to his disciples, "As the Father has sent me, I am sending you" (John 20:21). Our ministries have something in common with Jesus' ministry. Like Jesus, we are sent. We are authorized to speak on behalf of God. We have the Holy Spirit. We live and speak to make God's nature plain to those who already belong to God by right, to his creatures. We proclaim a message of grace and truth. And like Jesus, we are called to lay down our lives (Col 1:24).

No matter how much we seek to pattern our lives and ministries after Christ's, we should never do so in a way that minimizes his uniqueness. His role as creator is inseparable from his nature as God (Col 1:15–16). He is not merely the one in whose name we speak; he is the one whom we proclaim.

Gracious Father, thank you for exalting Jesus and giving him a Name above every name. Lord Jesus, thank you for your work of creation, making all that exists and making it to honour the Father. I acknowledge that I am accountable to you. Holy Spirit, thank you for opening my blind eyes that I might see the glory of God in the face of Jesus. Amen.

Day 3

> All the trees of the forest will know that I the LORD bring down the
> tall tree and make the low tree grow tall. I dry up the green tree
> and make the dry tree flourish. "I the LORD have spoken, and I will
> do it." (Ezek 17:24)

The Creator Has Power

There is a clear connection between God's being the sovereign Creator of all that exists and his ability to speak powerfully to his people and through his people to the world. Hear the word of the Lord:

> This is what God the LORD says –
> the Creator of the heavens, who stretches them out,
>   who spreads out the earth with all that springs from it,

> who gives breath to its people,
>   and life to those who walk on it:
> "I, the LORD, have called you in righteousness;
>   I will take hold of your hand.
> I will keep you and will make you
>   to be a covenant for the people
>   and a light for the Gentiles,
> to open eyes that are blind,
>   to free captives from prison
>   and to release from the dungeon those who sit in darkness.
> "I am the LORD; that is my name!
>   I will not yield my glory to another
>   or my praise to idols.
> See, the former things have taken place,
>   and new things I declare;
> before they spring into being
>   I announce them to you." (Isa 42:5–9)

God called his people Israel in righteousness and made them his covenant people. He led them by the hand and made them a light to the Gentiles. His word in them was powerful, just as his creating word was powerful. He gave them a message of freedom from captivity, a message that they were to embody.

The fact that his word created them as a holy nation was living proof that God, who spoke the world into existence, still speaks. (Deuteronomy 4:32–40 offers a vivid restatement of this truth.) His demonstrated ability to announce his people's future ahead of time was something only he, the sovereign Creator, could do. His words validate his claim to be the sovereign Creator, the giver of life and breath to all who walk on his earth. Because "the former things" had already taken place, God's people could be confident in his ability to predict "new things." He spoke and brought what he spoke to pass in order to wean his people from idols and reclaim the honour and glory that are rightfully his.

The Lord Jesus perfectly embodied Israel's role as "light to the nations," and he faithfully proclaimed Israel's message (Isa 61:1–3; Luke 4:14–21). Now Israel's mantle rests on us who are *in Christ* (1 Pet 2:9–12; Rev 1:6). We preach to our fellow creatures not merely because we have been created by God and for God but also because we have been re-created by God.

By God's grace we are more than God's creatures: we are his children and his heirs. But we are not less than his creatures. Take some time to thank God for what he has given you simply by creating you.

Gracious Lord, I owe you everything. Before you called me to preach you gave me a voice and eyes and a mind. You gave me ears to hear your voice and weaknesses to remind me that this world is not my home. Before you lavished grace gifts upon me, you endowed me with your likeness, placed me in a family and put me in this generation. Thank you! Amen.

Day 4

> The LORD has established his throne in heaven, and his kingdom rules over all. Praise the LORD, you his angels, you mighty ones who do his bidding, who obey his word. Praise the LORD, all his heavenly hosts, you his servants who do his will. Praise the LORD, all his works everywhere in his dominion. Praise the LORD, my soul. (Ps 103:19–22)

The Creator Acts Today

Christians are not deists, who think that God created the universe but has had nothing to do with it since then. God's active involvement in his world makes all the difference in how we approach the ministry of the word. A passage that clearly links God's work in creation to his work at present is Hebrews 1:1–2:4:

> In the past God spoke to our ancestors through the prophets at many times and in various ways, but in these last days he has spoken to us by his Son, whom he appointed heir of all things, and through whom also he made the universe. The Son is the radiance of God's glory and the exact representation of his being, sustaining all things by his powerful word. After he had provided purification for sins, he sat down at the right hand of the Majesty in heaven. So he became as much superior to the angels as the name he has inherited is superior to theirs.
>
> For to which of the angels did God ever say,

"You are my Son;
>> today I have become your Father"?

Or again,

>> "I will be his Father,
>>> and he will be my Son"?

And again, when God brings his firstborn into the world, he says,

>> "Let all God's angels worship him."

In speaking of the angels he says,

>> "He makes his angels spirits,
>>> and his servants flames of fire."

But about the Son he says,

>> "Your throne, O God, will last for ever and ever;
>>> a sceptre of justice will be the sceptre of your kingdom.
>> You have loved righteousness and hated wickedness;
>>> therefore God, your God, has set you above your companions
>>> by anointing you with the oil of joy."

He also says,

>> "In the beginning, Lord, you laid the foundations of the earth,
>>> and the heavens are the work of your hands.
>> They will perish, but you remain;
>>> they will all wear out like a garment.
>> You will roll them up like a robe;
>>> like a garment they will be changed.
>> But you remain the same,
>>> and your years will never end."

To which of the angels did God ever say,

>> "Sit at my right hand
>>> until I make your enemies
>>> a footstool for your feet"?

Are not all angels ministering spirits sent to serve those who will inherit salvation?

We must pay the most careful attention, therefore, to what we have heard, so that we do not drift away. For since the message spoken through angels was binding, and every violation and disobedience received its just punishment, how shall we escape if we ignore so great a salvation? This salvation, which was first announced by the Lord, was confirmed to us by those who heard him. God also testified to it by signs, wonders and various miracles, and by gifts of the Holy Spirit distributed according to his will.

The people who first heard these words were under pressure to stay out of sight and out of trouble. They needed a clear reminder that there was no going back to Judaism to find a haven from the storm of persecution that they were facing. So the writer of Hebrews reminded them (and us), that God has spoken his final word in Jesus. His ultimate word is no less powerful than the Word that created the universe and now upholds it. Jesus is not only the agent of creation; he is the radiance of God's glory, the exact representation of God's being. He is God whose throne will last forever (Heb 1:8).

When the pressure is on, it helps to recall that the word we have believed is not some private thought for a select group of people. When called to give up our safety, our health, our property, even our lives, for the cause of Christ, we can obey, knowing that the word that puts us at risk comes from God who not only created all things but sustains all things. He bears the world towards its intended goal, and no one is in a position to thwart him.

God's goal is to make sure that we grasp the source of this exalted word we have heard. It was not a message God entrusted to angels. All three persons of the Godhead participated in proclaiming the gospel. It was first "announced by the Lord," that is, Jesus; God the Father "testified to it by signs, wonders and various miracles"; and the Holy Spirit distributed gifts "according to his will" (Heb 2:3–4). All this was confirmed by eyewitnesses.

When a word powerful enough to uphold the universe is spoken by the triune God, we ought to pay attention! And when we speak in God's name, we speak God's word: "Remember your leaders, who spoke the word of God to you" (Heb 13:7a).

When you are tempted to retreat into privatized faith, to blend in with the surroundings, to let someone else pay the price of gospel obedience, remember that God himself has spoken definitively in Christ and has entrusted that word to you. Pay attention to it. Let it sound forth through you. Persevere in faith and obedience.

Father, you are worthy of our worship for you have not abandoned your creation or left us to ourselves. Instead you came to us in Jesus, and together with him you sent to us your life-giving Spirit. We offer you now the sacrifice of praise, the fruit of lips that openly profess your name. May the reminder of your steadfast love keep us from drifting away from what we have heard. Amen.

Day 5

One day Jesus said to his disciples, "Let us go over to the other side of the lake." So they got into a boat and set out. As they sailed, he fell asleep. A squall came down on the lake, so that the boat was being swamped, and they were in great danger. The disciples went and woke him, saying, "Master, Master, we're going to drown!" He got up and rebuked the wind and the raging waters; the storm subsided, and all was calm. "Where is your faith?" he asked his disciples. In fear and amazement they asked one another, "Who is this? He commands even the winds and the water, and they obey him." (Luke 8:22–25)

Christ Sustains and Redeems

Colossians 1:15–23 reminds us of Christ's creating, sustaining and redeeming work:

The Son is the image of the invisible God, the firstborn over all creation. For in him all things were created: things in heaven and on earth, visible and invisible, whether thrones or powers or rulers or authorities; all things have been created through him and for him. He is before all things, and in him all things hold together. And he is the head of the body, the church; he is the beginning and the firstborn from among the dead, so that in everything he might have the supremacy. For God was pleased to have all his fullness dwell in him, and through him to reconcile to himself all things, whether things on earth or things in heaven, by making peace through his blood, shed on the cross.

Once you were alienated from God and were enemies in your minds because of your evil behaviour. But now he has reconciled you by Christ's physical body through death to present you holy in his sight, without blemish and free from accusation – if you continue in your faith, established and firm, and do not move from the hope held out in the gospel. This is the gospel that you heard and that has been proclaimed to every creature under heaven, and of which I, Paul, have become a servant.

Like the writer of Hebrews, Paul wants his listeners to understand the supremacy of Christ. He is exalted over all things, including the invisible powers. As the source of everything (the Creator), the one who takes precedence over everything (he came before it), the one who is pre-eminent over everything (he stands above it) and the sustainer and goal of everything, he is uniquely qualified to be the head of the church. No being in all creation or at any time can countermand Christ's work of reconciliation. No accusation can stick against those he has declared not guilty. No bad news can derail or nullify the good news. No boundaries hold back its proclamation. It is the same gospel that is preached to every creature under heaven (1:23), for no creature is beyond the scope of Christ's reconciling power.

At the heart of much deficient preaching is an inadequate Christ. When we think of Jesus only as someone who soothes our fears, gives us a purpose in life, deals with our feelings of guilt and helps us with family problems, our preaching will never rise above the level of "assisted living." In Christ, we have *everything* we need for life and godliness (2 Pet 1:3), for the biblical Jesus is capable of providing a far greater salvation. Don't settle for a lesser Jesus! Pray these words adapted from Revelation 1:5–6:

Lord Jesus, faithful witness, firstborn from the dead, ruler of the kings of the earth, to you we offer our praise. You love us and have freed us from our sins by your blood, and have made us to be a kingdom and priests to serve our God and Father – to you be glory and power for ever and ever! Amen.

Day 6

For this reason I kneel before the Father, from whom every family in heaven and on earth derives its name. I pray that out of his glorious riches he may strengthen you with power through his Spirit in your inner being, so that Christ may dwell in your hearts through faith. And I pray that you, being rooted and established in love, may have power, together with all the Lord's holy people, to grasp how wide and long and high and deep is the love of Christ, and to know this love that surpasses knowledge – that you may be filled to the measure of all the fullness of God. (Eph 3:14–19)

Christ Works in Us

God calls us who preach to a robust task. Paul knew this because he understood the full power of Christ's person and his work, and this transformed his understanding of his own task. Colossians 1:24–2:5 is one of Paul's clearest statements of his theology of preaching:

Now I rejoice in what I am suffering for you, and I fill up in my flesh what is still lacking in regard to Christ's afflictions, for the sake of his body, which is the church. I have become its servant by the commission God gave me to present to you the word of God in its fullness – the mystery that has been kept hidden for ages and generations, but is now disclosed to the Lord's people. To them God has chosen to make known among the Gentiles the glorious riches of this mystery, which is Christ in you, the hope of glory.

He is the one we proclaim, admonishing and teaching everyone with all wisdom, so that we may present everyone fully mature in Christ. To this end I strenuously contend with all the energy Christ so powerfully works in me.

I want you to know how hard I am contending for you and for those at Laodicea, and for all who have not met me personally. My goal is that they may be encouraged in heart and united in love, so that they may have the full riches of complete understanding, in order that they may know the mystery of God, namely, Christ, in whom are hidden all the treasures of wisdom and knowledge. I tell you this so that no one may deceive you by fine-sounding arguments. For though I am absent from you in body, I am present with you in spirit and delight to see how disciplined you are and how firm your faith in Christ is.

Paul joyfully embraced a cruciform ministry. He readily supplemented Christ's final and complete sacrifice for our sins with his own sacrifices to get the gospel message out to the world and into the lives of his listeners. His message is that the risen Jesus indwelling the believer gives a lively hope of glory (1:27).

Paul sees himself as not merely a spokesman for this message but an example of its power. That is why he goes to great lengths to describe his labours and sufferings. What Christ commands, Paul embodies. He knows that when the power of the word is seen as well as heard, the word is made known in its fullness. So he gladly works hard to serve the church because he is commissioned by God (1:25) and because he has confidence that the indwelling Christ will bring his listeners to maturity.

I have to confess that too often I do not preach in faith. I preach as if the impact of the sermon rests on my skill and my homiletical tools. It is not that we should disregard any tools that will help people hear the message. As John Stott says, "If God cared enough to inspire every word of Scripture, we should work hard on every word of our sermons." But working hard and trusting our work are two different things.

Let me encourage you to ask the Holy Spirit to shed particularly bright light on those words in Colossians 1 and 2 that will help you trust Christ as you preach Christ. When we live *in Christ* we will be visual aids, demonstrating the power that we trust is also working in our listeners as they hear God's word and go forth to do God's will. This gospel is gloriously rich. Don't settle for a lesser task, derived from a lesser gospel, rooted in a lesser Jesus.

Now to him who is able to do immeasurably more than all we ask or imagine, according to his power that is at work within us, to him be glory in the church and in Christ Jesus throughout all generations, for ever and ever! Amen. (Eph 3:20–21)

God the Revealer

> God said to Moses, "I AM WHO I AM. This is what you are to say to the Israelites: 'I AM has sent me to you.'" (Exod 3:14)

God Reveals Himself

Any relationship worthy of the name involves mutual self-disclosure. God knows us completely, as Psalm 139 reminds us, but our knowledge of God is partial and imperfect. It is limited by what God does not disclose (Deut 29:29) and by what we cannot grasp (Isa 55:9). But 1 John 3:1–3 promises that at the end of time, his disclosure will be complete and our capacity to handle it will be sufficient:

> See what great love the Father has lavished on us, that we should be called children of God! And that is what we are! The reason the world does not know us is that it did not know him. Dear friends, now we are children of God, and what we will be has not yet been made known. But we know that when Christ appears, we shall be like him, for we shall see him as he is. All who have this hope in him purify themselves, just as he is pure.

As 1 Corinthians 13:12 puts it:

> For now we see only a reflection as in a mirror; then we shall see face to face. Now I know in part; then I shall know fully, even as I am fully known.

Then we will know fully. So what about now? God knows us as he knows everything, that is, he knows us completely and perfectly. To what extent may we know him? God is in control of how much he lets himself be known. Beyond general revelation (through nature and conscience), God reveals himself through historical acts; through the words that accompany and interpret his actions; through people, supremely the Lord Jesus in whom God speaks and acts in person; and through the Holy Spirit "who guides the chosen instruments of God, who fills the incarnate Son, who inspires the sacred records, and who bears His accompanying witness, so that the inward eyes and ears of people are opened to the God who is here made known, and reconciliation is brought to its objective fulfilment in repentance in faith."[1]

In other words, God has gone out of his way to make himself known to us, his creatures, not just by sending messengers but by coming himself in the persons of his Son and Spirit. He is committed to this relationship and eager to be known. He works through us and within us, and if necessary around us to see that his self-disclosure gets through to all people.

Thank you gracious Lord that amazingly you have made yourself known to us. We marvel that though our knowledge of you is not what it will be, it is sufficient, it is enough. You have mercifully given us everything we need for a godly life through the knowledge of you who called us by your own glory and goodness. Thank you. Amen.

Day 8

> But now, this is what the Lord says – he who created you, Jacob,
> he who formed you, Israel: "Do not fear, for I have redeemed you;
> I have summoned you by name; you are mine. When you pass
> through the waters, I will be with you; and when you pass through
> the rivers, they will not sweep over you. When you walk through
> the fire, you will not be burned; the flames will not set you ablaze.
> For I am the Lord your God, the Holy One of Israel, your Saviour;
> I give Egypt for your ransom, Cush and Seba in your stead."
> (Isa 43:1–3)

God Reveals His Holiness

Luke 5:1–11 combines four aspects of God's self-disclosure – historical acts, words, persons and the Holy Spirit:

> One day as Jesus was standing by the Lake of Gennesaret, the
> people were crowding around him and listening to the word

---

1. Geoffrey W. Bromiley, "God," in *The International Standard Bible Encyclopedia*, ed. Geoffrey W. Bromiley et al.; rev. ed. (Grand Rapids, MI: Eerdmans, 1982), 2:496.

of God. He saw at the water's edge two boats, left there by the fishermen, who were washing their nets. He got into one of the boats, the one belonging to Simon, and asked him to put out a little from shore. Then he sat down and taught the people from the boat.

When he had finished speaking, he said to Simon, "Put out into deep water, and let down the nets for a catch."

Simon answered, "Master, we've worked hard all night and haven't caught anything. But because you say so, I will let down the nets."

When they had done so, they caught such a large number of fish that their nets began to break. So they signalled their partners in the other boat to come and help them, and they came and filled both boats so full that they began to sink.

When Simon Peter saw this, he fell at Jesus' knees and said, "Go away from me, Lord; I am a sinful man!" For he and all his companions were astonished at the catch of fish they had taken, and so were James and John, the sons of Zebedee, Simon's partners.

Then Jesus said to Simon, "Don't be afraid; from now on you will fish for people." So they pulled their boats up on shore, left everything and followed him.

When Jesus spoke, the people heard the word of God. When he acted, they knew they were in the presence of the holy God. What the fishing partners heard and saw was enough to make them give up everything and follow him.

I am inclined to think the order of events here is significant. After Jesus has finished speaking to the crowds, he speaks to Peter, saying words that test Peter's faith. Peter chooses to act on the word of Christ, to do what he says, even though it is contrary to everything he knows by experience and observation. When Jesus' word is vindicated with a superabundant catch of fish, Peter instantly grasps that he and Jesus are not equals. This is not a peer relationship. Jesus is *Lord*. Undoubtedly, Peter does not yet fill the word "Lord" with all the meaning it will later come to have for him, but he already knows enough to feel undone in the presence of perfect holiness and yet be willing to leave everything to follow Jesus.

This paradox will always be a feature of a true relationship with the living God. We are attracted to him and yet we are in quaking, uncomfortable awe of him, an awe that asks him to leave. If we ever feel completely comfortable in his presence, our knowledge of him is not quite right. If we feel unable to come into his presence, the astonishing grace of the gospel hasn't quite sunk in.

People have sometimes complained to me that their preachers have no *gravitas*, no respectful solemnity that indicates they have been in the very presence of the living God. When we stand before the people with an open Bible, they should sense that we are all on holy ground. Our self-confidence as preachers will be utterly gone, but our expectation that God will speak will be high because we have already heard his voice. We, like Moses, will have taken off our sandals. We, like Isaiah, will have confessed ourselves unclean and have received an assurance of pardon.

How do people perceive you as God's representative? Does your demeanour reflect his holiness and power? Seek his face so that your hearers may note, as they did of Peter and John, that you have been with Jesus (Acts 4:13).

Gracious Father, I confess to you that too often I have sauntered casually into your presence without taking into account your awesome holiness. Please forgive me for Jesus' sake and remind me as often as I need it that you are utterly set apart from all other claimants to worship. You are holy. Thank you that in Jesus I may nevertheless have access to you. Amen.

God the Saviour

You, my brothers and sisters, were called to be free. But do not use your freedom to indulge the flesh; rather, serve one another humbly in love. (Gal 5:13)

God Frees Us to Serve

We are recalling things that God has done for us, not merely as preachers but more basically as Christians. Without the gospel we would have nothing to preach and no motive to preach it. We would be without hope and without God in the world. You know the gospel. If you are not clear about it, reread Romans! The gospel is more than our message. It is our life, our anchor, our worldview, our theology, our hope. The gospel is not only a message that justifies; it also establishes those who believe (Rom 16:25). For the Apostle Paul, it changed everything. For a sample of how the gospel shaped his life, read his words in 1 Corinthians 9:1–27:

> Am I not free? Am I not an apostle? Have I not seen Jesus our Lord? Are you not the result of my work in the Lord? Even though I may not be an apostle to others, surely I am to you! For you are the seal of my apostleship in the Lord.
>
> This is my defence to those who sit in judgment on me. Don't we have the right to food and drink? Don't we have the right to take a believing wife along with us, as do the other apostles and the Lord's brothers and Cephas? Or is it only I and Barnabas who lack the right to not work for a living?
>
> Who serves as a soldier at his own expense? Who plants a vineyard and does not eat its grapes? Who tends a flock and does not drink the milk? Do I say this merely on human authority? Doesn't the Law say the same thing? For it is written in the law of Moses: "Do not muzzle an ox while it is treading out the grain." Is it about oxen that God is concerned? Surely he says this for us,

doesn't he? Yes, this was written for us, because whoever ploughs and threshes should be able to do so in the hope of sharing in the harvest. If we have sown spiritual seed among you, is it too much if we reap a material harvest from you? If others have this right of support from you, shouldn't we have it all the more?

But we did not use this right. On the contrary, we put up with anything rather than hinder the gospel of Christ.

Don't you know that those who serve in the temple get their food from the temple, and that those who serve at the altar share in what is offered on the altar? In the same way, the Lord has commanded that those who preach the gospel should receive their living from the gospel.

But I have not used any of these rights. And I am not writing this in the hope that you will do such things for me, for I would rather die than allow anyone to deprive me of this boast. For when I preach the gospel, I cannot boast, since I am compelled to preach. Woe to me if I do not preach the gospel! If I preach voluntarily, I have a reward; if not voluntarily, I am simply discharging the trust committed to me. What then is my reward? Just this: that in preaching the gospel I may offer it free of charge, and so not make full use of my rights as a preacher of the gospel.

Though I am free and belong to no one, I have made myself a slave to everyone, to win as many as possible. To the Jews I became like a Jew, to win the Jews. To those under the law I became like one under the law (though I myself am not under the law), so as to win those under the law. To those not having the law I became like one not having the law (though I am not free from God's law but am under Christ's law), so as to win those not having the law. To the weak I became weak, to win the weak. I have become all things to all people so that by all possible means I might save some. I do all this for the sake of the gospel, that I may share in its blessings.

Do you not know that in a race all the runners run, but only one gets the prize? Run in such a way as to get the prize. Everyone who competes in the games goes into strict training. They do it to get a crown that will not last; but we do it to get a crown that will last forever. Therefore I do not run like someone running aimlessly; I do not fight like a boxer beating the air. No, I strike a blow to my body and make it my slave so that after I have preached to others, I myself will not be disqualified for the prize.

The gospel freed Paul from demanding his rights to comfort and a salary. It freed him to submit to God's call on his life. It enabled him to use his freedom to be a servant to all sorts of people. It fuelled and defined his ambitions and motivated his self-discipline. The gospel frees us to do the same.

Thank you, Jesus, for dying to set us free from all those things that enslave us. Please graciously enable me to live in that freedom today and to joyfully pour out all those liberated energies, passions, and hopes on the altar of other people's faith, to the glory of your great Name. Amen.

Day 10

He chose to give us birth through the word of truth, that we might be a kind of firstfruits of all he created. (Jas 1:18)

God Gives Life to the Dead

God devised the gospel. By giving his only Son to die in the place of guilty sinners he created "a righteous way of making the unrighteous righteous," to borrow a memorable phrase from John Stott. But that message on its own is not perceived as good news by rebels who hate God. The good news includes the message that God gives life to those who are dead in their trespasses and sins. Hear again what God has done for us helpless sinners:

As for you, you were dead in your transgressions and sins, in which you used to live when you followed the ways of this world and of the ruler of the kingdom of the air, the spirit who is now at work in those who are disobedient. All of us also lived among them at one time, gratifying the cravings of our flesh and following its desires and thoughts. Like the rest, we were by nature deserving of wrath. But because of his great love for us, God, who is rich in mercy, made us alive with Christ even when we were dead in transgressions – it is by grace you have been saved. And God raised us up with Christ and seated us with him in the heavenly realms in Christ Jesus, in order that in the coming ages he might show the incomparable riches of his grace, expressed in his kindness to us in Christ Jesus. For it is by grace you have been saved, through faith – and this is not from yourselves, it is the gift of God – not by works, so that no one can boast. For we are God's handiwork, created in Christ Jesus to do good works, which God prepared in advance for us to do. (Eph 2:1–10)

Our individual salvation is only a part of God's grand scheme. His purpose is to glorify himself on a cosmic scale (Eph 3:10) for all eternity (Eph 2:7). By saving unrighteous people like us, he effectively cuts the ground from under our boasting and rightfully takes the credit for restoring his image in us. It is God who enables us to do the good works we do, and it was God who prepared them for us ahead of time so that we couldn't boast about them.

God called us from death to life with his word. Listen to how Peter describes this:

For you have been born again, not of perishable seed, but of imperishable, through the living and enduring word of God. For,

"All people are like grass,
    and all their glory is like the flowers of the field;
the grass withers and the flowers fall,
    but the word of the Lord endures forever."

And this is the word that was preached to you. (1 Pet 1:23–25)

Though it is the Holy Spirit who gives people new birth into the kingdom of God, he uses a tool, "the living and enduring word of God." This word is normally heard through preaching. Therefore, what God did *for* us in calling us from death to life by his word, he now does *through* us when we preach that apostolic gospel.

Thank you gracious Lord for resurrection life freely given us in Jesus. What we could not do for ourselves or others you have generously done for us all. Thank you for entrusting your powerful word to us. May it have its life-giving power as the Holy Spirit uses it to quicken us and those to whom we preach. For the glory of your great Name. Amen.

Day 11

> We are not like Moses, who would put a veil over his face to
> prevent the Israelites from seeing the end of what was passing
> away. But their minds were made dull, for to this day the same veil
> remains when the old covenant is read. It has not been removed,
> because only in Christ is it taken away. Even to this day when
> Moses is read, a veil covers their hearts. But whenever anyone
> turns to the Lord, the veil is taken away. (2 Cor 3:13–16)

God Removes the Veil

Paul's work of preaching was deeply shaped by the miracle of his new birth.
Having renounced self-confidence in favour of confidence "through Christ
before God" (2 Cor 3:4), Paul speaks "in Christ . . . before God with sincerity,
as those sent from God" (2 Cor 2:17). This stance immediately rules out
some things:

> Therefore, since through God's mercy we have this ministry, we
> do not lose heart. Rather, we have renounced secret and shameful
> ways; we do not use deception, nor do we distort the word of God.
> On the contrary, by setting forth the truth plainly we commend
> ourselves to everyone's conscience in the sight of God. And even
> if our gospel is veiled, it is veiled to those who are perishing. The
> god of this age has blinded the minds of unbelievers, so that they
> cannot see the light of the gospel that displays the glory of Christ,
> who is the image of God. For what we preach is not ourselves,
> but Jesus Christ as Lord, and ourselves as your servants for Jesus'
> sake. For God, who said, "Let light shine out of darkness," made
> his light shine in our hearts to give us the light of the knowledge
> of God's glory displayed in the face of Christ. (2 Cor 4:1–6)

When we see our preaching ministry as being Christ's ministry
accomplished in and through us by his Spirit and word, and when we keep
in mind that we have this ministry not because we deserve it but because of
God's mercy, we do not use any unrighteous means or techniques that belie
the truthfulness of the word. Trickery, manipulation, deception, and anything
remotely like these are forbidden. No more stealing sermon material, even
though that practice goes back at least to Jeremiah's day (see Jer 23:30)!

What do we do instead? We simply set forth the truth plainly and let it speak for itself. We preach Christ as Lord and not ourselves. We preach *of him* (e.g. Acts 2:22–36; 2 Cor 4:5), *in him* (2 Cor 2:17; 12:19), *for him* (1 Cor 1:17) and *through him* (Heb 13:21; 1 Pet 4:11) – and he speaks *through us* (2 Cor 2:14; 13:3). In other words, we are really only qualified to preach because he lives in us and we live in him.

This keeps us from despairing when some listeners reject our message, for we understand that they do so because the gospel has been veiled to the perishing. Their rejection of the message is not a reflection on the power of the gospel or on our style of presenting it (as long as we have done nothing offensive). Understanding this theology of failure keeps us from shouldering responsibility for their rebellious hearts. But do we have a theology of success? Yes, we do. We know that the gospel successfully does its regenerating work precisely because the light has turned on for us. When the creator God made his light shine in our hearts, he gave us "the light of the knowledge of God's glory in the face of Christ" (2 Cor 4:6). Like Paul, we are convinced, by the miracle of our own rebirth and that of every other Christian, that God uses his word to open blind eyes and raise dead sinners. Like Paul, we believe and therefore we speak (2 Cor 4:13).

Gracious Father, may your gracious regenerating work in us remain a vivid encouragement to us as preachers. Enable me to say in my heart, "If God saved me – and he did – he can save others. If God has kept me – and he has – he can use his word to establish others." Help me this day to set forth the truth of your word plainly. Amen.

Day 12

Now I rejoice in what I am suffering for you, and I fill up in my flesh what is still lacking in regard to Christ's afflictions, for the sake of his body, which is the church. I have become its servant by the commission God gave me to present to you the word of God in its fullness – the mystery that has been kept hidden for ages and generations, but is now disclosed to the Lord's people. To them God has chosen to make known among the Gentiles the glorious riches of this mystery, which is Christ in you, the hope of glory.

He is the one we proclaim, admonishing and teaching everyone
with all wisdom, so that we may present everyone fully mature in
Christ. To this end I strenuously contend with all the energy Christ
so powerfully works in me. (Col 1:24–29)

God Calls Us into a Community

God calls individuals to himself by the gospel we preach. But he calls them
individually in order to create a single body, the church. Having marvelled at
God's plan to include Gentiles (Eph 2:14–22), Paul goes on to talk about how
this truth impacts his preaching:

> Surely you have heard about the administration of God's grace
> that was given to me for you, that is, the mystery made known
> to me by revelation, as I have already written briefly. In reading
> this, then, you will be able to understand my insight into the
> mystery of Christ, which was not made known to people in other
> generations as it has now been revealed by the Spirit to God's holy
> apostles and prophets. This mystery is that through the gospel
> the Gentiles are heirs together with Israel, members together of
> one body, and sharers together in the promise in Christ Jesus.
>
> I became a servant of this gospel by the gift of God's grace
> given me through the working of his power. Although I am less
> than the least of all the Lord's people, this grace was given me:
> to preach to the Gentiles the boundless riches of Christ, and to
> make plain to everyone the administration of this mystery, which
> for ages past was kept hidden in God, who created all things. His
> intent was that now, through the church, the manifold wisdom
> of God should be made known to the rulers and authorities in
> the heavenly realms, according to his eternal purpose that he
> accomplished in Christ Jesus our Lord. In him and through faith
> in him we may approach God with freedom and confidence.
> (Eph 3:2–12)

Paul sees himself as a steward of God's grace, which has been given to
him for others (3:2). Not only has it made him a servant of the gospel, but it
has also made him able to preach – to make the message plain to everyone
(3:7–9). There is something wonderful about Paul's astonishment that he, a
former blasphemer and persecutor of the church, is now allowed to preach
the message that creates the church. His role does not make him proud; it

humbles him, reminding him that he is the very least of God's people, indeed, as he says in 1 Timothy 1:15, the worst of sinners.

You and I will sometimes find that someone idolizes us because of our role as preachers or praises us because of the skill with which we fulfil that office. Regardless of whether this is so rare that we hunger for it or so common that we count on it, it is dangerous to our souls. We must remind ourselves that we have this ministry only by the grace of God. It is only "in him and through faith in him [that] we may approach God" (3:12). Approaching God to listen to him is the prerequisite for going to speak to people. The Israelites put this succinctly in their request to Moses, even if their promise was naively optimistic (Deut 5:27):

> Go near and listen to all that the LORD our God says. Then tell us whatever the LORD our God tells you. We will listen and obey.

That is our assignment: listen and tell. (It is also our listeners' task: listen and obey.) When we begin to presume that we have what it takes to preach good sermons, we and our congregations are in grave danger. All of us are then likely to hear only the best *we* can produce instead of the message *God* has entrusted to us as stewards.

The plurality of eldership within each local church is a built-in protection for those of us who preach. We should see ourselves not as the only ones who can preach, but as the ones designated to do so from among several who are "able to teach" (1 Tim 3:2). It is surely significant that arguably the first Christian sermon, preached on the day of Pentecost, was delivered by Peter who "stood up with the Eleven" (Acts 2:14). Even as the first among equals, Peter did not fly a solo mission on that day. Ministry teams were the rule throughout the early church, as they should also be today.

Take some time to thank God for his grace. Draw near to listen before you stand up to speak.

Father, we thank you again for your lavish grace. Its abundance dwarfs our gratitude. Cleanse us from all unrighteousness that we may draw near to you to listen. Help me to remain humbly in this listening posture until I see again your written word as your living word and embrace it and submit to it because I long to live in submission to you. Take away once more those idols that seek to usurp your rightful place or that I coddle. Replace them with a proper zeal for your glory so that I might faithfully speak in your name. Amen.

Day 13

Follow the way of love and eagerly desire gifts of the Spirit, especially prophecy. For anyone who speaks in a tongue does not speak to people but to God. Indeed, no one understands them; they utter mysteries by the Spirit. But the one who prophesies speaks to people for their strengthening, encouraging and comfort. Anyone who speaks in a tongue edifies themselves, but the one who prophesies edifies the church. I would like every one of you to speak in tongues, but I would rather have you prophesy. The one who prophesies is greater than the one who speaks in tongues, unless someone interprets, so that the church may be edified. (1 Cor 14:1–5)

God Calls Us to Build His Church

God's calling individuals to populate the church also reminds us that although individual obedience is always something we must pursue, there will normally be corporate dimensions to our obedience because God is building the church. Notice how Peter blends the two dimensions:

As you come to him, the living Stone – rejected by humans but chosen by God and precious to him – you also, like living stones, are being built into a spiritual house to be a holy priesthood, offering spiritual sacrifices acceptable to God through Jesus Christ. For in Scripture it says:

"See, I lay a stone in Zion,
    a chosen and precious cornerstone,
and the one who trusts in him
    will never be put to shame."

Now to you who believe, this stone is precious. But to those who do not believe,

"The stone the builders rejected
    has become the cornerstone,"
and,

"A stone that causes people to stumble
    and a rock that makes them fall."

> They stumble because they disobey the message – which is also what they were destined for.
>
> But you are a chosen people, a royal priesthood, a holy nation, God's special possession, that you may declare the praises of him who called you out of darkness into his wonderful light. Once you were not a people, but now you are the people of God; once you had not received mercy, but now you have received mercy.
>
> Dear friends, I urge you, as foreigners and exiles, to abstain from sinful desires, which wage war against your soul. Live such good lives among the pagans that, though they accuse you of doing wrong, they may see your good deeds and glorify God on the day he visits us. (1 Pet 2:4–12)

We come to Christ as individuals but God makes us into a people: a chosen people, a royal priesthood, a holy nation, a people who belong to God. Every stone is important, but the stones are being built into a spiritual house. This new identity is corporate. Our present alien status here is a corollary of our having a new corporate identity, citizenship in heaven. God not only indwells us individually, he dwells among us corporately in a way that goes beyond the sum of the parts.

When we preach in the assembly of God's people, we should certainly picture ourselves speaking to individuals because people can only hear with their own ears. But this does not mean that we speak only about individual matters. We should help our listeners think of themselves not as individual spiritual agents but as members of the body of Christ whose every action or inaction impacts every other part of the body, both locally and globally. Peter was practising this when he exhorted his readers in 1 Peter 5:8–9:

> Be alert and of sober mind. Your enemy the devil prowls around like a roaring lion looking for someone to devour. Resist him, standing firm in the faith, because you know that the family of believers throughout the world is undergoing the same kind of sufferings.

We can only be alert and sober minded as individuals, and we can only resist the devil and stand firm in the faith as individuals. But notice what Peter says Christians know. They know that other believers throughout the world are going through the same kind of sufferings. Their resolve to persevere in faith comes not merely from a growing knowledge of the trustworthiness of God but also from an awareness of their brothers and sisters close at hand

and around the globe. As preachers, we are to foster this awareness, and we can only do so when we are in touch with what is happening in the church. This is one of the reasons why the pastoral and preaching roles are linked in the New Testament. The best preachers are the best pastors and vice versa.

Father, we thank you for giving us brothers and sisters and for calling and gifting us to build up the body of Christ. Please give us eyes to see not only individuals in all their needs and potential but also the congregations to which you have assigned us. Help us see deformities and deficiencies and evidences of malnutrition that we may balance the diet with nourishment from your holy word. Remind us that we are indeed members of one another so that our health is intimately bound up with the spiritual health of everyone else in the fellowship. Please make us better physicians of the soul, for the health of the body of Christ and for your greater glory. Amen.

God the Giver

For when I preach the gospel, I cannot boast, since I am compelled to preach. Woe to me if I do not preach the gospel! If I preach voluntarily, I have a reward; if not voluntarily, I am simply discharging the trust committed to me. (1 Cor 9:16–17)

God Appoints Us Stewards of the Word

When we think of gifts, we tend to think of ourselves as the recipients of what is given to us. If someone gives me a sweater for Christmas, I am the one who enjoys it and wears it. But this pattern of thinking does not work when it comes to spiritual gifts. Yes, God gives gifts to his children, but he gives them for employment, not merely for enjoyment (1 Tim 6:17). We are not only consumers; we are also stewards. As people with the gift of preaching, we are fundamentally stewards of God's word. This fact informs Paul's view of his role in the church:

> This, then, is how you ought to regard us: as servants of Christ and as those entrusted with the mysteries God has revealed. Now it is required that those who have been given a trust must prove faithful. I care very little if I am judged by you or by any human court; indeed, I do not even judge myself. My conscience is clear, but that does not make me innocent. It is the Lord who judges me. Therefore judge nothing before the appointed time; wait until the Lord comes. He will bring to light what is hidden in darkness and will expose the motives of the heart. At that time each will receive their praise from God. (1 Cor 4:1–5)

The church should view us as servants of Christ and as stewards of the mysteries of God. We should think of ourselves in the same way. Since this is our role, faithfulness becomes our fundamental responsibility. Yet ultimately neither we nor our listeners can evaluate our faithfulness. Having a clear conscience proves nothing. We are all far too good at concealing our true motives. Only the Lord is qualified to judge. At his coming he will illuminate what we may have tried to hide, and he will praise (yes, the Lord will *praise*) those who by his grace warrant it.

These facts have significant practical implications. It is appropriate to publicly thank God for other believers (Derek Tidball calls this a eucharistic strategy in ministry; see Phil 2:20–22 or Col 4:12–13). But we should resist receiving (or giving to other preachers) the kind of affirmation that belies our role as servants. It is too early to judge, and furthermore it is not our place to judge, whether the Lord will pronounce one of his servants faithful.

Apparently, Paul could distance himself from affirmation and criticism, and from self-congratulation and self-deprecation. He worked to keep his conscience clean (Acts 24:16), but he did not trust its verdict. He had a profound grasp of the deceitfulness of sin and its lingering effects on even his regenerate heart.

May you know the freedom that comes with accountability to God himself. It is before our own Master that we stand or fall, and he is able to make us stand (Rom 14:4).

Master, I acknowledge that even if I were to do all you asked of me, on the last day, I should only say, "I am an unworthy servant." Unfortunately, I fall well below that standard. I long to hear your "Well done, good and faithful servant" on that day. Until then, by your mercies, equip me to be faithful in little things as well as bigger ones and especially in the stewardship you have given me to open your word to your people. Amen.

Day 15

> Keep watch over yourselves and all the flock of which the Holy
> Spirit has made you overseers. Be shepherds of the church of God,
> which he bought with his own blood. (Acts 20:28)

God Appoints Us to Protect His Body

When we think of God's gifts to preachers, we inevitably and correctly think of the gift of teaching. Paul instructed Timothy that an overseer must be "able to teach" (1 Tim 3:2). He told Titus that an elder "must hold firmly to the trustworthy message as it has been taught, so that he can encourage others by sound doctrine and refute those who oppose it" (Titus 1:9).

The capacity to encourage people by sound teaching and to refute those who oppose it is essential. It is not optional. This does not mean that every church elder needs to be comfortable teaching large groups, but every elder must know the Scriptures and be able to faithfully and clearly bring them to bear on a range of situations.

On rare occasions, I have known students who were preparing for ordination to pastoral ministry in the church but seemed incapable of understanding and explaining the meaning and applications of scriptural texts. They showed no aptitude to teach. When, with a good deal of trepidation, I questioned the validity of their call to pastoral ministry, they almost universally expressed relief. Most of them then changed their vocational course. In these cases, not only was the good of the student at stake, but so also was the future well-being of the church.

Some members of an earlier generation interpreted any clear touch of God's Spirit as a call to ministry and thus a call to preach (or be a missionary). When those who were not gifted to preach misheard in this way, the results were painful and destructive. Off-loaded from one small church to another, they strove to do something God had never asked or gifted them to do, and each church they served suffered for it.

If you are a bishop, district superintendent, or church chairman, or in any way responsible for looking after preachers, come alongside those who fail to show aptitude for preaching. Gently help them to find another ministry. Though this may not be easy, it is your duty and it benefits all concerned. Don't rely solely on your own discernment, but when the evidence is clear and sustained, provide the support and encouragement needed so the person can find his or her intended role in the body.

If you are doubting your own ability to teach, ask someone you trust to put the interests of the church above any personal desire for comfort or acceptance and speak the truth in love. Then listen openly, seek confirmation, and find your rightful place in God's economy.

I realize that some preachers have been grievously wounded by congregations that misunderstand what giftedness to minister the word entails. These churches have cast out preachers they should have embraced. But humbly seeking God's best for the church often leads to supportive realignment of a preacher's gifts and the church's expectations. That is a wonderful relief for everyone.

Father, I acknowledge great discomfort in telling someone that they are not gifted to preach. Indeed, I confess that this discomfort has sometimes led me to avoid confronting would-be preachers or steering them to a fitting ministry. Forgive me for elevating my own comfort above the good of your church. Grant me wisdom when I can see no evidence of aptitude to teach. Keep on raising up those to whom you have entrusted the ministry of the word. For the good of the church and the glory of your Name I pray. Amen.

Day 16

> Each of you should use whatever gift you have received to serve others, as faithful stewards of God's grace in its various forms. If anyone speaks, they should do so as one who speaks the very words of God. If anyone serves, they should do so with the strength God provides, so that in all things God may be praised through Jesus Christ. To him be the glory and the power for ever and ever. Amen. (1 Pet 4:10–11)

God Gives Gifts to Every Member of His Body

Not only does the Holy Spirit give spiritual gifts to individuals for the common good, but the ascended Christ gives gifted people to the body of Christ at large:

> But to each one of us grace has been given as Christ apportioned it. This is why it says:
>
> > "When he ascended on high,
> >   he took many captives
> >   and gave gifts to his people."
>
> (What does "he ascended" mean except that he also descended to the lower, earthly regions? He who descended is the very one who ascended higher than all the heavens, in order to fill the whole universe.) So Christ himself gave the apostles, the prophets, the evangelists, the pastors and teachers, to equip his people for works of service, so that the body of Christ may be built up until we all reach unity in the faith and in the knowledge

of the Son of God and become mature, attaining to the whole measure of the fullness of Christ.

Then we will no longer be infants, tossed back and forth by the waves, and blown here and there by every wind of teaching and by the cunning and craftiness of people in their deceitful scheming. Instead, speaking the truth in love, we will grow to become in every respect the mature body of him who is the head, that is, Christ. From him the whole body, joined and held together by every supporting ligament, grows and builds itself up in love, as each part does its work. (Eph 4:7–16)

God's goal for the church, as Ephesians 3:10 tells us, is to create a visual aid of his multifaceted wisdom, a living and breathing body that is plainly visible to those on earth and even to those in heaven. Such a body is well developed in every way. It is not a body whose feet have grown but whose torso has not!

God designed this growth to be predicated on three things. First, the body must be attached to its head (Col 2:19). Second, the equippers (apostles, prophets, evangelists, and pastor-teachers) must use their gifts to equip everyone in the church for service. Third, having been equipped, the members must use their gifts to build up the church in love. When these three things happen, the God-intended results follow. The church grows into unity in the faith and knowledge of the Son of God. It becomes mature, reflecting the measure of the stature of the fullness of Christ. It enjoys stability, no longer blown around by every wind of doctrine. And as a consequence, even the principalities and powers marvel at the multifaceted wisdom of God who could make something so beautiful out of such unpromising raw material.

Father, thank you for your many-faceted wisdom that designed the church to be as remarkable as the human body. Enable us called to equip the saints to serve so effectively as equippers that every part of the body of Christ will be enabled to minister as you intend. Amen.

Day 17

I thank God, whom I serve, as my ancestors did, with a clear conscience, as night and day I constantly remember you in my prayers. Recalling your tears, I long to see you, so that I may be filled with joy. I am reminded of your sincere faith, which first lived in your grandmother Lois and in your mother Eunice and, I am persuaded, now lives in you also. For this reason I remind you to fan into flame the gift of God, which is in you through the laying on of my hands. (2 Tim 1:3–6)

God Appoints Us to Equip Others

Spiritual gifts are wonderful things, but no gift comes fully developed. Recall 1 Corinthians 12:4–6:

There are different kinds of gifts, but the same Spirit distributes them. There are different kinds of service, but the same Lord. There are different kinds of working, but in all of them and in everyone it is the same God at work.

Gifts, service and working are inseparable. They are "three ways of looking at . . . 'manifestations' of the Spirit."[1] All three persons of the Godhead (described here as "Spirit," "Lord" and "God") are involved in enabling us to serve and build up the body of Christ, the church.

When we use our gifts, we engage in various kinds of service, doing various kinds of kingdom work. In each case, God is at work. In each case, we work. We serve. Or, to put it in the context of this book, there is no such thing as a gift of preaching without a preacher who preaches. A hoe is useless unless you use it. Gifts develop, or as the Puritans used to say, "improve" with use. Equipping happens when equippers offer teaching, explanations, examples, and opportunities for those being equipped to use their gifts and receive encouragement and feedback on how to improve.

Even preachers (equippers, described in Eph 4:11 as "pastor-teachers") need to be equipped. It is only a slight exaggeration to say that in some remote parts of the world anyone who owns a Bible automatically becomes the preacher, even if the person knows precious little about its message. This situation – having an unequipped equipper – produces predictably bad results. They are bad not because the preacher does not have the gift of preaching, but because no equipper has offered teaching, or modelling, or training to develop and encourage the person's gifts.

---

1. Gordon D. Fee, *The First Epistle to the Corinthians*, NICNT (Grand Rapids, MI: Eerdmans, 1987), 587.

Because God loves the church and wants to preserve her from error, he wonderfully enables many preachers who lack even rudimentary equipping to preach with astonishing accuracy and power. But God did not intend things to be this way. He gave gifted people to the church to equip us all – including preachers – to use our gifts so that the body of Christ would develop a mature and unified faith. In practice, this means that becoming a preacher is never a task undertaken in isolation. You may sense God's call to preach. But even if that is a bona fide call, it will always require that others, in one way or another, supply the outfitting you need to use the gifts God has given.

Who takes responsibility for this equipping? Too often, sadly, we leave the younger person who feels called to preach to seek out help. It is much better for the elders of the church to constantly look for those who could be entrusted with the gospel and who will be able to teach (2 Tim 2:2). John Owen is right when he asserts that the calling of pastors is the duty of the church.[2] How much heartache would be avoided if local churches affirmed and supported budding preachers early on! Church leaders should take it upon themselves to equip their young preachers and to supplement this with formal seminary training when possible.

If you are a church leader, ask the Lord to show you someone who appears to have the gift of preaching that needs to be stirred up. If you are not a leader but feel you have this gift, seek opportunities to use it. This is not being proud. Faithful service in little things will test your calling and gifting and help the church affirm them both as appropriate.

Father, thank you for those who saw nascent spiritual gifts in me and gave the opportunity to use them. Thank you for those who encouraged me to exercise those gifts when the evidence of promise must have been scant. Thank you for those who supported me through years of training and reined me in when I thought too highly of myself. Thank you for gracious congregations who exercised forbearance with me when I stubbornly spoke when I should have listened. Help me to be for the next generation what they were for me. Amen.

2. John Owen, *The True Nature of a Gospel Church and Its Government* (1689), abr. and ed. John Huxtable (Greenwood, SC: Attic, 1947), 56.

Day 18

> If anyone speaks, they should do so as one who speaks the very words of God. If anyone serves, they should do so with the strength God provides, so that in all things God may be praised through Jesus Christ. To him be the glory and the power for ever and ever. Amen. (1 Pet 4:11)

God Supplies the Message and the Messengers

Beginning with Genesis 1:3, God reveals himself as a talking God. Until Genesis 16:9, God speaks without an intermediary. There he speaks through the "angel [messenger] of the LORD." God certainly remains free to speak through any means (dreams, visions, even donkeys), but increasingly he speaks through prophets like Abraham (Gen 20:7), whose task is to speak in God's name to the people God sends them to.

Moses epitomizes God's ideal spokesman. He summarizes his role in receiving the Ten Commandments by saying, "I stood between the LORD and you to declare to you the word of the LORD" (Deut 5:5). In fact, Moses becomes the template for future prophets:

> The nations you will dispossess listen to those who practice sorcery or divination. But as for you, the LORD your God has not permitted you to do so. The LORD your God will raise up for you a prophet like me from among you, from your fellow Israelites. You must listen to him. For this is what you asked of the LORD your God at Horeb on the day of the assembly when you said, "Let us not hear the voice of the LORD our God nor see this great fire anymore, or we will die."
>
> The LORD said to me: "What they say is good. I will raise up for them a prophet like you from among their fellow Israelites, and I will put my words in his mouth. He will tell them everything I command him. I myself will call to account anyone who does not listen to my words that the prophet speaks in my name. But a prophet who presumes to speak in my name anything I have not commanded, or a prophet who speaks in the name of other gods, is to be put to death."

You may say to yourselves, "How can we know when a message has not been spoken by the LORD?" If what a prophet proclaims in the name of the LORD does not take place or come true, that is a message the LORD has not spoken. That prophet has spoken presumptuously, so do not be alarmed. (Deut 18:14–22)

What Moses forbids is perhaps as significant as what he predicts. The children of Israel were not to use human techniques (sorcery or divination) to attempt to gain knowledge of God and the power associated with such knowledge. God himself would provide a spokesman so that his followers could hear his voice. Like Moses, this prophet would go near to God to listen and then speak *all* and *only* what God instructed him to say.

God would supply the very words to the prophet, and these words would be authoritative. Whoever disregarded them would be disobedient by definition and would be held accountable. The prophet's words would be authenticated not by the prophet's *claim* to speak for God, but by virtue of his words coming to pass. Even when God speaks through people, his words are true and authoritative. This text is part of our warrant for considering Scripture to be verbally inspired (18:18), authoritative (18:19) and true (18:21).

Jesus fulfilled God's promise and was the ultimate prophet (Acts 3:22–23). Like everyone commissioned to speak in God's name, we should follow the pattern outlined in Deuteronomy:

1. We don't take the initiative – God does

2. We don't create the message – God gives it to us in Scripture

3. We don't lie – we speak the truth

4. We speak in God's name – we call people to hear God's voice and obey him

5. We tell people everything God commands us to say.

God authorizes people to speak in his name. Luke underscores this with Jesus' words that the "repentance for the forgiveness of sins" would be "preached in his name to all nations, beginning at Jerusalem" (Luke 24:47). As Acts attests, that is what happened (3:16; 4:7, 10, 30; 9:28–29). Authorization to speak in the name of Jesus was often explicit, as it was for Paul:

And for this purpose I was appointed a herald and an apostle –
I am telling the truth, I am not lying – and a true and faithful
teacher of the Gentiles. (1 Tim 2:7)

All three terms – preacher, apostle and teacher – bespeak Paul's authority.
He was a herald commissioned to announce the message of the one who sent
him; he was a "sent one," an apostle; and he was one authorized to teach only
the gospel message.

I urge you to reverently and seriously scrutinize your own preaching
programme. Ask the Lord to show you whether you genuinely follow the
pattern of the prophets.

*Thank you Father for supplying the messages I am to speak to your people on
your behalf. Thank you that I need not give my time and energy to coming up
with a message; I need only articulate clearly and faithfully the messages you
give me in your word. I rejoice that the message came before I did and will
last when I am no longer standing in the pulpit. Thank you that your love for
the church moves you to open my eyes to see what you have for your people
this week. Please make me scrupulously honest with your word and with the
people you have called me to serve. Amen.*

Day 19

"For I did not speak on my own, but the Father who sent me
commanded me to say all that I have spoken. I know that his
command leads to eternal life. So whatever I say is just what the
Father has told me to say." – Jesus (John 12:49–50)

God Authorizes Our Speech

Paul affirms that aspiring to be an overseer is a noble task (1 Tim 3:1). But we
do not choose this role, which is analogous to the priesthood. Even the Lord
Jesus did not put himself forward for his position:

And no one takes this honour on himself, but he receives it when
called by God, just as Aaron was.
In the same way, Christ did not take on himself the glory of
becoming a high priest. But God said to him,

> "You are my Son;
>> today I have become your Father." (Heb 5:4–5)

We preach because God charged us to speak for him; we derive our authority from him. Paul summarizes our position well:

> Unlike so many, we do not peddle the word of God for profit.
> On the contrary, in Christ we speak before God with sincerity, as
> those sent from God. (2 Cor 2:17)

When Paul, Silas, and Timothy preached in the synagogue in Thessalonica, they did not merely claim to have the authority to speak God's word ("we speak as those approved by God to be entrusted with the gospel" [1 Thess 2:4a]), but the listeners also acknowledged their authority:

> And we also thank God continually because, when you received
> the word of God, which you heard from us, you accepted it not
> as a human word, but as it actually is, the word of God, which is
> indeed at work in you who believe. (1 Thess 2:13)

God chooses and authorizes his representatives, but the actual power they wield is theirs by virtue of their message, not their title. We could put it even more strongly: the power comes because God stoops to speak through them (that is, through us). Paul says as much when he refers to himself as an ambassador of Christ:

> All this is from God, who reconciled us to himself through
> Christ and gave us the ministry of reconciliation: that God was
> reconciling the world to himself in Christ, not counting people's
> sins against them. And he has committed to us the message of
> reconciliation. We are therefore Christ's ambassadors, as though
> God were making his appeal through us. We implore you on
> Christ's behalf: Be reconciled to God. (2 Cor 5:18–20)

God himself makes his appeal through us. Peter puts it no less strongly:

> If anyone speaks, they should do so as one who speaks the very
> words of God. If anyone serves, they should do so with the
> strength God provides, so that in all things God may be praised
> through Jesus Christ. To him be the glory and the power for ever
> and ever. Amen. (1 Pet 4:11)

The apostles and their team members clearly believed that the word of God had a life of its own. They preached and taught, but their listeners heard the word of God:

> When the Gentiles heard this, they were glad and honoured the word of the Lord; and all who were appointed for eternal life believed. The word of the Lord spread through the whole region. (Acts 13:48–49)

Because God authorizes us to speak in his name and therefore speaks through us, we need to be like the apostles in giving prayer and the word the central place in our ministry:

> Brothers and sisters, choose seven men from among you who are known to be full of the Spirit and wisdom. We will turn this responsibility over to them and will give our attention to prayer and the ministry of the word. (Acts 6:3–4)

Receiving God's authorization to speak for him is both sobering and encouraging. It is sobering because being chosen humbles us, and so do the clear constraints placed on what we are to say as his representatives. It is encouraging because we do not speak with our own authority, which would not count for anything, but with the authority of God the Almighty, the Lord of Hosts.

When we go forth to speak in the name of the Lord Almighty, we can expect our listeners to know that there is a God and he still speaks through his word and those who submit to it.

Lord, I am under orders from you to say what you teach me to say, neither adding to it nor subtracting from it. Grant me such an awareness that my authority as a preacher comes from you that I tremble even to contemplate going beyond what stands written in your word. Amen.

God the Holy Spirit

Teach me to do your will, for you are my God; may your good
Spirit lead me on level ground. (Ps 143:10)

The Spirit Accompanies Us

We do not go forth alone or unaccompanied. God goes with us as he was with
Jeremiah and his other spokesmen in the Old Testament. Sometimes the Old
Testament writers even identify the Spirit's involvement in prophetic speech.
For instance, Micah, contrasting himself with false prophets, made this claim:

> But as for me, I am filled with power,
>> with the Spirit of the LORD,
>> and with justice and might,
> to declare to Jacob his transgression,
>> to Israel his sin. (Mic 3:8)

Even more famously, Isaiah linked his preaching and the work of the
Holy Spirit with words clearly fulfilled in Jesus' ministry (compare with
Luke 4:18–21):

> The Spirit of the Sovereign LORD is on me,
>> because the LORD has anointed me
>> to proclaim good news to the poor.
> He has sent me to bind up the broken hearted,
>> to proclaim freedom for the captives
>> and release from darkness for the prisoners,
> to proclaim the year of the LORD's favour
>> and the day of vengeance of our God,
> to comfort all who mourn,
>> and provide for those who grieve in Zion –
> to bestow on them a crown of beauty
>> instead of ashes,

the oil of joy
> instead of mourning,
and a garment of praise
> instead of a spirit of despair.
They will be called oaks of righteousness,
> a planting of the LORD
> for the display of his splendour. (Isa 61:1–3)

Joel 2:28–32 reaffirms and extends this connection between the Holy Spirit and prophetic speech, especially in the form in which it is quoted by Peter on the day of Pentecost in Acts 2:14–21:

> Then Peter stood up with the Eleven, raised his voice and addressed the crowd: "Fellow Jews and all of you who live in Jerusalem, let me explain this to you; listen carefully to what I say. These people are not drunk, as you suppose. It's only nine in the morning! No, this is what was spoken by the prophet Joel:
>
>> "*In the last days, God says,*
>>> I will pour out my Spirit on all people.
>> Your sons and daughters will prophesy,
>>> your young men will see visions,
>>> your old men will dream dreams.
>> Even on my servants, both men and women,
>>> I will pour out my Spirit in those days,
>>> and they will prophesy.
>> I will show wonders in the heavens above
>>> and signs on the earth below,
>>> blood and fire and billows of smoke.
>> The sun will be turned to darkness
>>> and the moon to blood
>>> before the coming of the great and glorious day of
>>> the Lord.
>> And everyone who calls
>>> on the name of the Lord will be saved."

These words follow the Septuagint closely, but drop a few lines from Joel's prophecy and add the words in italic type above. Peter clearly took this event as addressing Moses' longing: "I wish that all the LORD's people were prophets and that the LORD would put his Spirit on them!" (Num 11:29). Joel predicted the events that had come to pass at Pentecost.

The intentional repetition of "will prophesy" tells us that Peter sees this as of utmost significance. Not only do Joel's words explain the unusual phenomena of that day, but they also explain how an army of young and old, men and women would be able to take the gospel message to the world. Every believer has the Holy Spirit; everyone who calls on the name of the Lord will be saved. These are the last days, the days of preparation for judgment. Those who heard Peter's message evidently felt the urgency. Many repented and believed, and all who did so received the Holy Spirit as promised (Acts 2:37–38). Peter's sermon was the first fulfilment of Jesus' promise in Acts 1:8:

> But you will receive power when the Holy Spirit comes on you; and you will be my witnesses in Jerusalem, and in all Judea and Samaria, and to the ends of the earth.

Holy Spirit, though I usually pray "in" you and through the Lord Jesus to the Father, today I address you as God and thank you for enabling me to preach. Without your good work behind the scenes enabling me to see the truth of your word and to understand it and speak it clearly, I simply could not preach faithfully. So, I ask you, keep working in and around me to achieve your lofty calling of glorifying the Lord Jesus so that he in turn might give glory to the Father. Amen.

Day 21

> For we know, brothers and sisters loved by God, that he has chosen you, because our gospel came to you not simply with words but also with power, with the Holy Spirit and deep conviction. You know how we lived among you for your sake. (1 Thess 1:4–5)

The Spirit Gives Us Power

More of the Spirit's power was manifested after Pentecost. For example, when Peter and John and the rest of the apostles were "proclaiming in Jesus the resurrection of the dead" (Acts 4:2), the rulers wanted to know by what power they taught. Acts 4:8 records who enabled Peter to respond:

> Then Peter, filled with the Holy Spirit, said to them, "Rulers and elders of the people!"

When Peter and John were threatened and released, they returned to the church, reported what had happened, and united in prayer, asking for power to speak God's word with boldness. They received an amazing answer:

> After they prayed, the place where they were meeting was shaken. And they were all filled with the Holy Spirit and spoke the word of God boldly. (Acts 4:31)

Stephen, full of God's grace and power, was more than a match for his opponents who "could not stand up against the wisdom the Spirit gave him as he spoke" (Acts 6:10). The Holy Spirit did not abandon Stephen but gave him the capacity to preach fearlessly, even when the hostility reached its final ugly crescendo:

> When the members of the Sanhedrin heard this, they were furious and gnashed their teeth at him. But Stephen, full of the Holy Spirit, looked up to heaven and saw the glory of God, and Jesus standing at the right hand of God. "Look," he said, "I see heaven open and the Son of Man standing at the right hand of God."
>
> At this they covered their ears and, yelling at the top of their voices, they all rushed at him, dragged him out of the city and began to stone him. Meanwhile, the witnesses laid their coats at the feet of a young man named Saul.
>
> While they were stoning him, Stephen prayed, "Lord Jesus, receive my spirit." Then he fell on his knees and cried out, "Lord, do not hold this sin against them." When he had said this, he fell asleep. (Acts 7:54–60)

These passages show that preaching with power is not a matter of speaking loudly or impressively or doing anything to draw attention to ourselves. Rather, it means preaching boldly. When we preach with power, we take up the cross to suffer and sometimes even to die, for God's power is shown in our weakness. Resurrection power shines forth when the seed falls into the ground and dies (John 12:24–25). If signs are needed, God can provide them. Our task is to faithfully proclaim God's word.

May the God of hope fill you with all joy and peace as you trust in him, so that you may overflow with hope by the power of the Holy Spirit. (Rom 15:13)

Day 22

> But you will receive power when the Holy Spirit comes on you;
> and you will be my witnesses in Jerusalem, and in all Judea and
> Samaria, and to the ends of the earth. (Acts 1:8)

The Spirit Enables Us

Spectacular manifestations of the Spirit not only convinced outsiders, they also persuaded Jewish Christians that Gentiles were equal members in the church (Acts 10, 11, 15). Peter apparently believed that all Christian preaching, even preaching unaccompanied by remarkable signs, was from the Bible and by the Holy Spirit. Consider his words:

> Concerning this salvation, the prophets, who spoke of the grace
> that was to come to you, searched intently and with the greatest
> care, trying to find out the time and circumstances to which
> the Spirit of Christ in them was pointing when he predicted the
> sufferings of the Messiah and the glories that would follow. It
> was revealed to them that they were not serving themselves but
> you, when they spoke of the things that have now been told you
> by those who have preached the gospel to you by the Holy Spirit
> sent from heaven. Even angels long to look into these things.
> (1 Pet 1:10–12)

Follow the logic of this tightly-reasoned little paragraph. The prophets knew that the Spirit of Christ in them (the Holy Spirit) was pointing to the sufferings and glories of the predicted Messiah. They wanted to know more, as did the angels, but instead of giving more details, the Spirit revealed to them that they did not speak for their own benefit, but for the benefit of Peter's readers – the "you" of verse 12. The sufferings and subsequent glories of Christ that the prophets predicted are the very things Christian preachers spoke of when they preached the gospel "by the Holy Spirit" in the first century AD.

Peter's first readers, Christians scattered across Asia Minor, may have heard the gospel from one of the apostles, possibly Peter himself on the day of Pentecost, but this is far from certain. More likely, this description of gospel preaching applies to all Christian preaching, not just that of the apostles. If that is true, it reminds all of us who preach that it is the Holy Spirit who enables us to preach, and that his work is to take what he inspired in the Bible and help us see the gospel in it.

Father, thank you for providing your Spirit to us who are called to speak in your Name. Without him, we could not do so. Protect me from the sin of taking for granted the Spirit's ministry in and through me when I preach your word. Amen.

Day 23

> Jesus replied, "Very truly I tell you, no one can see the kingdom of God unless they are born again." "How can someone be born when they are old?" Nicodemus asked. "Surely they cannot enter a second time into their mother's womb to be born!" Jesus answered, "Very truly I tell you, no one can enter the kingdom of God unless they are born of water and the Spirit. Flesh gives birth to flesh, but the Spirit gives birth to spirit. You should not be surprised at my saying, 'You must be born again.' The wind blows wherever it pleases. You hear its sound, but you cannot tell where it comes from or where it is going. So it is with everyone born of the Spirit." (John 3:3–8)

The Spirit Regenerates Us

Our survey of the apostolic era would not be complete without calling attention to how Paul's preaching impacted the Thessalonians. His preaching received a mixed response:

> When Paul and his companions [Silas and Timothy] had passed through Amphipolis and Apollonia, they came to Thessalonica, where there was a Jewish synagogue. As was his custom, Paul went into the synagogue, and on three Sabbath days he reasoned with them from the Scriptures, explaining and proving that the Messiah had to suffer and rise from the dead. "This Jesus I am proclaiming to you is the Messiah," he said. Some of the Jews were persuaded and joined Paul and Silas, as did a large number of God-fearing Greeks and not a few prominent women.

But other Jews were jealous; so they rounded up some bad characters from the marketplace, formed a mob and started a riot in the city. They rushed to Jason's house in search of Paul and Silas in order to bring them out to the crowd. (Acts 17:1–5)

Notice carefully that Paul reasoned from the Scriptures. Laying the Old Testament open before his Jewish and (presumably some) God-fearing Gentile listeners, Paul spoke of the Messiah, proving that the Messiah had to suffer and rise from the dead. Having made his case from Scripture concerning these two pivotal events in the life of the Messiah, he set forth Jesus as the logical candidate for the role of Messiah, the Christ. The logic was powerful. Starting with what they knew and agreed on – the authority of the Hebrew Scriptures – Paul made a case his listeners would be hard-pressed to reject.

His reasoning persuaded some that Jesus was the Messiah, but not all were pleased (Acts 17:5–34), so Paul and his team had to run for their lives. When Paul explains in 1 Thessalonians why some people believed and were regenerated, he does not attribute his success on that occasion to his skill as a biblical interpreter or as a preacher:

> We remember before our God and Father your work produced by faith, your labour prompted by love, and your endurance inspired by hope in our Lord Jesus Christ.
>
> For we know, brothers and sisters loved by God, that he has chosen you, because our gospel came to you not simply with words but also with power, with the Holy Spirit and deep conviction. You know how we lived among you for your sake. You became imitators of us and of the Lord, for you welcomed the message in the midst of severe suffering with the joy given by the Holy Spirit. (1 Thess 1:3–6)

Paul's message was not just words. It came with power and conviction and joy, all evidences of the work of the Holy Spirit. The final proof of the reality of the Thessalonians' conversion was the faith, hope and love they manifested in the midst of suffering. They were not only imitators of the messengers; they were models to other churches. The point needs to be stressed. When we speak of the Holy Spirit's ministry in our preaching, we must underscore the fact that much of that work is not in us; it is in our listeners. We will come back to this in Part Three of this book.

For now, let's summarize what we can count on the Holy Spirit to do in relation to our preaching: The Holy Spirit has already inspired the Scriptures we preach; he regenerates people, opening blind eyes to see the glory of God in the face of Jesus Christ; he empowers his followers to bear witness; he may graciously give signs when we preach, as he did occasionally in Acts; he gives spiritual gifts; he baptizes us into the body of Christ; he deploys us to preach. What else should we expect?

Lord, I recall hearing the gospel many times before I actually heard your voice and saw your glory in the face of Jesus. Thank you for granting me new life. Give me patience with those whose eyes are still closed, those for whom my sermons are just words. Grant power to me as I preach and deep conviction to them as they hear your word. Amen.

Day 24

> For the one whom God has sent speaks the words of God, for God gives the Spirit without limit. (John 3:34)

The Spirit Ministers to Us

Since the Holy Spirit is always at work along with the Father and the Son, it seems wrong to focus on just a few specifics of his ministry. The Spirit brings glory to the Son and thus to the Father, but because he always shines the light on the other persons of the Trinity, we don't always notice what he is doing. Nevertheless, let me remind you of several overlapping ministries of the Holy Spirit that relate to preaching. Though not restricted to preachers, these ministries are indispensable if our preaching is to bear fruit. The Holy Spirit helps by teaching, illuminating Scripture, sanctifying believers by the word of God, and helping us to pray.

In preparing his followers for life after his departure, Jesus promised the Holy Spirit, referring to him as the Advocate (NIV), sometimes interpreted as helper, counsellor or comforter, or just transliterated as *Paraclete*, using the Greek term for someone called alongside to help. Read the following five passages introducing the Spirit's ministries in John, looking carefully for other descriptions of this Third Person of the Trinity.

> If you love me, keep my commands. And I will ask the Father, and he will give you another advocate to help you and be with you forever – the Spirit of truth. The world cannot accept him,

because it neither sees him nor knows him. But you know him, for he lives with you and will be in you. (14:15–17)

All this I have spoken while still with you. But the Advocate, the Holy Spirit, whom the Father will send in my name, will teach you all things and will remind you of everything I have said to you. (14:25–26)

When the Advocate comes, whom I will send to you from the Father – the Spirit of truth who goes out from the Father – he will testify about me. And you also must testify, for you have been with me from the beginning. (15:26–27)

But very truly I tell you, it is for your good that I am going away. Unless I go away, the Advocate will not come to you; but if I go, I will send him to you. When he comes, he will prove the world to be in the wrong about sin and righteousness and judgment: about sin, because people do not believe in me; about righteousness, because I am going to the Father, where you can see me no longer; and about judgment, because the prince of this world now stands condemned. (16:7–11)

I have much more to say to you, more than you can now bear. But when he, the Spirit of truth, comes, he will guide you into all the truth. He will not speak on his own; he will speak only what he hears, and he will tell you what is yet to come. He will glorify me because it is from me that he will receive what he will make known to you. All that belongs to the Father is mine. That is why I said the Spirit will receive from me what he will make known to you. (16:12–15)

It is crucial to recall that Jesus addressed these words to the Eleven in preparation for their ministry after the Lord Jesus' death, resurrection and ascension. The gift of the Holy Spirit enabled them to recall what Jesus taught, to grasp the truth of it (in a way they clearly had not grasped up to this point), and to take everything that Jesus is and does and place it in a larger context that glorifies the Father. Some of them wrote parts of the New Testament because of the Holy Spirit's ministries described here.

The Holy Spirit was promised to be with them forever (14:16). He remains "the Spirit of truth" (14:17; 15:26; 16:13). He lives in us, as he did in them. His primary task remains that of glorifying Jesus. So although his ministry to us who live now is not identical to his ministry to the Eleven, there is nevertheless a similarity because of his unchanging nature. The Spirit still continues the ministry of Jesus, extending and internalizing it.

Jesus emphasizes that the promised Holy Spirit will be given not to the world but "to you," that is, to Jesus' followers (16:7). (The phrase occurs twice in this verse.) Therefore, the Spirit's ministry to the world is a mediated ministry. By indwelling believers, the Spirit enables us corporately to show the world the reality of its sin, the emptiness of its righteousness and the necessity of its judgment. We do this by living and speaking in the power of the Holy Spirit. We function as the body of Christ, manifesting his nature in a way that reveals the world's sin. This is possible only by the power of the Holy Spirit, and is the sort of life that truly glorifies God, for it does not minimize our sin nor rest on our own righteousness. Neither does it gloss over the necessity of judgment. Instead, it merely affirms that our sins are acknowledged, our righteousness is a gift we received from Christ, and our just judgment has been taken by Christ.

Father, we long to live up to our calling as your children. By your Spirit, so conform us to the image of Christ that when the world sees us who make up the body of Christ now on earth, they will be convicted of sin, receptive to receiving your righteousness in Christ, and eager to run from the judgment to come. Amen.

Day 25

I will not leave you as orphans; I will come to you. Before long, the world will not see me anymore, but you will see me. Because I live, you also will live. On that day you will realize that I am in my Father, and you are in me, and I am in you. Whoever has my commands and keeps them is the one who loves me. The one who loves me will be loved by my Father, and I too will love them and show myself to them." Then Judas (not Judas Iscariot) said, "But, Lord, why do you intend to show yourself to us and not to the world?" Jesus replied, "Anyone who loves me will obey my teaching. My Father will love them, and we will come to them and make our home with them. Anyone who does not love me will not obey my teaching. These words you hear are not my own; they belong to the Father who sent me. All this I have spoken while still with you. But the Advocate, the Holy Spirit, whom the Father will send in my name, will teach you all things and will remind you of everything I have said to you." (John 14:18–26)

The Spirit Teaches Us

How does the Holy Spirit pursue this God-glorifying teaching ministry with us? He does so in a number of ways, which we will look at over the next few days. First, as we have seen, he gives gifted teachers to the church (Eph 4:11; 1 Tim 3:2; Titus 1:9). We learn from them in public and private, formally and informally. Second, the Holy Spirit places us in the body of Christ, and we are taught by its members individually and corporately. The writer to the Hebrews says to his readers, "by this time you ought to be teachers" (5:12), and the Lord Jesus affirms those who not only obey his word, but teach it:

> Therefore anyone who sets aside one of the least of these commands and teaches others accordingly will be called least in the kingdom of heaven, but whoever practises and teaches these commands will be called great in the kingdom of heaven. (Matt 5:19)

I am struck by how important the whole church is in helping us grasp the love of God:

> For this reason I kneel before the Father, from whom every family in heaven and on earth derives its name. I pray that out of his glorious riches he may strengthen you with power through his Spirit in your inner being, so that Christ may dwell in your hearts through faith. And I pray that you, being rooted and established in love, may have power, together with all the Lord's holy people, to grasp how wide and long and high and deep is the love of Christ, and to know this love that surpasses knowledge – that you may be filled to the measure of all the fullness of God. (Eph 3:14–19)

The Holy Spirit gives us the capacity to grasp the dimensions of God's love, but it is only "together with all the saints" that we see its dimensions. I don't think this merely means that all of us in the church will eventually understand God's love, but that the way we come to grasp it is by seeing it both received and manifested by the variety of people who make up the body of Christ.

Remember that God's love is often mediated, and thus we may experience it indirectly. Sometimes it comes through the sacrificial kindness of a parishioner, the generosity of a donor, or the valid criticism of a peer. We can even grasp a dimension of God's love when we and our family members are not the recipients but are seeing a brother or sister genuinely show love for another.

Now to him who is able to do immeasurably more than all we ask or imagine, according to his power that is at work within us, to him be glory in the church and in Christ Jesus throughout all generations, for ever and ever! Amen. (Eph 3:20–21)

Day 26

Who is wise and understanding among you? Let them show it by their good life, by deeds done in the humility that comes from wisdom. But if you harbour bitter envy and selfish ambition in your hearts, do not boast about it or deny the truth. Such "wisdom" does not come down from heaven but is earthly, unspiritual, demonic. For where you have envy and selfish ambition, there you find disorder and every evil practice. But the wisdom that comes from heaven is first of all pure; then peace-loving, considerate, submissive, full of mercy and good fruit, impartial and sincere. Peacemakers who sow in peace reap a harvest of righteousness. (Jas 3:13–18)

The Spirit Gives Us Wisdom and Knowledge

A third way the Holy Spirit teaches through us is by giving us gifts of wisdom and knowledge:

Now to each one the manifestation of the Spirit is given for the common good. To one there is given through the Spirit a message of wisdom, to another a message of knowledge by means of the same Spirit, to another faith by the same Spirit, to another gifts

> of healing by that one Spirit, to another miraculous powers, to
> another prophecy, to another distinguishing between spirits,
> to another speaking in different kinds of tongues, and to still
> another the interpretation of tongues. All these are the work of
> one and the same Spirit, and he distributes them to each one, just
> as he determines. (1 Cor 12:7–11)

The expressions "message of wisdom" and "message of knowledge" could be rendered "word of wisdom" and "word of knowledge." In other words, the Holy Spirit gives to some in the church insights and awareness *for speaking*. Therefore, when we grasp what the church needs to hear and say it for the good of the church, we manifest what the Spirit is doing. It is tempting to minimize these workings of the Spirit because of the excesses associated with them. Claims of a word from God that relate to a new building project or some ego-inflating ministry have nothing at all to do with these gifts. Instead, we should expect there to be people in the church who by virtue of the Holy Spirit's ministry can say things that help us understand God's wisdom and know what he is doing and what we should do. This sort of guidance will never contradict what the same Spirit led the authors of the Bible to write, but it may help us see what Scripture calls for in our specific situation.

One occupational hazard we face as preachers is the misguided notion that we no longer need to learn from others, especially from others whose academic credentials we consider inferior to our own. A particularly virulent, contemporary strain of this infection is the gender- or ethno-centric idea that we can only learn from people with whom we identify racially or socially, or in respect to age or gender. Surely this reflects not only arrogance but also unbelief, for it implies that God the Holy Spirit will (can?) only speak to us through people like ourselves. In fact, God seems to delight in using the foolish, the weak, the lowly, the despised, and the things that are not to bring to nothing the things that are, indeed, to humble the wise and knowledgeable (1 Cor 1:26–31).

The teaching ministry of the Holy Spirit includes what the Lord promises to those who are hauled into court for preaching the gospel:

> When you are brought before synagogues, rulers and authorities,
> do not worry about how you will defend yourselves or what you
> will say, for the Holy Spirit will teach you at that time what you
> should say. (Luke 12:11–12)

This promise should never be taken as an excuse not to prepare for preaching. But when an enforced opportunity to testify arises, this ministry of the Holy Spirit is a great comfort.

Gracious God, we thank you for giving your Holy Spirit not only to us, but to others. Remind me deeply today that others who have your word and Spirit can not only understand it, but can also explain it, teach it and apply it. Grant me a posture of humility that I may learn from them, even as I test all things by your word and hold fast to that which is good. Amen.

Day 27

> Send me your light and your faithful care, let them lead me; let them bring me to your holy mountain, to the place where you dwell. (Ps 43:3)

The Spirit Illuminates Scripture for Us

Another way the Holy Spirit teaches through us is by illuminating the Scriptures to help us see what they hold. In some ways, this ministry mirrors the Spirit's ministry as God's agent in inspiration. Having breathed out the word (2 Tim 3:16), the Spirit now sheds light on it. My experience at the theatre helps me keep in mind how important this is. When my wife and I go to watch a play, we find our seats in the theatre and wait for two things to happen. First, the curtain has to be lifted, that is, the stage has to be unveiled. Second, the lights have to be turned on. If either of these is not done, we will not be able to follow what is happening on the stage.

In a similar way, for the drama of redemption to be known, we need an unveiling – a revelation – and illumination. Revelation has come in written form as Scripture: we have the Bible. Illumination happens whenever by faith we read the Bible. The text most frequently associated with this work of the Holy Spirit is 1 Corinthians 2:6–16. As you read, notice that Paul speaks of his preaching ministry (2:6, 7, 13). The Spirit enables Paul and his colleagues (and us) to understand (2:8, 12, 14) and preach the gospel (2:13).

> We do, however, speak a message of wisdom among the mature, but not the wisdom of this age or of the rulers of this age, who are coming to nothing. No, we declare God's wisdom, a mystery that

has been hidden and that God destined for our glory before time began. None of the rulers of this age understood it, for if they had, they would not have crucified the Lord of glory. However, as it is written:

> "What no eye has seen,
>> what no ear has heard,
> and what no human mind has conceived" –
>> the things God has prepared for those who love him –

these are the things God has revealed to us by his Spirit. The Spirit searches all things, even the deep things of God. For who knows a person's thoughts except their own spirit within them? In the same way no one knows the thoughts of God except the Spirit of God. What we have received is not the spirit of the world but the Spirit who is from God, so that we may understand what God has freely given us. This is what we speak, not in words taught us by human wisdom but in words taught by the Spirit, explaining spiritual realities with Spirit-taught words. The person without the Spirit does not accept the things that come from the Spirit of God but considers them foolishness, and cannot understand them because they are discerned only through the Spirit. The person with the Spirit makes judgments about all things, but such a person is not subject to merely human judgments, for,

> "Who has known the mind of the Lord
>> so as to instruct him?"

But we have the mind of Christ.

In a nutshell, Paul's argument is this: We speak a message of wisdom, but not the worldly wisdom that human ingenuity can devise or human faculties can discover. Our message is the revealed wisdom of God that only those with God's Spirit can discern. The gospel of Christ crucified only makes sense as a way of salvation to those who have the mind of Christ, the capacity to discern God's ways. God gives us words to proclaim this gospel, that is, words to explain these spiritual realities. Stated negatively, an unbeliever (someone without the Holy Spirit and therefore without the mind of Christ) cannot understand the gospel (1 Cor 2:14–16a) and considers it foolishness. God gives us words to express this gospel that are appropriate to both the message and our listeners.

The blessing of illumination makes preaching fruitful in more than the obvious way. Obviously, we are in trouble if we try to explain something we cannot understand, which would be the case without the Holy Spirit's illuminating work. But it is equally important to remember that when we expound Scripture to Christians, we speak to people who can understand our message by virtue of the same ministry of the Spirit. Even unbelievers depend on the initial illumination that marks their move from darkness to the light, as 2 Corinthians 4:6 describes:

> For God, who said, "Let light shine out of darkness," made his light shine in our hearts to give us the light of the knowledge of God's glory displayed in the face of Christ.

Father, as I recall how I lived so long in the dark with the Bible available and yet practically invisible to me, I thank you that you turned the light on and I began to see Jesus in its pages and see myself in desperate need of the salvation that only he could supply. Please keep the light on. Please turn the light on for my listeners when I preach. I cannot do this, but you can. Thank you for this supernatural work without which no preaching could ever hope to achieve its purposes. Amen.

Day 28

> You, however, know all about my teaching, my way of life, my purpose, faith, patience, love, endurance, persecutions, sufferings – what kinds of things happened to me in Antioch, Iconium and Lystra, the persecutions I endured. Yet the Lord rescued me from all of them. In fact, everyone who wants to live a godly life in Christ Jesus will be persecuted, while evildoers and impostors will go from bad to worse, deceiving and being deceived. But as for you, continue in what you have learned and have become convinced of, because you know those from whom you learned it. (2 Tim 3:10–14)

The Spirit Sanctifies Us

The name we use to refer to the Holy Spirit implies another of his ministries: sanctification – the work of making us holy. The Lord Jesus prayed that all his followers would be sanctified by the word of truth (John 17:17), so we cannot separate the Spirit's ministry of sanctification from the ministry of the word of God, which has been entrusted to us. The moment we were baptized into the church by the Holy Spirit (reborn), we were set aside for God's purposes, made different by parentage and citizenship from the world around us. The Apostle Paul, addressing what was by no means a perfect church, did not hesitate to describe the Corinthians as "sanctified":

> To the church of God in Corinth, to those sanctified in Christ Jesus and called to be his holy people, together with all those everywhere who call on the name of our Lord Jesus Christ – their Lord and ours. (1 Cor 1:2)

The process of sanctification, begun at conversion, continues. Paul states as much in his prayer for the Thessalonians:

> May God himself, the God of peace, sanctify you through and through. May your whole spirit, soul and body be kept blameless at the coming of our Lord Jesus Christ. (1 Thess 5:23)

We could profit much from reviewing sanctification, but I limit myself to one insight based on Jesus' example. Jesus continues his high priestly prayer with these key words:

> As you sent me into the world, I have sent them into the world. For them I sanctify myself, that they too may be truly sanctified. My prayer is not for them alone. I pray also for those who will believe in me through their message. (John 17:18–20)

Here we see the pattern of Jesus sending us as he has been sent by the Father. This prayer is not only for the disciples who were physically present but for all of us who believe through their word (17:20). Jesus affirms that his followers' sanctification is predicated on *his* holiness. Being holy is necessary in Jesus' case, because he had to be a sinless sin-bearer, dying not for his own sin (since he had none) but for ours. For Jesus to have been a sinner would have rendered his death merely the just payment for his own sins, not the substitutionary atonement for ours.

This text invites the question: What is the relationship between our sanctification as preachers and that of our listeners? I suggest that we follow

Jesus' example. Our efforts to grow in holiness are not merely, or even primarily, for our personal benefit. We need to be able to say with Jesus, *"for them* I sanctify myself."* It is noteworthy how often Paul invites his readers and listeners to imitate him and others who are holy (see 1 Cor 4:16; 11:1; 2 Tim 3:10–14; Phil 3:17; 2 Thess 3:9). He readily defends his ministry by appealing to what his listeners can see and to what God alone can see in his heart (1 Thess 2:1–12).

We all know from experience that an entire ministry can be discredited by unholiness. It is worth reflecting on the positive role God intends holiness to play in our ministries. Love for our listeners can and should be a major motivation for doing the hard work of cooperating with the Holy Spirit in his sanctifying work (Phil 2:12–13). Part of pouring out our lives as sacrifices on the altar of their faith (Phil 2:17) is ensuring that we as sacrifices are acceptable and pleasing to God (Heb 12:28–13:16). When we pursue holiness for the praise of God and the good of our listeners, we will enjoy its benefits. Since "without holiness no one will see the Lord" (Heb 12:14), we should not expect intimacy with God when we neglect sanctification. But when we pursue God for godly reasons, a clearer vision of him will permeate our preaching.

Father, there are days when I wish my own holiness were not so integral to my preaching. That would feel easier. I could merely speak a message and neglect the non-verbal component of the gospel. I might even be tempted to think that my lack of holiness displays your grace. Protect me from all such self-deceptions, I pray, and strengthen my will to do your will from the heart in reliance upon your Holy Spirit. Help me this day to take the steps of gospel obedience you have prepared for me, and to rejoice that you can proclaim the gospel through me. Amen.

Day 29

But when the set time had fully come, God sent his Son, born of a woman, born under the law, to redeem those under the law, that we might receive adoption to sonship. Because you are his sons, God sent the Spirit of his Son into our hearts, the Spirit who calls out, "Abba, Father." (Gal 4:4–6)

The Spirit Helps Us Pray

Of all the ways the Holy Spirit ministers to us as preachers, we consider only one more: he helps us pray. We know that the Lord Jesus is actively interceding for us (Rom 8:34; Heb 7:25), but in a complementary way, the Holy Spirit also intercedes for us:

> In the same way, the Spirit helps us in our weakness. We do not know what we ought to pray for, but the Spirit himself intercedes for us through wordless groans. And he who searches our hearts knows the mind of the Spirit, because the Spirit intercedes for God's people in accordance with the will of God. (Rom 8:26–27)

We all suffer from weakness and ignorance. We lack strength to pray and insight into what specifically we ought to ask in prayer. Just as the Spirit supports us in our painful wait for glory (Rom 8:18–25), so he helps us by compensating for the deficiencies that hinder our prayers. Yes, he gives strength and insight, but the focus here is not on remedying our shortcomings but on what the Spirit does despite them. He who is not limited to human words deeply identifies with us in our groaning and prays for us. He does so according to God (as the last phrase might be rendered, more literally). He does know God's mind, and he does not lack stamina, knowledge or words. He asks for the things that he knows God wants and that glorify him.

This is wonderful good news because it means that our living in these days between the ascension and the Parousia is not limited by the quality or quantity of our prayers. The Spirit prompts us to pray (Eph 2:18) and pray we will, but in the final analysis, our ability to pray does not put a ceiling on God's ability to answer.

Clearly, this ministry of the Spirit is no substitute for our prayers or the prayers of those we enlist to intercede for us. We should follow Paul's example and request others to pray for our preaching:

> Devote yourselves to prayer, being watchful and thankful. And pray for us, too, that God may open a door for our message, so that we may proclaim the mystery of Christ, for which I am in chains. Pray that I may proclaim it clearly, as I should. (Col 4:2–4)

Father, teach me to pray more like the Apostle Paul did [as recorded in 2 Thessalonians 1:11–12], the sort of Christ-exalting, God-honouring prayers that can only be prompted by the Holy Spirit: "With this in mind, we constantly pray for you, that our God may make you worthy of his calling, and that by his power he may bring to fruition your every desire for goodness and your every deed prompted by faith. We pray this so that the name of our Lord Jesus may be glorified in you, and you in him, according to the grace of our God and the Lord Jesus Christ."

God the Father

But the Lord said to Ananias, "Go! This man is my chosen instrument to proclaim my name to the Gentiles and their kings and to the people of Israel. I will show him how much he must suffer for my name." (Acts 9:15–16)

God Selects Our Place

We sometimes see gifted preachers who do not flourish or see much fruit in one setting, but whose ministry the Lord blesses in another setting. I often reflect on how the people of Salem Free Church in Fargo, North Dakota, allowed me to use the gifts I had without insisting that I manifest skills or traits I did not have. In another setting with different expectations, my ministry may not have been "favourably received" (Rom 15:31).

Many variables can account for apparent success, and it may not be wise or helpful to seek them out, much less assume that what we see at the time is all God is doing. But one gift God gives to preachers that we often neglect is the gift of deployment, of putting us in just the place he has designed for us.

Jesus went through all the towns and villages, teaching in their synagogues, proclaiming the good news of the kingdom and healing every disease and sickness. When he saw the crowds, he had compassion on them, because they were harassed and helpless, like sheep without a shepherd. Then he said to his disciples, "The harvest is plentiful but the workers are few. Ask the Lord of the harvest, therefore, to send out workers into his harvest field." (Matt 9:35–38)

Jesus' compassion for the helpless crowds moves him to propose an indirect solution to their plight rather than a direct intervention. First, Jesus underscores the obvious disparity between the amount of work to be done and the number of hands to do it, illustrating this with a familiar agricultural image. There is a huge harvest; there are few workers. The metaphor implies that time is limited. The grain won't stand in the field forever.

Notice that Jesus does not say the workers are *too* few. God is not wringing his hands in heaven because of insufficient human resources. Given the expanse of the opportunity – the crowds – and the comparatively few workers, Jesus invites his disciples to pray. The remedy would not be of human origin. The prayer is to be addressed to "the Lord of the harvest," that is, to God in whose field the labourers toil. This matters because God is sovereign by virtue of his ownership. He is able to bring the harvest in with many hands or few, to add more workers, or, as in the case of Gideon's "army," to deliberately use a few. The request itself, the earnest asking, is that he as Lord of the harvest will push people out into *his* harvest field. Though not wrong in itself, we should not ask for more workers, but that the few available will be deployed by God himself.

An army of workers is not the answer to vast human need, for then the results would look like a brilliant human strategy of effective recruiting. God's plan is for all who name his name to work in his field in the places where he sends them. Though God can and does increase the numbers daily, as he has since Pentecost (Acts 2:47), it is the deployment of those workers – all of us – in the fields of his choice that makes the difference. He gives spiritual gifts to each worker. He superintends the shaping of each personality. He orchestrates the experiences of every labourer.

When we ask him, he pushes us into his field. His more or less forceful pushing into our places of labour should be thought of as an answer to prayer, even when the location, geographically or sociologically, isn't what we might have preferred. Sometimes, God seems to delight in preparing people who are completely at home in their place of ministry in terms of background, race, culture, and education. In other cases, he drops people into environments that could scarcely be more alien to them. He receives glory in either case. We are not wise to strategize for him about these things; we are to pray, and prayer includes listening.

Thank you Lord that as you were sent, so you send. Thank you also that the place you send each of us is perfect, even when it is difficult. Make me like the seed that is willing to fall into the ground and die so that it does not remain alone but bears much fruit. Amen.

Day 31

"For I know the plans I have for you," declares the Lord, "plans
to prosper you and not to harm you, plans to give you hope and a
future." (Jer 29:11)

God Plans Our Opportunities

Acts 13:1–3 records one of the clearest and most instructive examples of
deployment in the New Testament:

Now in the church at Antioch there were prophets and teachers:
Barnabas, Simeon called Niger, Lucius of Cyrene, Manaen (who
had been brought up with Herod the tetrarch) and Saul. While
they were worshipping the Lord and fasting, the Holy Spirit said,
"Set apart for me Barnabas and Saul for the work to which I have
called them." So after they had fasted and prayed, they placed
their hands on them and sent them off.

Notice what sort of men these were: leaders whose gifts had already been
recognized by the church; prophets and teachers; a group in the church at
Antioch, not independent contractors or spiritual entrepreneurs; of different
cultures, as their names attest; and disciplined, in that they were fasting
and praying.

While worshipping, the men received the Holy Spirit's instruction to set
apart two of their number (Barnabas and Saul) for the work to which he, the
Holy Spirit, had called them. Their worship consisted not only of praising
God, but also of listening to God. Having heard this word of instruction,
all five men fasted and prayed, laid hands on Barnabas and Saul, and sent
them off.

The text does not say whether they fasted and prayed to seek confirmation
about the guidance from the Holy Spirit or to dedicate themselves to their
respective tasks. I am inclined to believe it was the latter since the word from
the Holy Spirit is reported without any question concerning its authenticity
or clarity. In any case, the result was immediate and apparently unquestioning
obedience by those who stayed in Antioch and by those who went. The
laying on of hands did not impart something that was not already there, but
it did reaffirm the solidarity that existed between the sending church and
the missionaries.

Here was a diverse group of gifted leaders ministering in a church where their ministries were recognized. They all heard the same word from the Holy Spirit. Two were to be deployed elsewhere, and three were to stay where they were. This is instructive. Deployment does not always mean a move any more than a flight over seawater makes a person a missionary. God has his own perfect reasons for sending those he sends and deploying others close to home.

Notice especially that deployment entails human and divine cooperation. We pray, and God answers. We obey, and we, as the church, send. God is glorified, for his workers are thus deployed to locations and tasks for which God, who knows all things, has uniquely suited them.

I have enjoyed watching students see the pearl of great price and sell everything to follow Jesus wherever he leads. But occasionally I am disappointed when graduating students set limits on what God might reasonably expect them to do or where he might expect them to serve. I am not against using our God-given minds to assess our gifts, strengths, weaknesses and passions and to explore ministry callings accordingly. I am not even against a realistic assessment based on how one handles a hot or cold climate or perpetually grey skies. But it is sad to see some students limit their universe to no more than a day's journey away from their parents. God may have much greater opportunities planned for them.

Trusting God means more than trusting him with our eternal destinies. It means trusting him with our daily lives. I hope that as a pastoral leader you make it your regular practice to fast and pray with fellow leaders, asking God to deploy proven, gifted leaders from your midst even when such deployments represent a significant sacrifice to the local fellowship you serve.

Father, thank you that discerning your will for where we use the gifts you have given is not something we must do alone. Please bring into all our lives those with whom we can worship and listen for your directives. Attune our ears to your still, small voice, even when and perhaps especially when you speak through others. Amen.

Day 32

This mystery is that through the gospel the Gentiles are heirs together with Israel, members together of one body, and sharers together in the promise in Christ Jesus. (Eph 3:6)

God Prepares Our Inheritance

Any review of the good gifts God has given us must include gifts promised but not yet given. Built into the gospel is the good news of a future hope. Paul's cascade of praise to the triune God for every spiritual blessing includes not just what the Father did in eternity past (planning, purposing, choosing), or what the Son did in history (redeeming us by his blood), or what the Holy Spirit does in each generation (including us in Christ), but also what each of those provisions means for the future:

> Praise be to the God and Father of our Lord Jesus Christ, who has blessed us in the heavenly realms with every spiritual blessing in Christ. For he chose us in him before the creation of the world to be holy and blameless in his sight. In love he predestined us for adoption to sonship through Jesus Christ, in accordance with his pleasure and will – to the praise of his glorious grace, which he has freely given us in the One he loves. In him we have redemption through his blood, the forgiveness of sins, in accordance with the riches of God's grace that he lavished on us. With all wisdom and understanding, he made known to us the mystery of his will according to his good pleasure, which he purposed in Christ, to be put into effect when the times reach their fulfilment – to bring unity to all things in heaven and on earth under Christ.
>
> In him we were also chosen, having been predestined according to the plan of him who works out everything in conformity with the purpose of his will, in order that we, who were the first to put our hope in Christ, might be for the praise of his glory. And you also were included in Christ when you heard the message of truth, the gospel of your salvation. When you believed, you were marked in him with a seal, the promised Holy Spirit, who is a deposit guaranteeing our inheritance until the

redemption of those who are God's possession – to the praise of his glory. (Eph 1:3–14)

The Holy Spirit not only guarantees that there will be a future inheritance; he also seals us for it. Read Peter's description of this:

Praise be to the God and Father of our Lord Jesus Christ! In his great mercy he has given us new birth into a living hope through the resurrection of Jesus Christ from the dead, and into an inheritance that can never perish, spoil or fade. This inheritance is kept in heaven for you, who through faith are shielded by God's power until the coming of the salvation that is ready to be revealed in the last time. (1 Pet 1:3–5)

The inheritance is kept for us; we are kept for the inheritance. Since our salvation is one glorious package, those parts not yet ours are as good as ours already. We know this because God is the giver of the whole package, even if he does not give all of it at one time.

Thank you gracious Father for including me as an heir and for guarding both me and the inheritance until the day it is mine. I rejoice that this is one thing in this fallen world that I can count on. Amen.

Day 33

In that day this song will be sung in the land of Judah: We have a strong city; God makes salvation its walls and ramparts. Open the gates that the righteous nation may enter, the nation that keeps faith. You will keep in perfect peace those whose minds are steadfast, because they trust in you. Trust in the LORD forever, for the LORD, the LORD himself, is the Rock eternal. (Isa 26:1–4)

God Secures Us

Consider Paul's description of God's promise to us:

And we know that in all things God works for the good of those who love him, who have been called according to his purpose. For those God foreknew he also predestined to be conformed to the image of his Son, that he might be the firstborn among many brothers and sisters. And those he predestined, he also called; those he called, he also justified; those he justified, he also glorified.

What, then, shall we say in response to these things? If God is for us, who can be against us? He who did not spare his own Son, but gave him up for us all – how will he not also, along with him, graciously give us all things? Who will bring any charge against those whom God has chosen? It is God who justifies. Who then is the one who condemns? No one. Christ Jesus who died – more than that, who was raised to life – is at the right hand of God and is also interceding for us. Who shall separate us from the love of Christ? Shall trouble or hardship or persecution or famine or nakedness or danger or sword? As it is written:

> "For your sake we face death all day long;
>   we are considered as sheep to be slaughtered."

No, in all these things we are more than conquerors through him who loved us. For I am convinced that neither death nor life, neither angels nor demons, neither the present nor the future, nor any powers, neither height nor depth, nor anything else in all creation, will be able to separate us from the love of God that is in Christ Jesus our Lord. (Rom 8:28–39)

Although there are texts in virtually every book of the New Testament that offer similar reassurance, I want to emphasize these verses because they speak so powerfully to our vulnerability as preachers. If we foolishly build our sense of well-being on how well we are received, what share of the world's wealth we attain, the comfort or safety that our role or performance secures for us, or our reputation among our peers, we are destined to be perpetually insecure. We have been called not only to believe in Jesus, but also to suffer for his sake (Phil 1:29). "In fact, everyone who wants to live a godly life in Christ Jesus will be persecuted" in one form or another (2 Tim 3:12). We are among those who can rejoice at being allowed to share the disgrace of our Master (Acts 5:41), who see it as our clear calling to fill up in our flesh what is lacking in Christ's afflictions (Col 1:24). This is what it means to take up the cross.

We who can expect such challenges often need a deep drink from Romans 8. We must get our minds around the unbreakable chain from eternity past to eternity future. We need to glory in the logic of verse 32: If God gave what was dearest to him – his unique Son – and he did, can we actually imagine that having made that investment he would withhold anything good from those he is bringing to glory? Of course we need to define "good" as God does in verse 28, but the promise is still astonishing and, better yet, rock solid, because the God of the universe stands behind it and we already have evidence that he is at work.

Father, I confess that too often I have sought security in things that are by nature insecure and unstable. Forgive me for exalting the works of my own hands to places they should never occupy. Restore me, I pray, to deep and abiding confidence in your ability to keep me in the hollow of your hand. Amen.

Day 34

> Very rarely will anyone die for a righteous person, though for
> a good person someone might possibly dare to die. But God
> demonstrates his own love for us in this: While we were still
> sinners, Christ died for us. (Rom 5:7–8)

God Loves Us

How then would we sum up God's relationship with us? God loves us. John 3:16 still deserves to be the most well-known verse in the Bible:

> For God so loved the world that he gave his one and only Son,
> that whoever believes in him shall not perish but have eternal life.

Not surprisingly, God's people express their innermost thoughts concerning God's love in the Bible's songbook. God's love governs all his actions towards us. In utter despair at the opposition he faced from wicked and deceitful men, David asks God to deal with them severely in Psalm 109. Nevertheless, he asks God to deliver him from them on the basis of God's covenant faithfulness, his love:

> Help me, LORD my God; save me according to your unfailing
> love. (Ps 109:26)

For God's people, his love is better than life itself. Psalm 63:3–5 paints a vivid picture for us:

Because your love is better than life,
    my lips will glorify you.
I will praise you as long as I live,
    and in your name I will lift up my hands.
I will be fully satisfied as with the richest of foods;
    with singing lips my mouth will praise you.

God's love is wonderful. It begets love in response:

Praise be to the LORD,
    for he showed me the wonders of his love
    when I was in a city under siege.
In my alarm I said,
    "I am cut off from your sight!"
Yet you heard my cry for mercy
    when I called to you for help.
Love the LORD, all his faithful people!
    The LORD preserves those who are true to him,
    but the proud he pays back in full. (Ps 31:21–23)

Indeed, God's love is beyond description:

Your love, LORD, reaches to the heavens,
    your faithfulness to the skies. (Ps 36:5)
You, Lord, are forgiving and good,
    abounding in love to all who call to you. (Ps 86:5)

God's love is gracious:

The LORD is compassionate and gracious,
    slow to anger, abounding in love.
He will not always accuse,
    nor will he harbour his anger forever;
he does not treat us as our sins deserve
    or repay us according to our iniquities.
For as high as the heavens are above the earth,
    so great is his love for those who fear him;
as far as the east is from the west,
    so far has he removed our transgressions from us.
As a father has compassion on his children,
    so the LORD has compassion on those who fear him;
for he knows how we are formed,

he remembers that we are dust. (Ps 103:8–14)

God's love endures forever, as Psalm 136 reminds us twenty-six times. Moreover, God's love is rightly called "unfailing":

> But I trust in your unfailing love;
>> my heart rejoices in your salvation. (Ps 13:5)

His love is permanent. We can count on it, as Ethan the Ezrahite sings:

> I will sing of the Lord's great love forever;
>> with my mouth I will make your faithfulness known
>> through all generations.
> I will declare that your love stands firm forever,
>> that you have established your faithfulness in heaven itself.
> (Ps 89:1–2)

Because God's unfailing love rests on his unchanging character and is suffused with his mercy, we can hope in him:

> Israel, put your hope in the Lord,
>> for with the Lord is unfailing love
>> and with him is full redemption. (Ps 130:7)

Father, thank you for your sacrificial and perfect love for me. You created me to know you and to experience that love. I rejoice that you enabled me to see you as you are, the lover of my soul. Amen.

Our Response of Faith and Love

Day 35

The fool says in his heart, "There is no God." They are corrupt,
their deeds are vile; there is no one who does good. (Ps 14:1)

We Acknowledge God's Reality

It is now time to think more about our response to God's love. As you start
this second section of meditations on our relationship with God, I encourage
you to reread the introduction on page 1 to refresh your memory of our
shared goal.

At a very basic level, it is logical that we respond to God with faith:

And without faith it is impossible to please God, because anyone
who comes to him must believe that he exists and that he rewards
those who earnestly seek him. (Heb 11:6)

We can't please God if we doubt his existence! The facts of the gospel
have to be true or we are in serious trouble as believers and as preachers. Paul
goes to the heart of this concern in 1 Corinthians 15, his famous chapter on
the resurrection:

But if it is preached that Christ has been raised from the dead,
how can some of you say that there is no resurrection of the
dead? If there is no resurrection of the dead, then not even Christ
has been raised. And if Christ has not been raised, our preaching
is useless and so is your faith. More than that, we are then found
to be false witnesses about God, for we have testified about God
that he raised Christ from the dead. But he did not raise him
if in fact the dead are not raised. For if the dead are not raised,
then Christ has not been raised either. And if Christ has not been
raised, your faith is futile; you are still in your sins. Then those
also who have fallen asleep in Christ are lost. If only for this life

we have hope in Christ, we are of all people most to be pitied. (15:12–19)

The argument is straightforward. Paul and all Christian preachers preached that Christ was raised from the dead. If, in fact, resurrection from the dead is not a reality, then several things follow. Christ is not risen. Our preaching is empty and useless. Our listeners' faith is equally empty, and they, like us, are still in sin. Those Christians who have died are lost, and clearly have no hope of resurrection. Hearers and preachers are the most pitiful people, for we preach and believe something that has no basis in reality. We as preachers are false witnesses about God, since we testify in our preaching that God raised Jesus from the dead, which of course he could not have done if, as a matter of principle, the dead are not raised.

Notice that there is not the slightest hint here that faith is a mental principle, a matter of perspective, some sort of auto-suggestion, a mind-set that helps us cope with daily life. Paul is talking of external, objective, verifiable reality. His claim is that the message he (and we) preach corresponds to that reality. If it does not, all the dire consequences mentioned come into play. So faith is never pictured as creating reality, only as acknowledging reality as it is and has been revealed by God. Saving faith involves more than this, but never less.

Thank you gracious Lord that true faith rests on unshakeable and unchangeable reality, that from everlasting to everlasting, you are God. Thank you that because I know you, I live in the real world. Amen.

Day 36

May your unfailing love come to me, LORD, your salvation, according to your promise; then I can answer anyone who taunts me, for I trust in your word. (Ps 119:41–42)

We Trust in God's Word

Because we do not create reality but rather acknowledge the reality that God has revealed, our faith in God is inseparable from faith in God's word. Twice in Psalm 56 David juxtaposes his trust in God with his trust in God's word. Read verses 3–11 and notice especially the beginning and end of the quotation:

When I am afraid, I put my trust in you.
    In God, whose word I praise – in God I trust and am not afraid.
    What can mere mortals do to me?
All day long they twist my words;
    all their schemes are for my ruin.
They conspire, they lurk,
    they watch my steps,
    hoping to take my life.
Because of their wickedness do not let them escape;
    in your anger, God, bring the nations down.
Record my misery;
    list my tears on your scroll –
    are they not in your record?
Then my enemies will turn back
    when I call for help.
    By this I will know that God is for me.
In God, whose word I praise,
    in the LORD, whose word I praise –
in God I trust and am not afraid.
    What can man do to me?

The repetitions and their placement here are significant. Some might decry this praising of God's word as the sort of Bible worship they expect from evangelicals. But David exalts God's word because God himself exalts it, as David says in Psalm 138:2, "I will bow down towards your holy temple and give thanks to your name for your steadfast love and your faithfulness, for you have exalted above all things your name and your word" (ESV).

There is no way God's word will not reflect God's integrity. God means what he says. The role God's word plays in our lives is intensely personal. We know God by his direct action in our lives, but we recognize that those actions are his only because he has revealed his nature and ways to us in his word. Otherwise, we would not understand that what happens to us comes from his hand. Trust in God and trust in his word are inseparable because God's speech is the means God uses to reveal that he is trustworthy. If God lies – something Titus 1:2 says he is incapable of doing – he denies himself, something equally impossible (2 Tim 2:13).

Thank you, Father, for your sure and certain word. Its truth, power, balance, wisdom, and clarity make it more than worthy of every minute I spend seeking to plumb its depths. Renew my hunger for it and enable me to meet you in its pages today. Amen.

Day 37

> What good is it, my brothers and sisters, if someone claims to
> have faith but has no deeds? Can such faith save them? Suppose
> a brother or a sister is without clothes and daily food. If one of
> you says to them, "Go in peace; keep warm and well fed," but does
> nothing about their physical needs, what good is it? In the same
> way, faith by itself, if it is not accompanied by action, is dead. (Jas
> 2:14–17)

We Demonstrate Our Trust

When we recall that our goal is not merely intellectual assent to God's reality but a growing relationship, the word *trust* better suits what we are discussing. As preachers, we have to preach in faith, trusting God to be and do all he has revealed and claimed.

2 Chronicles 20 describes a time when Jehoshaphat king of Judah faced a vast army of traditional enemies. Hearing that this invading force was approaching, Jehoshaphat, though alarmed, inquired of the Lord, proclaimed a fast and gathered his people to seek the Lord. His prayer reveals refreshing humility, candour and faith:

> "LORD, the God of our ancestors, are you not the God who is in
> heaven? You rule over all the kingdoms of the nations. Power and
> might are in your hand, and no one can withstand you. Our God,
> did you not drive out the inhabitants of this land before your
> people Israel and give it forever to the descendants of Abraham
> your friend? They have lived in it and have built in it a sanctuary
> for your Name, saying, 'If calamity comes upon us, whether the
> sword of judgment, or plague or famine, we will stand in your
> presence before this temple that bears your Name and will cry
> out to you in our distress, and you will hear us and save us.'
>
> "But now here are men from Ammon, Moab and Mount
> Seir, whose territory you would not allow Israel to invade when
> they came from Egypt; so they turned away from them and did

not destroy them. See how they are repaying us by coming to drive us out of the possession you gave us as an inheritance. Our God, will you not judge them? For we have no power to face this vast army that is attacking us. We do not know what to do, but our eyes are on you." (20:6b–12)

The people stood before the Lord. God answered through Jahaziel, a Levite:

He said: "Listen, King Jehoshaphat and all who live in Judah and Jerusalem! This is what the LORD says to you: 'Do not be afraid or discouraged because of this vast army. For the battle is not yours, but God's . . . You will not have to fight this battle. Take up your positions; stand firm and see the deliverance the LORD will give you, Judah and Jerusalem. Do not be afraid; do not be discouraged. Go out to face them tomorrow, and the LORD will be with you.'" (20:15, 17)

Faith did not mean inaction; it meant the very opposite – obedience. Notice Jehoshaphat's response:

Jehoshaphat bowed down with his face to the ground, and all the people of Judah and Jerusalem fell down in worship before the Lord. Then some Levites from the Kohathites and Korahites stood up and praised the Lord, the God of Israel, with a very loud voice.

Early in the morning they left for the Desert of Tekoa. (2:18–20a)

Jehoshaphat's instructions are especially important in light of our focus:

Listen to me, Judah and people of Jerusalem! Have faith in the LORD your God and you will be upheld; have faith in his prophets and you will be successful. (20:20b)

Notice that the king invites faith in God *and in God's prophets*! The parallelism that so often characterizes writing in Hebrew seems to be in use here. Faith in God and faith in his prophets go hand in hand because God speaks through his prophets. When we speak for God – as we do as preachers – the very faith of our listeners necessitates faith in us because God charged us to speak for him.

The Israelites had little choice but to trust the prophets because God's speech through them was more or less exclusive. The people did not have direct access to God's written word. In our case, faithful parishioners can read for themselves what God has spoken when their preachers are not faithful transmitters of biblical truth. Nevertheless, the principle stands. When we trust God, he reveals himself to us for the benefit of others who trust in us.

Father, it is such a weighty thing to know that those to whom we preach trust us to be faithful to your word. It would be unbearable to think that we misled them or compromised their faith by our faithlessness. May I so study and so preach that I faithfully re-speak your word and so that my listeners' trust in me as preacher is always warranted. Amen.

Day 38

> Moses answered the people, "Do not be afraid. Stand firm and you will see the deliverance the LORD will bring you today. The Egyptians you see today you will never see again. The LORD will fight for you; you need only to be still." (Exod 14:13–14)

We Rest in God's Sufficiency

When facing a vast army of enemies, Jehoshaphat, though king of Judah, did not use his authority to lord it over the people. God had spoken. The people had responded well. Jehoshaphat had exhorted them to faith and had promised success. With all this, he still consults the people before appointing the "choral attack force!" The rest, as they say, is history.

> After consulting the people, Jehoshaphat appointed men to sing to the LORD and to praise him for the splendour of his holiness as they went out at the head of the army, saying:
>
>> "Give thanks to the LORD,
>>   for his love endures forever."
>
> As they began to sing and praise, the LORD set ambushes against the men of Ammon and Moab and Mount Seir who were invading Judah, and they were defeated. The Ammonites and Moabites rose up against the men from Mount Seir to destroy and annihilate them. After they finished slaughtering the men from Seir, they helped to destroy one another.

When the men of Judah came to the place that overlooks the desert and looked towards the vast army, they saw only dead bodies lying on the ground; no one had escaped. So Jehoshaphat and his men went to carry off their plunder, and they found among them a great amount of equipment and clothing and also articles of value – more than they could take away. There was so much plunder that it took three days to collect it. On the fourth day they assembled in the Valley of Berakah, where they praised the LORD. This is why it is called the Valley of Berakah to this day. (2 Chr 20:21–26)

Despite the centuries and settings that separate us from the original participants in this story, the lesson is that our faith must always rest in God's complete sufficiency. The reason many of us do not preach as if everything depended upon God's voice being heard in the assembly is that we don't really believe it. In our unbelief, we look for other means of meeting the needs of the church and our preaching inevitably suffers.

Our lack of faith translates into neglect. Why put hours into understanding and preaching a text of Scripture when we are just conveying some ideas that may be better than others, but are helpful only insofar as they help people adjust their consciousness or correct their thinking? We tell ourselves there are other ways to move people to give, recruit them to serve, help them to cope. Why not use those strategies? But the corollary of God's complete sufficiency is our insufficiency to do what God really wants done. We can do all sorts of things, but we cannot give life to the spiritually dead; we cannot turn sinners into saints; we cannot grow the body of Christ. Astonishingly, God has committed himself to do these things through us who preach, but he is the one who acts, as the story of Jehoshaphat underscores.

Lord, I believe; help my unbelief. Help me to trust you enough to wait upon you to open my eyes to see you in your word. Then help me to trust you to show me how to word your word for the listeners to whom you have called me to speak on your behalf. Amen.

Day 39

Hear me, my people, and I will warn you – if you would only listen to me, Israel! You shall have no foreign god among you; you shall

not worship any god other than me. I am the LORD your God, who
brought you up out of Egypt. Open wide your mouth and I will fill
it. But my people would not listen to me; Israel would not submit
to me. So I gave them over to their stubborn hearts to follow their
own devices. If my people would only listen to me, if Israel would
only follow my ways, how quickly I would subdue their enemies
and turn my hand against their foes! Those who hate the LORD
would cringe before him, and their punishment would last forever.
But you would be fed with the finest of wheat; with honey from the
rock I would satisfy you. (Ps 81:8–16)

We Listen to God's Word

Power in preaching comes not from any technique but from faithfulness,
speaking words that are authoritative because they faithfully present God's
thinking, actions, ways and intentions. Reliance upon something other than
God is not a new problem. Isaiah addressed this misplaced dependence:

> Woe to those who go down to Egypt for help,
>   who rely on horses,
> who trust in the multitude of their chariots
>   and in the great strength of their horsemen,
> but do not look to the Holy One of Israel,
>   or seek help from the Lord.
> Yet he too is wise and can bring disaster;
>   he does not take back his words.
> He will rise up against that wicked nation,
>   against those who help evildoers.
> But the Egyptians are mere mortals and not God;
>   their horses are flesh and not spirit.
> When the LORD stretches out his hand,
>   those who help will stumble,
> those who are helped will fall;
>   all will perish together. (31:1–3)

The arm of flesh will fail us, but we may not recognize that it is failing us
until it is too late. The problem is not that we preach and obey nothing when
we refuse to hear God's word, but that we preach and obey other words –

counterfeit words. In Jeremiah's day, the Lord had to rebuke his people for failing to listen to his word. Jeremiah 6:16–19 is a representative sample:

This is what the LORD says:

> "Stand at the crossroads and look;
>> ask for the ancient paths,
> ask where the good way is, and walk in it,
>> and you will find rest for your souls.
>> But you said, 'We will not walk in it.'
> I appointed watchmen over you and said,
>> 'Listen to the sound of the trumpet!'
>> But you said, 'We will not listen.'
> Therefore hear, you nations;
>> you who are witnesses,
>> observe what will happen to them.
> Hear, you earth:
>> I am bringing disaster on this people,
>> the fruit of their schemes,
> because they have not listened to my words
>> and have rejected my law."

Father, grant me ears to hear your word. Amen.

Day 40

Now the serpent was more crafty than any of the wild animals the LORD God had made. He said to the woman, "Did God really say, 'You must not eat from any tree in the garden'?" The woman said to the serpent, "We may eat fruit from the trees in the garden, but God did say, 'You must not eat fruit from the tree that is in the middle of the garden, and you must not touch it, or you will die.'" "You will not certainly die," the serpent said to the woman. (Gen 3:1–4)

We Avoid Distorting God's Word

Judah's rebellion as reflected in yesterday's reading from Jeremiah, was rooted in failure to listen. But the problem was not that simple. Read what the Lord instructs Jeremiah to say to the people of Judah:

> This is what the LORD Almighty, the God of Israel, says: Reform your ways and your actions, and I will let you live in this place. *Do not trust in deceptive words* and say, "This is the temple of the Lord, the temple of the Lord, the temple of the Lord!" If you really change your ways and your actions and deal with each other justly, if you do not oppress the foreigner, the fatherless or the widow and do not shed innocent blood in this place, and if you do not follow other gods to your own harm, then I will let you live in this place, in the land I gave your ancestors for ever and ever. But look, *you are trusting in deceptive words that are worthless.*
>
> Will you steal and murder, commit adultery and perjury, burn incense to Baal and follow other gods you have not known, and then come and stand before me in this house, which bears my Name, and say, "We are safe" – safe to do all these detestable things? Has this house, which bears my Name, become a den of robbers to you? But I have been watching! declares the LORD. (Jer 7:3–11)

God's people cloaked their idolatry and wicked behaviour with worthless words, religious slogans, and probably even affirmations of their salvation. Where did these deceptive words come from? We need not look far. Read Jeremiah's continued proclamation:

> Even the stork in the sky
>   knows her appointed seasons . . .
> But my people do not know
>   the requirements of the Lord.
> How can you say, "We are wise,
>   for we have the law of the LORD,"
> when actually *the lying pen of the scribes
>   has handled it falsely?* . . .
> Since [the wise] have rejected the word of the LORD,
>   what kind of wisdom do they have? . . .
> From the least to the greatest,

all are greedy for gain;
prophets and priests alike,
all practice deceit.
They dress the wound of my people
as though it were not serious.
"Peace, peace," they say,
when there is no peace. (8:7–11)

The people's failure to know what the Lord requires was the direct result of the way the scribes mishandled his word. Their lying pens distorted the message – perhaps the very words – so that the people rejected the word of the Lord, possibly without realizing the gravity of their offence. They thought of themselves as religious, and so they were, but their religion was not faith in the living God.

The scribes' failure of faithfulness produced a failure of faith in their listeners. Priests and prophets were therefore deceivers and deceived, painting the national catastrophe in rosy colours. There is surely a word of warning here for those of us who train others for ministry, who handle Scripture "professionally." If our pens lie, those we train will lie too, and the results will be disastrous in the churches they serve.

We may feel uncomfortable recalling that we do everything in the sight of God, but Isaiah warns that those who act as if God is blind become blind to his word and deaf to his voice (ch. 29). God's watchful eye provides much-needed accountability.

Fortunately, God *has* spoken and acted, and he does not change. If failure to trust God leads to disaster for preacher and people, resting in him is the secret of healthy, stable fruitfulness. These promises should encourage us as preachers:

Trust in the Lord with all your heart
and lean not on your own understanding;
in all your ways submit to him,
and he will make your paths straight. (Prov 3:5–6)

Those who trust in the Lord are like Mount Zion,
which cannot be shaken but endures forever. (Ps 125:1)

Do not let your hearts be troubled. You believe in God; believe
also in me. (John 14:1)

Paul's wish for his friends in Rome is conditional upon trust in God:

> May the God of hope fill you with all joy and peace *as you trust in him*, so that you may overflow with hope by the power of the Holy Spirit. (Rom 15:13)

This is what God wants for us, too.

Gracious Lord, protect me from the temptation to twist your word, to add to it or subtract from it, to emphasize any part of it in a way that distorts any other part of it. Enable me to believe that you can be trusted completely to say what you mean and mean what you say. Amen.

Day 41

> Dear friends, let us love one another, for love comes from God. Everyone who loves has been born of God and knows God. (1 John 4:7)

We Love God and Others

Moses made it plain that loving God is a fundamental command when he said, "Love the LORD your God with all your heart and with all your soul and with all your strength" (Deut 6:5). The Lord Jesus made these words the first half of his own summary of the entire law when asked which was the greatest commandment:

> "The most important one," answered Jesus, "is this: 'Hear, O Israel: The Lord our God, the Lord is one. Love the Lord your God with all your heart and with all your soul and with all your mind and with all your strength.' The second is this: 'Love your neighbour as yourself.' There is no commandment greater than these." (Mark 12:29–31)

Love for others is not unrelated to our love for God nor our faith to obedience, as the Apostle John reminds us:

> And he has given us this command: Anyone who loves God must also love their brother and sister.
>
> Everyone who believes that Jesus is the Christ is born of God, and everyone who loves the father loves his child as well.

This is how we know that we love the children of God: by loving
God and carrying out his commands. In fact, this is love for God:
to keep his commands. And his commands are not burdensome,
for everyone born of God overcomes the world. This is the
victory that has overcome the world, even our faith. Who is it
that overcomes the world? Only the one who believes that Jesus
is the Son of God. (1 John 4:21–5:5)

Because we believe, we obey. The commands we obey include the
commands to love the Father and his children. The proof of our love for the
Father includes our love for his children.

The command to love both Father and his children is not burdensome
for faith enables us to do it. Faith opens the door to the rebirth that both
demands and enables love for the Son, as Jesus pointed out to those who
claimed God as their Father:

Jesus said to them, "If God were your Father, you would love me,
for I came here from God. I have not come on my own; God sent
me." (John 8:42)

Perhaps this is a good time to do some soul-searching. Imagine Jesus
repeatedly asking you the same question he asked Peter: "Do you love me?"
Imagine Jesus telling you, "Feed my lambs . . . Take care of my sheep . . . Feed
my sheep . . . Follow me!" (John 21:15–19).

Jesus could have asked whether Peter trusted him, was ready to obey
him, or was committed to serving him. Instead, he asked whether Peter loved
him. The proof of Peter's love would not be his profession of love but his
faithfulness in feeding and tending Christ's flock. That faithfulness would
cost Peter his life, but it would glorify God.

Our circumstances and callings are not identical to Peter's, but the
questions the Saviour asks and the instructions he gives still apply. Do you
love Jesus? Verbal assurances that you do are of value only insofar as they
reflect the truth that Christ already knows. If you do love Jesus and you are
called to minister the word of God, then get on with it, even though it costs
you everything.

Lord Jesus, if you kept track of my sin, how could I stand in your presence? You
know my heart. As much as I say I love you, I can only imagine how far short
of the ideal I fall. Thank you that your grace is not merely sufficient but is in
fact abundant. I am counting on that. As I seek to heed your calling on my life

to feed your sheep, please protect me from imagining that I could ever do so without loving the sheep you call me to feed. Amen.

Our Response of Obedience

Day 42

If you love me, keep my commands. (John 14:15)

Whoever has my commands and keeps them is the one who loves me. (John 14:21a)

We Love and Obey

Several texts of Scripture suggest that loving God and obeying him are virtually interchangeable. Deuteronomy 11:1 says, "Love the LORD your God and keep his requirements, his decrees, his laws and his commands always," and verse 22 links them so they function as a single precondition for the Lord's dispossessing the nations in the promised land.

Loving God and obeying him are linked not merely by obedience being an expression of love for God ("this is love for God: to keep his commands" – 1 John 5:3a), but also by God's command that we do both. Consider Joshua's exhortation:

> But be very careful to keep the commandment and the law that Moses the servant of the LORD gave you: to love the LORD your God, to walk in obedience to him, to keep his commands, to hold fast to him and to serve him with all your heart and with all your soul. (Josh 22:5)

In the context, Joshua affirms that some of the tribes have been obedient to Moses and himself, and that God has kept his promise to them. Now Joshua exhorts the people to keep on loving God, walking in his ways, obeying his commands, serving him and clinging to him. All this is to be pursued with their whole being, their whole heart and soul. We may think that commanding someone to love takes the heart out of doing it, but Joshua clearly did not think so (nor did the Apostle John). Take time to memorize verse 5, or failing that, print or write it out and keep it before your eyes. The verse marries duty and relationship in the same way that Jesus does.

Thank you, Jesus, for giving us a concrete definition of love. Amen.

Day 43

Today, if only you would hear his voice, "Do not harden your hearts as you did at Meribah, as you did that day at Massah in the wilderness, where your ancestors tested me; they tried me, though they had seen what I did. For forty years I was angry with that generation; I said, 'They are a people whose hearts go astray, and they have not known my ways.' So I declared on oath in my anger, 'They shall never enter my rest.'" (Ps 95:7b–11)

We Listen and Obey

Time and again, the Bible speaks of listening to God as indistinguishable from obeying him. We who preach have to take special note of this. We want more than merely auditory awareness from those who listen to the word of God as it comes through our lips. We want liberating, blessed, obedient hearing that leads to doing what God requires. So we need to be praying that our hearers will humbly receive the word planted in them. Read these words from James:

Do not merely listen to the word, and so deceive yourselves. Do what it says. Anyone who listens to the word but does not do what it says is like someone who looks at his face in a mirror and, after looking at himself, goes away and immediately forgets what he looks like. But whoever looks intently into the perfect law that gives freedom and continues in it – not forgetting what they have heard but doing it – they will be blessed in what they do. (1:22–25)

The link between hearing and action is clear in Solomon's famous prayer of dedication for the temple (1 Kings 8:23–42), although there God was the one called on to hear and act. Meditate on part of that prayer:

Hear the supplication of your servant and of your people Israel when they pray towards this place. Hear from heaven, your dwelling place, and when you hear, forgive. . . .

When the heavens are shut up and there is no rain because your people have sinned against you, and when they pray towards this place and give praise to your name and turn from their sin because you have afflicted them, then hear from heaven and forgive the sin of your servants, your people Israel. Teach them the right way to live, and send rain on the land you gave your people for an inheritance.

> When famine or plague comes to the land, or blight or mildew, locusts or grasshoppers, or when an enemy besieges them in any of their cities, whatever disaster or disease may come, and when a prayer or plea is made by anyone among your people Israel – being aware of the afflictions of their own hearts, and spreading out their hands towards this temple – then hear from heaven, your dwelling place. Forgive and act; deal with everyone according to all they do, since you know their hearts (for you alone know every human heart), so that they will fear you all the time they live in the land you gave our ancestors. (1 Kgs 8:30, 35–40)

The request that God hear is tantamount to asking that he act (see also Exod 22:23–24; Pss 17:1, 6; 27:7; 28:2; 30:10; 54:2; 140:6). Other verses make evident that for us, too, listening means responding to what is heard:

> If you listen carefully to what he says and do all that I say [literally, "If hearing you hear my voice, and do all I say"], I will be an enemy to your enemies and will oppose those who oppose you. (Exod 23:22)

> But if you will not listen to me and carry out all these commands . . . (Lev 26:14)

Truly hearing God's voice and acknowledging it as such leads to obeying God. When Jesus spoke the words the Father had given him, he wanted fruitful, obedient hearing (Mark 4:9). When John spoke in Jesus' name from Patmos, his refrain echoed Jesus' words: "Whoever has ears, let them hear what the Spirit says to the churches" (Rev 2:7a; see also 2:11, 17, 29; 3:6, 15, 22). Of course, not everyone has ears to hear. But we who preach must have such ears, and we are to heartily and immediately obey God's word.

I hope that a basic part of your daily routine is opening the Bible and inviting the living God to speak to you from it. Let him show you his nature, his ways, your sins and idols, and his ideals for you, for the church and for the world. Sometimes what you read will evoke worship. At other times you may feel a need to confess. Or you may feel a need to dig deeper into Scripture to see what else God is saying to you on a certain subject. Often, when the text describes God's will, you will simply begin to take steps of obedience.

Lord, protect me from stubborn, hard-heartedness that rebels against you and your word. Make me eager to hear your voice and instant in obedience, for the glory of your Name. Amen.

Day 44

> Teach me, LORD, the way of your decrees, that I may follow it to
> the end. Give me understanding, so that I may keep your law and
> obey it with all my heart. (Ps 119:33–34)

We Learn as We Obey

Obedience is often the fruit of hearing and the precondition for further learning
and growth. Recall what Jesus said to resistant Jews in the temple courts:

> Not until halfway through the Festival did Jesus go up to the
> temple courts and begin to teach. The Jews there were amazed
> and asked, "How did this man get such learning without having
> been taught?"
>
> Jesus answered, "My teaching is not my own. It comes from
> the one who sent me. *Anyone who chooses to do the will of God
> will find out whether my teaching comes from God or whether I
> speak on my own.* Whoever speaks on their own does so to gain
> personal glory, but he who seeks the glory of the one who sent
> him is a man of truth; there is nothing false about him. Has not
> Moses given you the law? Yet not one of you keeps the law. Why
> are you trying to kill me?" (John 7:14–19)

Verse 17 (which I italicized) states the principle: If anyone is willing to do
God's will, he or she will recognize God's truth. Jesus' detractors illustrate this
truth negatively. They failed to keep the law of Moses and, consequently, were
unable to recognize Jesus as the Messiah; indeed they even sought to kill him.
Jesus illustrates the truth positively. Instead of speaking "on his own" (and
thereby gaining honour only for himself), Jesus seeks the honour of the one
who sent him (the Father) and thereby reveals himself to be a man of truth.
He is able to receive truth from God and to accurately proclaim it. Others
who submit to God's word will recognize his true teaching for what it is and
accept the messenger who brings it.

Colossians 1:9–14 states the same principle: obedience to what we already
know from God enables further learning and more obedience. Paul loved to
report his prayers to express his gratitude to God and teach the churches
what was closest to his heart. Not only does God answer such prayers, but the
prayers reveal how God works.

For this reason, since the day we heard about you, we have not stopped praying for you. We continually ask God to fill you with the knowledge of his will through all the wisdom and understanding that the Spirit gives, so that you may live a life worthy of the Lord and please him in every way: bearing fruit in every good work, growing in the knowledge of God, being strengthened with all power according to his glorious might so that you may have great endurance and patience, and giving joyful thanks to the Father, who has qualified you to share in the inheritance of his holy people in the kingdom of light. For he has rescued us from the dominion of darkness and brought us into the kingdom of the Son he loves, in whom we have redemption, the forgiveness of sins. (Col 1:9–14)

Underneath all God-honouring obedience is the saving work of Christ (v. 13). His work bears fruit (such as the faith, hope and love that Paul thanks God for in Colossians 1:3–4). That visible evidence of God's work emboldens Paul to keep asking God to grant his readers true knowledge of God's will, knowledge that is inseparable from wisdom and spiritual insight.

People with these characteristics are able (in answer to prayer) to walk worthily of the Lord and to please him in every way in all kinds of good works. In this obedience, they bear fruit and experience the ability to joyfully and patiently endure, and they are grateful to God for his work in their lives. At the same time, they grow in their knowledge of God.

As preachers, because we handle the word of God every day and preach it every week, we face the real danger that we may cease to take it seriously and to listen for God's voice thundering or reassuring us. Once we develop the habit of opening the word professionally, keeping it at arm's length, we increasingly lose our capacity to hear it.

When we are not hearing God's voice ourselves, it becomes much more difficult to help others hear it. The remedy? One option is to preach fewer times each week, letting others share the load. Another is to use additional required preaching times to build on aspects of a single, main preaching text for the week. Or, we can take shorter texts that allow us to spend more time thinking through what obedience will mean rather than spending the bulk of our time covering the content of the text. But more to the point, we should ask God, who knows our situations and responsibilities, to help us to take his word seriously each time we open it, and to respond in faith and obedience to what it says.

Today the psalmist's words from Psalm 119:97–104 are my prayer:

*"Oh, how I love your law! I meditate on it all day long. Your commands
are always with me and make me wiser than my enemies. I have more
insight than all my teachers, for I meditate on your statutes. I have more
understanding than the elders, for I obey your precepts. I have kept my feet
from every evil path so that I might obey your word. I have not departed from
your laws, for you yourself have taught me. How sweet are your words to
my taste, sweeter than honey to my mouth! I gain understanding from your
precepts; therefore I hate every wrong path."*

Day 45

> You are my portion, LORD; I have promised to obey your words.
> I have sought your face with all my heart; be gracious to me
> according to your promise. I have considered my ways and have
> turned my steps to your statutes. I will hasten and not delay to
> obey your commands. Though the wicked bind me with ropes, I
> will not forget your law. At midnight I rise to give you thanks for
> your righteous laws. I am a friend to all who fear you, to all who
> follow your precepts. The earth is filled with your love, LORD; teach
> me your decrees. (Ps 119:57–64)

We Encounter God as We Obey

Having and keeping God's commands shows our love for God, but also opens
the door to a more intimate relationship with him. John 14:15–21 captures
the essence of obedience as a response to God's love:

> If you love me, keep my commands. And I will ask the Father,
> and he will give you another advocate to help you and be with
> you forever – the Spirit of truth. The world cannot accept him,
> because it neither sees him nor knows him. But you know him,
> for he lives with you and will be in you. I will not leave you as
> orphans; I will come to you. Before long, the world will not see
> me anymore, but you will see me. Because I live, you also will
> live. On that day you will realize that I am in my Father, and you

are in me, and I am in you. Whoever has my commands and keeps them is the one who loves me. The one who loves me will be loved by my Father, and I too will love them and show myself to them.

The Eleven who heard these words the night before Jesus was crucified had no real grasp of what was about to happen. Within hours, the situation would become far worse than they could imagine, and within days, things would be far better than they could ever have hoped for. What they needed to know was that love calls for obedience, and obedience is the precondition for a growing relationship with God. Notice that all three persons of the Trinity minister to those who show their love for Christ by obeying his commands (v. 21). The Son asks the Father to send the Spirit of truth – and he does (vv. 16–17). The Son promises to come to the Eleven – and he does. Because the Son lives, the disciples live (vv. 18–19). He mutually indwells the Father and us, and his Spirit helps us understand that concept (v. 20). The Father loves us as does the Son, who shows himself to us (v. 21).

Our relationship with God is not something to take for granted or treat as a relationship with our peers. Rather, it is an astonishing gift that should continue to amaze and thrill us!

Father, please remind me whenever I need it that if you who love me ask me to do things that are for your glory and my good, I must not imagine that it makes no difference to you if I disregard your directives. Give me a delight in doing your will that propels me to obedience, especially when the enemy of my soul is feeding me lies about the benefits of sin. I ask it that your Name may be honoured. Amen.

Our Response of Service

In the same way, count yourselves dead to sin but alive to God in
Christ Jesus. Therefore do not let sin reign in your mortal body so
that you obey its evil desires. Do not offer any part of yourself to
sin as an instrument of wickedness, but rather offer yourselves to
God as those who have been brought from death to life; and offer
every part of yourself to him as an instrument of righteousness.
For sin shall no longer be your master, because you are not under
the law, but under grace. (Rom 6:11–14)

We Serve with All We Are

Serving God is not the private domain of full-time pastors. It is the heartfelt
reflex of all those who grasp who God is and what he has done. A magnificent
passage in Romans makes this clear, although the chapter divisions sometimes
cause us to miss the connection:

> Oh, the depth of the riches of the wisdom and knowledge of God!
>   How unsearchable his judgments, and his paths beyond
>   tracing out!
> "Who has known the mind of the Lord?
>   Or who has been his counsellor?"
> "Who has ever given to God,
>   that God should repay them?"
> For from him and through him and for him are all things.
>   To him be the glory forever! Amen.

Therefore, I urge you, brothers and sisters, in view of God's
mercy, to offer your bodies as a living sacrifice, holy and pleasing
to God – this is your true and proper worship. Do not conform to
the pattern of this world, but be transformed by the renewing of

your mind. Then you will be able to test and approve what God's will is – his good, pleasing and perfect will. (Rom 11:33–12:2)

When we see the glories of the gospel (Rom 1–11), the appropriate, immediate response is verbal praise like that of the doxology in 11:33–36. But our response was never meant to stop there. Having expressed our praise with our lips, we are now urged to do so with our whole bodies, including our minds. This is our reasonable service, our appropriate worship.

Christ has been sacrificed for us. The sacrifice we now bring makes no atonement. Yet this living sacrifice of our whole selves – body and mind – is the only reasonable response to Christ's sacrificial purchase of us. We are no longer our own; we are his. Having been bought with a price, we glorify God with our bodies as his servants.

Lord, I am filled with wonder when I contemplate the fact that I can become an acceptable sacrifice to you! Thank you for declaring me not guilty and sanctifying me. I consecrate myself to you – my thoughts, my emotions, my attitudes, my eyes, hands, feet and every other part of me from head to toe. Take me and use me for your purposes and glory. Amen.

Day 47

Therefore if you have any encouragement from being united with Christ, if any comfort from his love, if any common sharing in the Spirit, if any tenderness and compassion, then make my joy complete by being like-minded, having the same love, being one in spirit and of one mind. Do nothing out of selfish ambition or vain conceit. Rather, in humility value others above yourselves, not looking to your own interests but each of you to the interests of the others. In your relationships with one another, have the same mind-set as Christ Jesus. (Phil 2:1–5)

We Serve Humbly

Jesus Christ is our Saviour, and our preaching flows from our identity "in Christ" (2 Cor 2:17; 12:19). Our message does not spring from what we have done but from what Christ has done for us on the cross and from what he does for us now in heaven. Thus we should not enter the pulpit relying on the extent of our sanctification or the quality of our training, and we should never contemplate inviting someone to follow Jesus based on our spiritual track record. Paradoxically, our weakness is our boast.

Besides being our Saviour, Jesus Christ is also our example. He manifested God's love towards us by coming to serve us. His disciples needed to learn this.

> Then James and John, the sons of Zebedee, came to him. "Teacher," they said, "we want you to do for us whatever we ask."
>
> "What do you want me to do for you?" he asked.
>
> They replied, "Let one of us sit at your right and the other at your left in your glory."
>
> "You don't know what you are asking," Jesus said. "Can you drink the cup I drink or be baptized with the baptism I am baptized with?"
>
> "We can," they answered.
>
> Jesus said to them, "You will drink the cup I drink and be baptized with the baptism I am baptized with, but to sit at my right or left is not for me to grant. These places belong to those for whom they have been prepared."
>
> When the ten heard about this, they became indignant with James and John. Jesus called them together and said, "You know that those who are regarded as rulers of the Gentiles lord it over them, and their high officials exercise authority over them. Not so with you. Instead, whoever wants to become great among you must be your servant, and whoever wants to be first must be slave of all. For *even the Son of Man did not come to be served, but to serve*, and to give his life as a ransom for many." (Mark 10:35–45)

The criterion of greatness in the kingdom and the church is sacrificial service. The standard is Jesus himself. Both those who seek privilege and recognition and those who become indignant when others do so need to learn from Jesus.

One lesson in this regard was not sufficient, so Jesus also provided an object lesson:

> The evening meal was in progress, and the devil had already prompted Judas, the son of Simon Iscariot, to betray Jesus. Jesus knew that the Father had put all things under his power, and that he had come from God and was returning to God; so he got up from the meal, took off his outer clothing, and wrapped a towel

around his waist. After that, he poured water into a basin and began to wash his disciples' feet, drying them with the towel that was wrapped around him.

He came to Simon Peter, who said to him, "Lord, are you going to wash my feet?"

Jesus replied, "You do not realize now what I am doing, but later you will understand."

"No," said Peter, "you shall never wash my feet."

Jesus answered, "Unless I wash you, you have no part with me."

"Then, Lord," Simon Peter replied, "not just my feet but my hands and my head as well!"

Jesus answered, "Those who have had a bath need only to wash their feet; their whole body is clean. And you are clean, though not every one of you." For he knew who was going to betray him, and that was why he said not every one was clean.

When he had finished washing their feet, he put on his clothes and returned to his place. "Do you understand what I have done for you?" he asked them. "You call me 'Teacher' and 'Lord,' and rightly so, for that is what I am. Now that I, your Lord and Teacher, have washed your feet, you also should wash one another's feet. I have set you an example that you should do as I have done for you. Very truly I tell you, no servant is greater than his master, nor is a messenger greater than the one who sent him. Now that you know these things, you will be blessed if you do them." (John 13:2–17)

Our commission to preach does not license us to domineer or lord it over others. Instead, it makes each of us a servant of the body, the church. It humbles us rather than elevates us.

Father, thank you for Jesus who had every reason in heaven and on earth to insist on his rights and rank, but humbled himself and became not merely a man, but also a servant; and not only a servant, but an obedient servant; and not only an obedient servant, but an obedient-to-death servant; and not only an obedient-to-death servant, but an obedient-to-death-on-the-cross sort of servant. Please keep working to make me like him. Amen.

Day 48

This, then, is how you ought to regard us: as servants of Christ and as those entrusted with the mysteries God has revealed. (1 Cor 4:1)

We Serve as Slaves

Servants of God serve those the Master calls them to serve. Colossians 1:24–25 captures the dynamic of this relationship:

> Now I rejoice in what I am suffering for you, and I fill up in my flesh what is still lacking in regard to Christ's afflictions, for the sake of his body, which is the church. I have become its servant by the commission God gave me to present to you the word of God in its fullness.

We serve the church and the world because we are commissioned servants of God. We have this position not because of any decision we made, but because Christ has bought us. Paul did not hesitate to describe himself as a servant or slave of Christ (Rom 1:1; Titus 1:1), and insisted that this lowly position was something he had been given (1 Cor 3:5; 1 Tim 1:12; Acts 20:24; 2 Cor 5:18). He encouraged the church to think of him and his fellow ministers "as servants of Christ and as those entrusted with the mysteries God has revealed" (1 Cor 4:1).

Significantly, Luke uses the Greek word for "servant" in his record of Paul's account of his conversion and call:

> Then I asked, "Who are you, Lord?"
> "I am Jesus, whom you are persecuting," the Lord replied. "Now get up and stand on your feet. I have appeared to you to appoint you as *a servant* and as a witness of what you have seen and will see of me." (Acts 26:15–16)

Paul saw himself as Jesus saw him. That was his identity from that day on.

Being a servant entails following Jesus, not just calling ourselves by the name he gives us:

> Whoever serves me must follow me; and where I am, my servant also will be. My Father will honour the one who serves me. (John 12:26)

In context, following Jesus means following Jesus to the cross. As always in the New Testament, suffering is the way to glory and the Father honours those who serve Jesus.

Serving Jesus also entails accountability. In Luke 12:35–48 Jesus lays out two scenarios involving servants and masters. In the first, the master returns from a wedding banquet to find his servants watching and ready. He then dons the clothing of a slave and serves them! In the second, a servant is given responsibility for feeding the other servants. If the master returns to find that servant doing as directed, the master will reward him with a promotion and greater responsibility. If, however, the servant has used his position of power to oppress his fellow servants and indulge his passions, then the master's surprise return will unleash severe punishment.

Being a servant of Jesus thus has consequences for our behaviour. Paul lays down that, "the Lord's servant must not be quarrelsome but must be kind to everyone, able to teach, not resentful" (2 Tim 2:24). But avoiding quarrelling is only one quality of many that are required:

> Rather, as servants of God we commend ourselves in every way: in great endurance; in troubles, hardships and distresses; in beatings, imprisonments and riots; in hard work, sleepless nights and hunger; in purity, understanding, patience and kindness; in the Holy Spirit and in sincere love; in truthful speech and in the power of God; with weapons of righteousness in the right hand and in the left; through glory and dishonour, bad report and good report; genuine, yet regarded as impostors; known, yet regarded as unknown; dying, and yet we live on; beaten, and yet not killed; sorrowful, yet always rejoicing; poor, yet making many rich; having nothing, and yet possessing everything. (2 Cor 6:4–10)

No wonder Paul could say he served God with a clear conscience (2 Tim 1:3).

Finally, being a servant of God is not just a matter of duties and responsibilities. We have already noted the promise of honour (John 12:26) and of opportunity for greater service. Servanthood also brings the blessing of fellowship, as when Paul calls Epaphras his fellow servant (Col 1:7). And there is comfort in the knowledge that the Master looks after his servants, as Paul's testimony in Acts 27:23 reflects: "Last night an angel of the God to whom I belong and whom I serve stood beside me." This support is not merely, or even necessarily, physical. What the early church asked God to provide was spiritual support: "Now, Lord, consider their threats and enable your servants to speak your word with great boldness" (Acts 4:29).

Father, candidly there are days when I wish words in the English language did not lose earlier meanings. I was ordained to the gospel ministry. A minister is supposed to be a servant but that term seems to have lost that meaning. Now it can refer to a position of privilege, even of power. Help me to so feed on your word that when our words lose their meaning, I will notice it and embrace my calling as you define it and not as my culture does. I ask this in Jesus' Name, Amen.

Day 49

> For I am the least of the apostles and do not even deserve to be
> called an apostle, because I persecuted the church of God. But
> by the grace of God I am what I am, and his grace to me was not
> without effect. No, I worked harder than all of them – yet not
> I, but the grace of God that was with me. Whether, then, it is I
> or they, this is what we preach, and this is what you believed.
> (1 Cor 15:9–11)

We Serve by Grace

Seeing ourselves as God's servants provides a clear basis for our own relationships. We see this in the way Paul relates to two groups of believers. One group is able to enjoy freedom in a matter about which there is some dispute, and on which Scripture does not clearly rule. Those in the other group have conscience qualms if they engage in that behaviour. Paul reminds them that they are both servants of God:

> Accept the one who is weak in faith, without quarrelling over
> disputable matters. One person's faith allows them to eat anything,
> but another person, whose faith is weak, eats only vegetables.
> The one who eats everything must not treat with contempt the
> one who does not, and the one who does not eat everything must
> not judge the one who does, for God has accepted them. Who
> are you to judge someone else's servant? To their own master,

servants stand or fall. And they will stand, for the Lord is able to
make them stand. (Rom 14:1–4)

This threefold affirmation of how we relate to our Master is deeply
reassuring. First, in such cases our role is not to judge someone else's servant.
Second, each of us stands before our own Master; our standing is not any
other servant's concern. Third, our Master is able to make us stand, and he
will do so! His grace is sufficient; he has accepted us, and he can make those
he has accepted stand before him.

In the final analysis, we trust not in our capacity to work nor in the
quality of our relationship with God but in Christ's faithfulness to keep us
and present us blameless at his return.

Paul's benedictory prayer for his beloved Thessalonians is my prayer today:

*May God himself, the God of peace, sanctify you through and through. May
your whole spirit, soul and body be kept blameless at the coming of our Lord
Jesus Christ. The one who calls you is faithful, and he will do it. (1 Thess
5:23–24)*

Part Two

Our Relationship with Scripture

The thesis of these meditations is that the neglect of any of three key relationships – with God, with Scripture, with our listeners – will negatively impact our preaching. Or, stated positively, a growing relationship with God, a more biblical attitude towards his word, and a more thoroughly scriptural approach to our listeners will all enhance our preaching. These three relationships are intertwined, but our relationship with God, by definition, takes precedence. That is why we have focused on it for so long. Attend to this relationship and the others will follow. Now, however, it is time to turn our attention to our relationship with Scripture.

"Relationship" may seem like a strange word to use to describe how people interact with a book, more specifically with the sixty-six canonical books of the Old and New Testaments. Yet most preachers are self-confessed bibliophiles, card-carrying lovers of books. The offer of a free book at a pastor's conference can cause a stampede. So we know in principle that a relationship with books is possible. Yet our relationship with the Bible has to be in a category by itself because the Bible claims to be and do far more than any other book.

As in any relationship, knowledge of the other party to the relationship is vital. If our view of the Bible is faulty, we will not interact with it wisely. So in the meditations that follow we will review how the Bible describes itself and consider the explicit or implicit implications of each description. Most of the lessons learned will apply to any Christian; others will apply specifically to us who are called to preach.

There are many texts I could cite, but for this book I will focus on those that have the clearest implications for preaching. There will be some repetition, and I encourage you not to chafe at this. Where Scripture is repetitive, we should dare to be repetitive too! A message is not always heard and received the first time it is stated. Remember, our goal is not to hear new ideas but to let Scripture shape our thinking, and thus our lives and our preaching. Each description, characteristic or metaphor for the Bible contributes to a weight of evidence that I hope and pray will be a useful antidote to our arch-enemy's ancient question: "Did God really say?" (Gen 3:1).

The Basics

Day 50

All Scripture is God-breathed and is useful for teaching, rebuking,
correcting and training in righteousness, so that the servant
of God may be thoroughly equipped for every good work.
(2 Tim 3:16–17)

Our Attitude to Scripture

To set the tone for our interaction with the word, we go first to a key passage
where a biblical writer sings about his relationship with the Bible. Psalm
119 is an acrostic poem with one section for each letter of the Hebrew
alphabet. Each line of every section begins with the section's letter. I suggest
you read the psalm through once without stopping and then read it again
slowly, making three lists: (1) synonyms for the Bible or descriptions of it;
(2) responses to God's word that the psalmist either asks for or claims to have;
and (3) expectations or outcomes relating to what was claimed or requested.
Below is the start of my own list, covering only the first few verses.

Verse	Description/Synonym	Response/Request	Expectation/Outcome
1	law of the LORD	obedience	blessed
2	his statutes	keep, seek God wholeheartedly	blessed
4	precepts	fully obey	
5	decrees	obedience	steadfast ways
6	commands	consider	not put to shame
7	righteous laws	learn	praise with an upright heart
8	decrees	obey, do not forsake	
9	your word	living according to	purity

Now, it is your turn to follow through with verses 10 through 176. When you have completed your review of Psalm 119, count the repetitions in each column to see what is being emphasized. Notice how often the psalmist seeks and expects greater closeness with God. He also expects God to deal with his opponents. Be careful how you apply this as a pastor!

Consider writing your own psalm reflecting your aspirations and expectations concerning God's word. Be honest, but also have faith. Be honest about your current position and request God's intervention and help, as the psalmist did.

What does what you have written tell you about your relationship with the Bible? My own writing on this exercise spurred me to do what the psalmist did – pray.

Lord, my love for your word is not what I want it to be, but it is greater than it was before I fed on this part of your word. Thank you for feeding me on this rich fare. Accept my praise and strengthen my resolve to obey all your precepts. Amen.

Day 51

Jesus performed many other signs in the presence of his disciples, which are not recorded in this book. But these are written that you may believe that Jesus is the Messiah, the Son of God, and that by believing you may have life in his name. (John 20:30–31)

The Purpose of Scripture

The Apostle Paul warned Timothy about terrible times to come, when even some within the church would love self, money and pleasure instead of God (2 Tim 3:1–9). Such people are disciples, that is, learners, but they are not able to come to knowledge of the truth. In fact, they oppose it. The apostolic prescription for leaders faced with this situation is clear. Timothy is to continue in what he has learned because he knows those who taught it to him (Lois, Eunice and Paul), and because he knows Scripture's power to make people wise for salvation through Jesus Christ.

The lives of messengers of the gospel will always either reinforce or undermine the truth we teach. Timothy's teachers authenticated their message by their willingness to suffer persecution for it. Alongside that contemporary validation of the message is the enduring authority of Scripture. Timothy's first-hand experience of the eye-opening power of Scripture was not a fluke. The very source of the Bible dictates its nature, and its nature determines its use:

> All Scripture is God-breathed and is useful for teaching, rebuking, correcting and training in righteousness, so that the servant of God may be thoroughly equipped for every good work. In the presence of God and of Christ Jesus, who will judge the living and the dead, and in view of his appearing and his kingdom, I give you this charge: Preach the word; be prepared in season and out of season; correct, rebuke and encourage – with great patience and careful instruction. (2 Tim 3:16–4:2)

Why did God go to the trouble of breathing out his word? Paul gives four reasons: (1) to teach the church; (2) to rebuke those in it who have gone astray; (3) to correct them; and (4) to train all of us in righteousness. The long-term aim is to thoroughly equip all God's people for every good work. God's ultimate goal, though unstated in these verses, is to receive glory for himself when corporately and individually we reflect his nature to the world and the principalities and powers (Eph 3:10).

The connection with preaching is clear and explicit. When Paul exhorts Timothy to "preach the word," the specific charges that follow correspond directly to the purposes for which Scripture was given by God. Timothy is to correct, rebuke, encourage and patiently instruct. The correspondence of purpose could hardly be greater without repeating all of the same words – and Paul does repeat two of them. Take some time now to evaluate the purposes of your preaching by this standard.

Father, forgive me when I have tried to use Scripture for my purposes in preaching at the expense of your purposes for inspiring it. Help me as I study to preach to submit to the biblical text in every respect, bowing the knee to its content and intent, its truths and its purposes. Amen.

Day 52

> When Paul and his companions had passed through Amphipolis
> and Apollonia, they came to Thessalonica, where there was
> a Jewish synagogue. As was his custom, Paul went into the
> synagogue, and on three Sabbath days he reasoned with them from
> the Scriptures, explaining [literally 'opening'] and proving that
> the Messiah had to suffer and rise from the dead. "This Jesus I am
> proclaiming to you is the Messiah," he said. (Acts 17:1–3)

The Preaching of Scripture

Sadly, there are pastors of evangelical churches who have been biblical preachers for a season but wearied of the task when they did not see immediate results. They now use the Bible as a source book for ideas and stories to promote their own agendas. Young preachers are especially susceptible to this temptation. So was Timothy, which is why Paul needed to address the issue. Paul writes in 2 Timothy 4:3–5:

> For the time will come when people will not put up with sound
> doctrine. Instead, to suit their own desires, they will gather
> around them a great number of teachers to say what their itching
> ears want to hear. They will turn their ears away from the truth
> and turn aside to myths. But you, keep your head in all situations,
> endure hardship, do the work of an evangelist, discharge all the
> duties of your ministry.

When preparing a sermon, a preacher is a fool to disregard the audience. Preachers are, after all, speaking to people, not just spewing words into the air. But the greater danger most face today is not that of neglecting the audience but of exalting them. A so-called reader-centred hermeneutic makes this temptation even more attractive because it puts the listener in charge. The Bible is treated as a prompt to elicit the listener's stories as opposed to an authoritative word from God.

Our task is not to tell our listeners what they want to hear, but what God has said and how that relates to them. We will always have to decide where to start that process (whether, for instance, we describe the problem first and then articulate the biblical answer to it, or present the biblical ideal first, which will draw people towards it). We also need to decide what part of

Scripture should be expounded at this point in time. But our goal must be to be able to look back on our ministries as Paul did and say, "For I have not hesitated to proclaim to you the whole will of God" (Acts 20:27).

We are like our listeners in that we too are tempted to cling to cultural and subcultural myths. When people with itching ears want a preacher who reinforces cherished but flawed beliefs, we usually resonate with them somewhat, for we too are drawn to half-truths and distortions. What could be more comfortable than mutual admiration between a complacent congregation, steeped in faulty ideas, and a preacher who affirms them and their thinking? The best way out of this deadly situation is for preachers to take the lead, keep their heads and keep preaching the word.

We have to let the Bible itself continually reform *our* thinking, challenge *our* worldview, correct *our* subcultural assumptions, and give *us* God's perspective. As this happens, we will be able to teach, convince, rebuke, encourage and exhort our fellow Christians to move in the right direction. I urge you to resolve to let the Bible set the agenda for your preaching because you are convinced that God himself has ordained it – properly understood and proclaimed in the power of the Holy Spirit – as the means of achieving what he wants for his church.

Biblical preaching is not a programme to try for a year or two to see how it works. It is a life-long faith commitment by someone who has become convinced that this is what God wants. Though there are many ministries of the word (including Bible studies, Christian literature and higher education), biblical exposition from the pulpit gives voice to God's written word and models careful handling of the Bible, setting the tone and providing ongoing training for all other ministries of the word in the local church.

I thank you, Father, that by deciding primarily to expound biblical books,
I was freed from many hours of anxiously trying to devise clever preaching
series to make your word more appealing to my listeners. Thank you for the
freedom to simply "open" your word to my listeners. Amen.

Day 53

For the message of the cross is foolishness to those who are
perishing, but to us who are being saved it is the power of God.
(1 Cor 1:18)

The Power of Scripture

Astonishingly, we can expect the word of God to do even more than just what we have seen from Psalm 119 and 2 Timothy 3:16–17. A number of the texts we will be looking at over the next few weeks have implications for the church, and should challenge your aspirations for the church you are called to serve. James 1:17–18 is one such text. It speaks of God using the word of truth to bring about his greatest gift to us – rebirth:

> Every good and perfect gift is from above, coming down from the Father of the heavenly lights, who does not change like shifting shadows. He chose to give us birth through the word of truth, that we might be a kind of firstfruits of all he created.

Second Timothy 3:15 conveys the same idea from a slightly different angle. Paul speaks of the two factors that should help Timothy continue in what he has learned – the people who taught Timothy the word and the power of the word itself:

> [F]rom infancy you have known the Holy Scriptures, which are able to make you wise for salvation through faith in Christ Jesus.

The Scriptures have the ability to make us wise unto salvation. Peter makes the same point when he speaks about the means of the new birth:

> For you have been born again, not of perishable seed, but of imperishable, through the living and enduring word of God. For,
>
> > "All people are like grass,
> >   and all their glory is like the flowers of the field;
> > the grass withers and the flowers fall,
> >   but the word of the Lord endures forever."
>
> And this is the word that was preached to you. (1 Pet 1:23–25)

The preached word has life in itself just like a seed does. But the words of the Bible are not perishable like plant, animal or human seeds, for they are eternal, the words of God. Preaching itself does not cause this life to sprout – the word does – but preaching is the delivery system that impresses the word into the heart.

Consider how the Apostle Paul explains the genesis of faith in Romans 10:12–17:

> For there is no distinction between Jew and Greek; for the same Lord is Lord of all, bestowing his riches on all who call on him.

For "everyone who calls on the name of the Lord will be saved." How then will they call on him in whom they have not believed? And how are they to believe in him of whom they have never heard? And how are they to hear without someone preaching? And how are they to preach unless they are sent? As it is written, "How beautiful are the feet of those who preach the good news!" But they have not all obeyed the gospel. For Isaiah says, "Lord, who has believed what he has heard from us?" So faith comes from hearing, and hearing through the word of Christ. (Rom 10:12–17 ESV)

It is the word of Christ that enables hearing and creates faith. First Corinthians 1:21 reinforces this truth:

For since in the wisdom of God the world through its wisdom did not know him, God was pleased through the foolishness of what was preached to save those who believe.

Once again, it is the preached word that God uses to save. In this passage, Paul deliberately takes on the role of a herald as opposed to that of a persuader.[1] He does this because the message he communicates brings with it the power to save. It does not require a professional orator's skills to make it effective; all that is required is faithful proclamation.

Thank you Lord for the astonishing power of your word, powerful enough to break up the rock of my own soul and make it a soft heart, receptive to more of your word. Amen.

---

1. Duane Litfin, "Swallowing Our Pride: An Essay on the Foolishness of Preaching" in *Preach the Word: Essays on Expository Preaching in Honour of R. Kent Hughes* (ed. Leland Ryken and Todd Wilson; Wheaton, IL: Crossway, 2007), 106–126.

Our Calling

> Therefore, I declare to you today that I am innocent of the blood of
> any of you. For I have not hesitated to proclaim to you the whole
> will of God. (Acts 20:26–27)

Proclaim All of God's Word

Early in the life of the church, the angel of the Lord delivered the apostles
from the common prison in Jerusalem and commissioned them to go back
to the temple and speak literally "all the words of this life." We read about this
in Acts 5:17–20:

> Then the high priest and all his associates, who were members
> of the party of the Sadducees, were filled with jealousy. They
> arrested the apostles and put them in the public jail. But during
> the night an angel of the Lord opened the doors of the jail and
> brought them out. "Go, stand in the temple courts," he said, "and
> tell the people all about this new life."

The implication is that preaching the bare minimum message required
to be reborn is not enough. The people need to learn "*all* about this new life."
Church leaders should attend to that need, proclaiming all the words that
God has given.

Colossians 1:24–25 makes it plain that this proclamation involves more
than just words:

> Now I rejoice in what I am suffering for you, and I fill up in my
> flesh what is still lacking in regard to Christ's afflictions, for the
> sake of his body, which is the church. I have become its servant
> by the commission God gave me to present to you the word of
> God in its fullness.

Paul saw himself as the servant of the church by the commission of God.
His specific assignment was, literally, "to fill out the word of God." He did this

by living a life that reflected the cross, giving immediate, tangible expression to a life transformed by that word. Paul also filled out the word of God by continuing to expound the mystery of Christ in us, the hope of glory. That is, he obeyed his commission, as verses 28–29 go on to say:

> He is the one we proclaim, admonishing and teaching everyone with all wisdom, so that we may present everyone fully mature in Christ. To this end I strenuously contend with all the energy Christ so powerfully works in me.

Thank you Father for the sheer comprehensiveness of your gospel. Because you love the whole world, you sent your only son that whoever believes in him should not perish but have eternal life. You inspired the whole of your word, both testaments and every word, so that none should be lost but that all might come to repentance. Make me more faithful in mining the riches of every word of it that I may do my part to faithfully preach every part of the message to every creature under heaven. Amen.

Day 55

> The Levites – Jeshua, Bani, Sherebiah, Jamin, Akkub, Shabbethai, Hodiah, Maaseiah, Kelita, Azariah, Jozabad, Hanan and Pelaiah – instructed the people in the Law while the people were standing there. They read from the Book of the Law of God, making it clear and giving the meaning so that the people understood what was being read. (Neh 8:7–8)

Explain God's Word

Paul's ministry to fill out the word of God is inevitably a ministry of making things plain, of clarifying God's purposes. In Ephesians 3:7–9, Paul elaborates on his calling:

> I became a servant of this gospel by the gift of God's grace given me through the working of his power. Although I am less than the least of all the Lord's people, this grace was given me: to preach to the Gentiles the boundless riches of Christ, and to make plain to

everyone the administration of this mystery, which for ages past was kept hidden in God, who created all things.

Notice that Paul sees himself as a servant of the church, as we saw in Colossians 1:25, and a servant of the gospel. We serve the gospel when we make the story of God's salvation plain, not merely to those we like or who we think like us, but *to everyone*. What God has revealed, we are to bring to light so that everyone can see it. Every text we preach sheds some light on God's plan and purpose for calling the nations to the obedience of faith. Our joyful duty is to let the text we expound do what it was placed in the Bible to do.

The first Christian preachers had Jesus himself as their model of how to preach "the unsearchable riches of Christ" from the Bible:

> And beginning with Moses and all the Prophets, he *explained* to them what was said in all the Scriptures concerning himself. (Luke 24:27)

> They asked each other, "Were not our hearts burning within us while he talked with us on the road and *opened the Scriptures* to us?" (Luke 24:32)

> Then he *opened their minds* so they could *understand* the Scriptures. (Luke 24:45)

Christ's dual opening – the opening of the Scriptures and the opening of their minds to understand the Scriptures – is what we prayerfully seek every time we preach. But prayer does not absolve us from our responsibility to explain until minds understand and hearts burn.

Gracious Lord, grant me open eyes to see the truths of your word as you mean them to be seen, that not only may my own mind understand and my own heart burn, but that other minds may be opened and other flames kindled when I preach. Amen.

Day 56

So I will always remind you of these things, even though you know them and are firmly established in the truth you now have. I think it is right to refresh your memory as long as I live in the tent of this body, because I know that I will soon put it aside, as our Lord Jesus

Christ has made clear to me. And I will make every effort to see that after my departure you will always be able to remember these things. (2 Pet 1:12–15)

Remind People of God's Word

Sometimes the Bible's ministry of supplementing what we have been taught exists primarily to remind us to obey the word, for by obeying we open ourselves to further insight. The Thessalonians who responded to the gospel were an early example of the success and power of God's word. Their case also reminds us that very early in the building up of the body of Christ the ethical implications of the gospel were stressed. Paul instructed the Thessalonians how to live even though he and his companions were in Thessalonica for less than a month. When it became evident that they needed to be reminded of what they had been taught and given, Paul did not hesitate. As you read his words to them, notice the tense of the verbs in italics:

> As for other matters, brothers and sisters, *we instructed you* how to live in order to please God, as in fact you are living. Now we ask you and urge you in the Lord Jesus to do this more and more. For *you know what instructions we gave you* by the authority of the Lord Jesus.
>
> It is God's will that you should be sanctified: that you should avoid sexual immorality; that each of you should learn to control your own body in a way that is holy and honourable, not in passionate lust like the pagans, who do not know God; and that in this matter no one should wrong or take advantage of a brother or sister. The Lord will punish all those who commit such sins, *as we told you and warned you before*. For God did not call us to be impure, but to live a holy life. Therefore, anyone who rejects this instruction does not reject a human being but God, the very God who gives you his Holy Spirit.
>
> Now about your love for one another we do not need to write to you, *for you yourselves have been taught by God* to love each other. And in fact, you do love all of God's family throughout Macedonia. Yet *we urge you*, brothers and sisters, to do so more and more. (1 Thess 4:1–10)

The apostolic team preached and instructed by the authority of the Lord Jesus. The living God himself taught their listeners through their words and carried on the ministry after the team had left, for the word of God went to work in them (1 Thess 2:13). Now the Thessalonians are not to reject this instruction (for to do so is to reject God). Their duty is to grow in obedience and live so as to please God "more and more."

Your preaching, and mine, may on occasion feel painfully repetitive. It will probably also sound redundant to our listeners unless we keep our aim in mind. But we should use repetition when necessary to secure growing obedience. Our emphasis should be on the *intent* of the passage, as well as the *content*. We should constantly ask ourselves, "Why is this truth in the Bible?" When we answer this question, we have licence to re-speak the truth for purposes that align with the answer.

Father, thank you for reminding me of things about you and things about your ways and things about myself that I too easily forget. Keep it up, in your mercies, lest I forget them. Amen.

Day 57

Sanctify them by the truth; your word is truth. (John 17:17)

What, after all, is Apollos? And what is Paul? Only servants, through whom you came to believe – as the Lord has assigned to each his task. I planted the seed, Apollos watered it, but God has been making it grow. So neither the one who plants nor the one who waters is anything, but only God, who makes things grow. The one who plants and the one who waters have one purpose, and they will each be rewarded according to their own labour. (1 Cor 3:5–8)

Allow God's Word to Work in Believers

The experience of the Thessalonians demonstrates a truth that Paul makes explicit:

[W]hen you received the word of God, which you heard from us, you accepted it not as a human word, but as it actually is, the word of God, which is indeed at work in you who believe. (1 Thess 2:13)

The truth is that the word of God goes to work in those who believe because it is living and active (Heb 4:12). This fact is wonderfully liberating for the preacher. In preaching, as indeed in much of church life, the temptation is to "make things happen." We design programmes with this purpose in mind. If our purpose is to put people in a position to hear the word and grow in faith and obedience, we do well. But if our aim is lower or something other than that, we may be cluttering people's lives and wasting our efforts. God himself is at work by his word in those who believe it and trust him to use it. Our task is to respond by faith in joyful obedience to what he has revealed and to expect further knowledge, faith and obedience to follow.

When we preach in faith that this can happen, it relieves some of the pressure for immediate results. We don't expect immediate results any more than vegetable gardeners expect to eat carrots the day they plant the carrot seeds. We want lasting fruit, which is the true evidence that the seed was planted and went to work in those who believed and continue to believe. The relaxed preacher prays and preaches Scripture, and in so doing conveys a hope that God will complete what he has begun (Phil 1:6).

Gracious Lord, grant me faith to believe that if I faithfully proclaim your word, it will go to work in those who believe. Like a seed with life in it, let me be content to plant and water it and watch you give the increase. Amen.

The Work of God's Word

So then, brothers and sisters, stand firm and hold fast to the
teachings we passed on to you, whether by word of mouth or by
letter. (2 Thess 2:15)

God's Word Establishes Believers

When Paul said farewell to the Ephesian elders, he entrusted them to God
and God's word:

> Now I commit you to God and to the word of his grace, which
> can build you up and give you an inheritance among all those
> who are sanctified. (Acts 20:32)

The word of God has power to achieve God's purposes by building us
up and giving us an inheritance among those who are sanctified. God's word
and his work go together. Notice, too, that the word of God is described as
the "word of his grace." When we preach, our messages will always be a word
of God's grace, even if what we are communicating is a rebuke or warning. As
preachers, we do God's bidding when we let his word expose sin so that it may
be recognized as sin and mourned over and repented of in joyful expectation
of receiving grace and mercy.

Notice also that the gift of our inheritance is granted in the company of
others who like us are sanctified (and, we might add, are being sanctified).
Preaching always looks for the corporate dimension of the text, whether
stated or implied. Romans 16:25–27 is a doxology that ties together many
themes of Romans:

> Now to Him who is able to establish you according to my gospel
> and *the preaching of Jesus Christ*, according to the revelation of the
> mystery which has been kept secret for long ages past, but now
> is manifested, and by the Scriptures of the prophets, according
> to the commandment of the eternal God, has been made known

to all the nations, leading to obedience of faith; to the only wise God, through Jesus Christ, be the glory forever. Amen. (NASB)

Notice that the gospel and "the preaching of Christ" are nearly synonymous and that they are known through the prophetic writings – the Bible Paul preached. By means of this preached message, now revealed to Gentiles as well as Jews, God himself not only saves Christians but also establishes them. We need to keep preaching the gospel to ourselves and our fellow believers. Then the churches we serve will be solidly grounded, firmly established, and God will be glorified.

What a blessing it is, Lord, to be established, to be able to stand firm and not be blown around by every wind of doctrine. Help me enable others to experience this blessing by actively establishing them by the preaching of your holy word. Amen.

Day 59

So Christ himself gave the apostles, the prophets, the evangelists, the pastors and teachers, to equip his people for works of service, so that the body of Christ may be built up until we all reach unity in the faith and in the knowledge of the Son of God and become mature, attaining to the whole measure of the fullness of Christ. (Eph 4:11–13)

God's Word Equips Believers

God's word thoroughly equips Christians "for every good work" (2 Tim 3:16–17). The writer to the Hebrews gives us a sample of what should be our foundational teaching of the word and an indication of how we know our listeners are ready to build on that foundation:

We have much to say about this, but it is hard to make it clear to you because you no longer try to understand. In fact, though by this time you ought to be teachers, you need someone to teach you the elementary truths of God's word all over again. You need milk, not solid food! Anyone who lives on milk, being still an infant, is not acquainted with the teaching about righteousness.

But solid food is for the mature, who by constant use have trained
themselves to distinguish good from evil.

Therefore let us move beyond the elementary teachings
about Christ and be taken forward to maturity, not laying again
the foundation of repentance from acts that lead to death, and
of faith in God, instruction about cleansing rites, the laying on
of hands, the resurrection of the dead, and eternal judgment.
(Heb 5:11–6:2)

The basic teachings about Christ and righteousness include such things
as repentance, faith, cleansing rites (baptisms?), the laying on of hands
(commissioning for service?), the resurrection (Christ's and ours?) and
eternal judgment. When these teachings have been consistently appropriated
and there is evidence of a capacity for ethical discernment, our listeners are
ready to move towards maturity, no longer feeding on the milk of the word
but on more solid food.

As we have already seen, the Bible was given to us to be believed and obeyed.
When we fail to obey the Bible, we are not able to hear more of it. Therefore,
whenever we expound Scripture, we should aim not just for understanding
but for the obedience of faith that enables further understanding, which
grows faith and further God-glorifying obedience. My own relationship with
the Bible is dependent upon this dynamic and so is yours and that of our
listeners. So, don't skip the basics, but build on them. Let the word of God
establish your listeners as discerning followers of Jesus.

*Thank you, Lord, for those who came alongside me to equip me for ministry
and especially for those who did the extra work of equipping me to equip
others. Thank you that I have the privilege of having that ministry with
others. Amen.*

Day 60

Keep your lives free from the love of money and be content with
what you have, because God has said, "Never will I leave you;
never will I forsake you." So we say with confidence, "The Lord is
my helper; I will not be afraid. What can mere mortals do to me?"
(Heb 13:5–6)

God's Word Teaches Us about Himself

That God's word teaches God's nature and ways is a truism, but it is still worth saying. Sometimes his nature will be stated explicitly, as in Psalm 46:1 which straightforwardly declares: "God is our refuge and strength, an ever-present help in trouble." More often, the biblical text is equally unambiguous, but God's attribute is only mentioned in passing, as in this passage from Paul's letter to Titus:

> Paul, a servant of God and an apostle of Jesus Christ to further
> the faith of God's elect and their knowledge of the truth that
> leads to godliness – in the hope of eternal life, which *God, who
> does not lie*, promised before the beginning of time, and which
> now at his appointed season he has brought to light through the
> preaching entrusted to me by the command of God our Saviour.
> (Titus 1:1–3)

This little section says much more about God than that he does not lie. The careful expositor will look for such statements and also for valid inferences about his nature and ways. For instance, in this passage we notice that God calls and equips servants (1:1); he makes and keeps promises (1:2); he is eternal (1:2); he works according to a plan that has a timetable (1:3); he entrusts the task of preaching to his servants (1:3); and he chooses people to be saved (1:1). We could mention even more.

Because the Bible is God's gracious self-disclosure and through it we gain knowledge of him, it makes sense to ask him to show us what he wants us to learn or remember about himself from each passage we preach.

*So, Lord, please help me read and study every text of your word theologically.
Open my eyes to see wonderful things about you yourself. Amen.*

Day 61

> Jesus answered, "Those who have had a bath need only to wash
> their feet; their whole body is clean. And you are clean, though not
> every one of you." (John 13:10)

God's Word Cleanses Us

In Ephesians 5:22–33, Paul uses the marriage relationship as an analogy for the relationship between Christ and the church:

> Wives, submit yourselves to your own husbands as you do to the Lord. For the husband is the head of the wife as Christ is the head of the church, his body, of which he is the Saviour. Now as the church submits to Christ, so also wives should submit to their husbands in everything.
>
> Husbands, love your wives, just as Christ loved the church and gave himself up for her to make her holy, *cleansing her by the washing with water through the word*, and to present her to himself as a radiant church, without stain or wrinkle or any other blemish, but holy and blameless. In this same way, husbands ought to love their wives as their own bodies. He who loves his wife loves himself. After all, no one ever hated their own body, but they feed and care for their body just as Christ does the church – for we are members of his body. "For this reason a man will leave his father and mother and be united to his wife, and the two will become one flesh." This is a profound mystery – but I am talking about Christ and the church. However, each one of you also must love his wife as he loves himself, and the wife must respect her husband.

In his instructions to husbands (5:25–27), Paul reminds them that Christ's love for his bride, the church, was manifested by his giving himself up for her. This self-giving was purposeful – to make the church holy, to sanctify her. Christ achieved this by "cleansing her by the washing with water through the word." The aim of that cleansing was to present her – perfect – to himself.

If we take this washing as referring primarily to our baptism as the outward sign of what Christ did in our regeneration, then our cleansing has already happened and it sets us apart (sanctifies us) for Christ. But since the aim of that cleansing is something that remains in the future, namely our perfecting, it does not seem to be too much to expect that the word may continue to do for us day by day what it did for us at the outset.

Notice the italicized words from John 15:1–8 that link the role of Christ's word in our initial cleansing with our responsibility to abide in him:

> I am the true vine, and my Father is the gardener. He cuts off every branch in me that bears no fruit, while every branch that

does bear fruit he prunes so that it will be even more fruitful. *You are already clean because of the word I have spoken to you.* Remain in me, as I also remain in you. No branch can bear fruit by itself; it must remain in the vine. Neither can you bear fruit unless you remain in me.

I am the vine; you are the branches. If you remain in me and I in you, you will bear much fruit; apart from me you can do nothing. If you do not remain in me, you are like a branch that is thrown away and withers; such branches are picked up, thrown into the fire and burned. *If you remain in me and my words remain in you*, ask whatever you wish, and it will be done for you. This is to my Father's glory, that you bear much fruit, showing yourselves to be my disciples.

Discipleship involves no less than letting Christ's cleansing words remain in us. We rest in the forgiveness, the cleansing we have already experienced by his word. However, this rest is not a sign of complacency but of faith, a faith that enables us to abide in Christ and makes us eager to have his sanctifying word dwell in us (John 17:17). When it does, we will ask for what his word commends and turn away from what his word condemns. Or, to put this cleansing function in terms of 2 Timothy 3:16–17, the word will convict and rebuke us for sin, from which we will turn, and show us the correct way, which we will embrace. We all need this washing of our feet despite having had the "bath" of regeneration (John 13:10).

Thank you, Lord, for forgiving me and for cleansing me from all unrighteousness when I confess my sins. Thank you for designing your word to show me what sins I need to confess. Amen.

The Nature of the Bible

Do not add to what I command you and do not subtract from it,
but keep the commands of the LORD your God that I give you.
(Deut 4:2)

The Bible Is Necessary and Sufficient

The texts we have reviewed so far have told us a few of the things the Bible does because it is the word of God. The implication is that God has not supplied another means of achieving these aims in our lives individually and corporately. To put this in other words, Scripture is necessary and sufficient. Read Psalm 19:7–11.

> The law of the LORD is perfect,
> > refreshing the soul.
> The statutes of the LORD are trustworthy,
> > making wise the simple.
> The precepts of the LORD are right,
> > giving joy to the heart.
> The commands of the LORD are radiant,
> > giving light to the eyes.
> The fear of the LORD is pure,
> > enduring forever.
> The decrees of the LORD are sure,
> > and all of them are righteous.
> They are more precious than gold,
> > than much pure gold;
> they are sweeter than honey,
> > than honey from the honeycomb.
> By them your servant is warned;
> > in keeping them there is great reward.

It is because of what God's word is (perfect, trustworthy, right, radiant, sure and altogether righteous, more precious than much pure gold, sweeter than honey) that it can do what God created it to do (revive the soul, make the simple wise, give joy to the heart and light to the eyes, warn God's servants and give great reward to those that keep it). And because the Bible is God's means of achieving these things (2 Tim 3:16–17), we need not look elsewhere to experience these blessings. Indeed, we must not look elsewhere, at least in the sense that we must not add to what he has said any more than we would subtract from it. Of course we look to God, but in doing so we trust the means he has given to achieve his purposes.

The Bible is clear that it does not need to be supplemented. Moses says this upon sending the Israelites into the promised land, where the danger of syncretism was acute:

> Now, Israel, hear the decrees and laws I am about to teach you. Follow them so that you may live and may go in and take possession of the land that the LORD, the God of your ancestors, is giving you. Do not add to what I command you and do not subtract from it, but keep the commands of the LORD your God that I give you. (Deut 4:1–2)

> The LORD your God will cut off before you the nations you are about to invade and dispossess. But when you have driven them out and settled in their land, and after they have been destroyed before you, be careful not to be ensnared by inquiring about their gods, saying, "How do these nations serve their gods? We will do the same." You must not worship the LORD your God in their way, because in worshipping their gods, they do all kinds of detestable things the LORD hates. They even burn their sons and daughters in the fire as sacrifices to their gods.
>
> See that you do all I command you; do not add to it or take away from it. (Deut 12:29–32)

Notice that God's word must neither be supplemented nor abridged. But it must be implemented; it must be obeyed. Agur gave similar counsel in Proverbs:

> Every word of God is flawless;
>   he is a shield to those who take refuge in him.
> Do not add to his words,
>   or he will rebuke you and prove you a liar. (30:5–6)

Any addition to Scripture is functionally a subtraction from Scripture, for to add to what God has given us implies that what he has given is not enough. Paul's aspiration, as told to the Ephesian elders, was "to finish the race and complete the task the Lord Jesus has given me – the task of testifying to the good news of God's grace" (Acts 20:24). As he looked back on his ministry among the Ephesians, Paul felt vindicated because his intention "to proclaim the whole will of God" (Acts 20:27) matched God's provision in Scripture.

I hope this aspiration and example shape your goals for ministry. When you and I review our teaching ministries to date, we should each see a good-faith effort to proclaim the whole will of God. There should be no glaring omissions or painful examples of topics we have too frequently addressed. Proclaiming the whole of God's word presupposes a love-relationship with it that moves us to eagerly submit to it daily and learn from its every page. We will keep track of where we have been in our personal reading to make sure that whatever plan we follow, the whole book is read periodically.

Lord, please protect me from so favouring parts of your word that I functionally dismiss other parts. Keep me from adding my own ideas as an overlay with the result that in practice I am adding to your word. As always, I need your help to get this right since I am often blind to my own biases. Amen.

Day 63

For we do not write you anything you cannot read or understand.
(2 Cor 1:13a)

The Bible Can Be Understood

The sufficiency of Scripture does not mean merely that the Bible covers all the topics Christians need to know about or merely that the Bible exhorts us to obey, gives us sufficient examples to follow, provides supernatural power to live the Christian life, and ultimately points us to the all-sufficient God. It also means that the Bible is sufficiently clear to be understood. The Westminster Divines put this truth well:

All things in Scripture are not alike plain in themselves, nor alike clear unto all (2 Pet 3:16); yet those things which are necessary to be known, believed, and observed, for salvation, are so clearly propounded and opened in some place of Scripture or other, that not only the learned, but the unlearned, in a due use of ordinary means, may attain unto a sufficient understanding of them (Ps 119:105, 130).[1]

The Bible explains itself well enough that even when other resources such as commentaries, Bible dictionaries, and books on theology are not available, we can understand it well enough to trust God and obey him and well enough to make his word plain to others. This is not to say that we should neglect such secondary sources any more than carpenters can work without their tools, but we should remember that these tools are secondary and should be treated as such.

Our assignment is to become thoroughly versed in the Bible. The more we study the entire Bible, the clearer it becomes. Our memories will never take the place of a good concordance, but the more we fill our minds with biblical content, the less dependent we will be on such tools. Clear passages will shed light on less clear ones. Straightforward teaching passages will illuminate less obvious lessons in narratives. More literal texts will provide a safety net under our interpretations of poetic, prophetic and apocalyptic passages.

If you have an abundance of books and access to high quality materials on the World Wide Web, thank God for the gifts he has given to the church and use them humbly and discerningly as if the gifted people who wrote or compiled them were teaching you in person. If your access is limited or non-existent, don't let that handicap you. You are part of a fellowship of faithful preachers who have served the church through much of its history. We must not glory in ignorance, but neither do we let it enslave us as long as we have access to the Scriptures themselves.

Thank you Lord for making your word plain enough and clear enough that I can understand it if and when I am willing to read it carefully and prayerfully. Help me today to see what each text I read is saying and doing. Amen.

---

1. Robert Shaw, *An Exposition of the Westminster Confession of Faith* (Fearn, Scotland: Christian Heritage, 1998), chap. 1, sec. 7.

Day 64

> But we have this treasure in jars of clay to show that this all-
> surpassing power is from God and not from us. (2 Cor 4:7)

The Bible Is a Storehouse of Treasure

After having offered and explained several parables of the kingdom (as recorded in Matt 13:1–50), Jesus asks a question and gives an instructive generalization in verses 51 and 52.

> "Have you understood all these things?" Jesus asked.
> "Yes," they replied.
> He said to them, "Therefore every teacher of the law who has become a disciple in the kingdom of heaven is like the owner of a house who brings out of his storeroom new treasures as well as old."

Understanding brings responsibility. When we become "teachers of the law," literally, scribes discipled in the kingdom of heaven, we should think of ourselves as stewards, yet as more than stewards. Stewards serve others with what is not their own but has only been entrusted to them. That is true of us (1 Cor 4:1–5; 9:17; Eph 3:8). But Jesus' words here put us in the category of the home owner, the master of the house who draws out of his treasure things new and old.

It would be unwise to over-interpret the distinction between steward and owner, but given the context and the disciples' profession of understanding, the idea seems to be that when we grasp something from Scripture, that truth becomes ours in the sense that it is available now to be brought out of the storehouse for the benefit of others. We have stored some treasures more recently and others a long time ago; both kinds of treasure need to be brought out.

The natural questions for us who preach are "Am I letting myself be discipled in the kingdom?" and "Is the Bible shaping my thinking so that some truths are 'sticking' and are therefore available for the benefit of others?" God himself is a rich store of salvation, wisdom and knowledge. The fear of him is the key to this treasure, as Isaiah 33:6 reminds us. Nevertheless, God's wisdom and knowledge have been written down for our benefit (1 Cor 10:11).

Once we value the treasure as our own, we need not fear losing it by proclaiming it. Indeed, few strategies for securing an idea surpass attempting to teach it. If you approach Bible study with the eagerness of a diamond miner or gold prospector, seeking to fill your mind with its treasures, you will never lack riches to distribute. Teaching the Bible is not merely a matter of distributing gems, much less of casting pearls! It is both the privilege and the responsibility of the instructed.

Father, please give me the key to the storehouse today. Help me live in the fear of yourself and treat your holy word with the reverence it deserves, submitting to its teaching because I bow the knee to you. Amen.

Day 65

> Hilkiah the high priest said to Shaphan the secretary, "I have found the Book of the Law in the temple of the Lord." He gave it to Shaphan, who read it. Then Shaphan the secretary went to the king and reported to him: "Your officials have paid out the money that was in the temple of the Lord and have entrusted it to the workers and supervisors at the temple." Then Shaphan the secretary informed the king, "Hilkiah the priest has given me a book." And Shaphan read from it in the presence of the king. When the king heard the words of the Book of the Law, he tore his robes. He gave these orders to Hilkiah the priest, Ahikam son of Shaphan, Akbor son of Micaiah, Shaphan the secretary and Asaiah the king's attendant: "Go and inquire of the Lord for me and for the people and for all Judah about what is written in this book that has been found. Great is the Lord's anger that burns against us because those who have gone before us have not obeyed the words of this book; they have not acted in accordance with all that is written there concerning us." (2 Kgs 22:8–13)

The Bible Is God's Mirror

James was eager that the scattered Christians to whom he wrote would benefit from the Bible. He expected the Bible to be God's means of granting rebirth by the Spirit's working (Jas 1:18), which meant receiving the word humbly, repenting of all moral filth and evil (1:19–21), and looking into the word of truth as one looks into a mirror:

> Do not merely listen to the word, and so deceive yourselves. Do what it says. Anyone who listens to the word but does not do what it says is like someone who looks at his face in a mirror and, after looking at himself, goes away and immediately forgets what he looks like. But whoever looks intently into the perfect law that gives freedom, and continues in it – not forgetting what they have heard, but doing it – they will be blessed in what they do. (Jas 1:22–25)

James begins by citing an example of what he does *not* encourage. The person who hears the word but does not obey it is like someone who looks in a mirror and instead of combing her unkempt hair or shaving his stubbly face walks away and forgets that some repair work was called for!

The Bible, as we have seen from 2 Timothy 3:16–17, shows us what needs correcting. Every time we read the Bible and every time we preach it faithfully, we hold up before ourselves and our listeners a remarkable mirror. Instead of merely reflecting the externals that anyone can see, the Bible reveals those things about us that God can see, and they do not make a pretty picture: remnants of the works of the flesh, footholds of the devil, flirtations with the world, even hypocrisy and idols. When we disregard these insights and move away from the mirror to get on with daily life, we are not treating the Bible according to its God-given nature.

In verse 25, James describes how we *should* relate to the Bible. Because it is perfect and gives freedom, we have nothing to lose and everything to gain by stooping down to take a closer look at what it reveals. It will not only reveal what needs correction but will show us the way of repentance, obedience and blessing. Instead of forgetting what the Bible says to us, we should keep it in mind, and by doing so walk in obedience as those who know they walk by faith in God's grace.

When I preach, I often hold my Bible up before the congregation with its open pages facing them. I tell my listeners it is God's mirror, perfectly designed to help them see themselves as God does. Then I invite them to be hearers who remember and continue in the Bible's instruction and so expect by faith to be blessed in their obedience.

Many contemporary listeners confuse disciplined gospel obedience with legalism. They wrongly think that if they seriously resolve to do what God has commanded, they are somehow relying on their works for salvation. We may need to explain that good works are very much a part of our response to God – not as the basis of our relationship with him but as the fruit and evidence of it.

A related misconception is that good works follow automatically, without any effort on the part of the believer. But that is not the case. Recall Paul's words in Philippians 2:12–13:

> Therefore, my dear friends, as you have always obeyed – not only in my presence, but now much more in my absence – continue to work out your salvation with fear and trembling, for it is God who works in you to will and to act in order to fulfil his good purpose.

It is because God is at work in us by his Spirit that we are able to obey, but the command to obey stands as one that is to be, well, obeyed! Naturally, we cannot expect others to take the commands of Scripture seriously if we are not doing so ourselves. We who preach do our listeners a great service by reinforcing the reality of our faith by doing what the Bible asks. Consistent obedience matters.

Thank you, Lord, for helping me see myself as you see me. Grant me repentance from thinking of myself more highly than I ought to think or discounting the progress your Spirit has already made in my life. Thank you that no matter how much necessary renovation the mirror reveals, there is ample grace and mercy to accomplish it. Amen.

Day 66

> And I will give you shepherds after my own heart, who will feed you with knowledge and understanding. (Jer 3:15 ESV)

The Bible Is the Bread of Life

In John 6, Jesus describes himself using the metaphor of bread. He is indeed the bread of life who comes from heaven and gives life to the world (John 6:33). Nothing I am about to say is meant to detract from that truth. Nevertheless, the word of God is described using the same metaphor by the biblical writers and Jesus himself. When Satan tempted Jesus to turn stones into bread, the Lord Jesus responded by citing Deuteronomy 8:3:

> Jesus answered, "It is written: 'Man shall not live on bread alone,
> but on every word that comes from the mouth of God.'" (Matt 4:4)

While Jesus is the Word of God par excellence (Heb 1:1–4), the word of God in Scripture is also a source of life-giving nourishment. I hope you noticed the eating imagery in Psalm 119:103:

> How sweet are your words to my taste,
> sweeter than honey to my mouth!

Those who have been reborn have an appetite for the delicious, sustaining sweetness of God's words. Psalm 19 uses the same image and spells out what these words can mean to us who feed upon them:

> They are more precious than gold,
> than much pure gold;
> they are sweeter than honey,
> than honey from the honeycomb.
> By them your servant is warned;
> in keeping them there is great reward. (19:10–11)

The word we have been given is wonderfully sweet and active when we respond to it with faith (Heb 4:2). Then we won't resist its warnings but welcome them as we do the words of a good friend who cares enough to speak frankly about some shortcoming in our life. We don't discount the word's promises but act in faith in order to experience them.

Our privilege and duty as preachers is first to model a healthy, appreciative appetite for Scripture, taking it in hungrily, heeding its warnings and believing its promises, and secondly, to help our listeners feed upon that word. We are responsible for helping our listeners get beyond a buffet mentality when it comes to feeding on the Bible. We may be tempted to survey the beautiful array of rich fare and choose what we like, perhaps that with which we are familiar, and leave the rest. But selectivity when it comes to the Bible is disobedience. We must feed on and live by *every* word that proceeds from the mouth of God. Neither we nor our listeners are free to disregard any text of Scripture, even those whose original application has been made obsolete by the coming of Christ.

Preachers are stewards of the bread of life (think waiters in a restaurant). Our task is to spread a fresh and attractive meal before our listeners. We don't add to what is served or take away from it. Presentation – what the food looks like – matters, as does its freshness. If your sermons feel stale and outdated, don't be surprised if your listeners show no enthusiasm for the meal you set before them.

Freshness and relevance are the reasons I recommend you don't recycle tired illustrations from books or Web sources. This practice has a surprisingly long history, and no doubt some stories will always get a reaction. Nevertheless, it is better to use the illustrations of others only as a spur to encourage you to find your own word pictures and examples. Draw your examples from your listeners' circumstances, not from times and places as foreign to them as the world of the Bible itself.

If a story can be verified and truly sheds light on your text, use it, but always attribute it to your source. If it cannot be verified, acknowledge that it may be apocryphal.

God's kitchen has delicious, nourishing fare of the widest possible variety. Your task is not to present the same food at every meal but to draw from the wonderful variety within the canon of Scripture. Even your favourite food would become unappealing if it were the only kind you ever ate! Therefore, make sure your preaching plan includes thoughtful expositions of the gospels and the epistles and poetic, apocalyptic, historical and narrative Scriptures. Draw from the Old Testament and the New. Unpack longer and shorter texts. Be true to the tone of the text so that sometimes your sermons will be affirming and encouraging and at other times searching and challenging.

When those you serve express satisfaction with the meal, make sure you pass the compliments on to the Chef! After all, preaching is letting God's voice be heard in the assembly. When his word nourishes, he should receive the credit.

Lord, please give me an appetite for those parts of your word I now find hard to swallow, if not downright distasteful. Educate my spiritual taste buds to feed on those parts that are an acquired taste, as well as those to which I naturally return, so that I may feed your people a balanced diet. Amen.

Day 67

> For this command is a lamp, this teaching is a light, and correction
> and instruction are the way to life. (Prov 6:23)

The Bible Is a Lamp

The old chorus *Thy Word* has wonderfully impressed Psalm 119:105 on many
of our hearts:

> Your word is a lamp to my feet
>   and a light for my path.

God gave us the Bible to show us the path, the way of obedience. Although
the lamp imagery is not limited to this ethical use, it is primary in Psalm 119
and elsewhere.

Many of us take for granted the blessing of artificial light, but I have stayed
in enough out-of-the-way camps, hotels, conference centres and hostels to
know how dangerous it is to be unable to see where you are going in the
middle of the night in unfamiliar surroundings. We are aliens and strangers
(1 Pet 2:11) living in a dark world (Eph 6:12), but we have been called out of
darkness into light (1 Pet 2:9). We are to walk in the light (1 John 1:7), and it
is the Bible that shows us how to do that. It reveals the next step of obedience
that we are to take.

However, light does us no good if we disregard it. Peter cautions his
readers against inattention.

> We also have the prophetic message as something completely
> reliable, and you will do well to pay attention to it, as to a light
> shining in a dark place, until the day dawns and the morning star
> rises in your hearts. (2 Pet 1:19)

Some preachers don't do justice to the ethical content of the Bible because
of a fear of legalism and a misunderstanding of the place of gospel obedience.
I suspect others of us fail to let the light of Scripture shine on the paths of
our listeners because we don't have a clear understanding of how to use the
legal material in the Old Testament. We fear exalting something that, in the
language of Hebrews 8:13, is obsolete, having been supplanted by the work
of Christ.

Although the distinction between the moral law, the civil law and the
ceremonial law may help here, the distinctions are not always easy to make,

and in any case they run the risk of leading us to completely abandon parts of the Bible. Guided by some Protestant reformers, I find it helpful to expect the law to do three things: reveal the character of God, be a schoolmaster to bring people to Christ, and guide us in obedience. So, for instance, God still hates idolatry. Whenever we see it creeping back into the life of God's people, we should examine ourselves to see if we are guilty of it. Paul's willingness to see greed as a species of idolatry in Colossians 3:5 reflects this handling of the Old Testament.

Every time we preach, we should expect the Bible to expose sin, to bring it to light. Therefore, no matter how positive your text, unpack the sins implied by its descriptions of righteousness. Warnings and rebukes in the text make that easier to do because no inferences are necessary, only contextualization. Then, having given the bad news about sin, help people get back on the path of gospel obedience.

Lord, protect me from being like those who seek darkness and not light because their deeds are evil. Instead, draw me to the light so that when it exposes my sins, I may confess them as sin and repent of them. Amen.

Day 68

> Repent therefore! Otherwise, I will soon come to you and will fight against them with the sword of my mouth. (Rev 2:16)
>
> The rest were killed with the sword coming out of the mouth of the rider on the horse, and all the birds gorged themselves on their flesh. (Rev 19:21)

The Bible Is the Sword of the Spirit

The Bible is not our only weapon in the fight for holiness. The Apostle Paul wants the Ephesians to put on the complete armour of God (Eph 6:11, 13, 14). We can't go out to preach in an unprotected state and expect to prevail.

The necessity of using every piece of this armour is reinforced by Paul's reference to all three persons of the Trinity: we are to be strong in the Lord, put on the whole armour of God, wield the sword of the Spirit, and pray in the Spirit.

Because the Father has exalted the Son to his right hand and has given us the Spirit, we are in a heavenly position as we confront our spiritual adversaries. Each piece of armour is God's, and we withstand attacks by virtue of our position in Christ and being indwelt by the Spirit. Read how Paul develops his case:

> Finally, be strong in the Lord and in his mighty power. Put on the full armour of God, so that you can take your stand against the devil's schemes. For our struggle is not against flesh and blood, but against the rulers, against the authorities, against the powers of this dark world and against the spiritual forces of evil in the heavenly realms. Therefore put on the full armour of God, so that when the day of evil comes, you may be able to stand your ground, and after you have done everything, to stand. Stand firm then, with the belt of truth buckled around your waist, with the breastplate of righteousness in place, and with your feet fitted with the readiness that comes from the gospel of peace. In addition to all this, take up the shield of faith, with which you can extinguish all the flaming arrows of the evil one. Take the helmet of salvation and the sword of the Spirit, which is the word of God.
>
> And pray in the Spirit on all occasions with all kinds of prayers and requests. With this in mind, be alert and always keep on praying for all the Lord's people. (Eph 6:10–18)

Paul's comparison of the word of God to a sword draws on Old Testament imagery like that found in one of the servant songs in Isaiah:

> Listen to me, you islands;
>> hear this, you distant nations:
> Before I was born the LORD called me;
>> from my mother's womb he has spoken my name.
> He made my mouth like a sharpened sword,
>> in the shadow of his hand he hid me;
> he made me into a polished arrow
>> and concealed me in his quiver. (49:1–2)

Israel was God's servant and the Lord Jesus took this role upon himself, filling it to perfection. He came to speak powerfully on behalf of the Father. Our task as preachers is to let his voice be heard when we speak in his name and on his behalf.

But what, specifically, does the sword image add to what we have already discovered about God's word? The answer can be found in Hebrews 4:12, which also speaks of God's word as a sword. The context is a lengthy exhortation to heed God's voice today:

> For the word of God is alive and active. Sharper than any double-edged sword, it penetrates even to dividing soul and spirit, joints and marrow; it judges the thoughts and attitudes of the heart. Nothing in all creation is hidden from God's sight. Everything is uncovered and laid bare before the eyes of him to whom we must give account. (Heb 4:12–13)

Because the word is alive and active, it acts. Because it is sharp, indeed sharper than any "two-mouthed" sword, it penetrates to the deepest recesses of the human mind and personality. Because God knows everything, his word can reveal anything. When we preach with this conviction in mind, we will expect the word itself to unearth what we could not imagine, to reveal what is hidden from us but not from God.

As preachers, we need this scalpel-like ministry of the word in our own lives before we wield it in the lives of others. We need the Bible to show us what needs to be cut out and repented of, and then repair what is defective. This is why devotional reading of the Bible is so critical for us. Until we have gone under the knife ourselves, we have a very limited view of what the passage wants to expose or repair in our listeners. What the text exposes in our hearts can help us preach with greater wisdom, depth and reality. This means we must not begin preparing to preach too late. No Saturday night specials!

When the Bible searches out and exposes our faults, you might think we go into the pulpit feeling disqualified to preach. On the contrary. Accusation and disqualification are the devil's work. The word humbles us, washes us, establishes us and restores to us the joy of our salvation so that we go into the pulpit overflowing with the grace of God, which then spills out on those who listen to us.

Lord, let your sword wound my listeners now that they may repent lest your word of judgment slay them on the last day. And help me lead the way in repentance and faith. Amen.

Day 69

> What, after all, is Apollos? And what is Paul? Only servants,
> through whom you came to believe – as the Lord has assigned to
> each his task. I planted the seed, Apollos watered it, but God has
> been making it grow. So neither the one who plants nor the one
> who waters is anything, but only God, who makes things grow.
> The one who plants and the one who waters have one purpose,
> and they will each be rewarded according to their own labour.
> (1 Cor 3:5–8)

The Bible Is Imperishable Seed

When Peter wanted to encourage scattered Christians to live up to their new status as children of God, he recalled their rebirth and what God used to accomplish it:

> Now that you have purified yourselves by obeying the truth so
> that you have sincere love for each other, love one another deeply,
> from the heart. For you have been born again, not of perishable
> seed, but of imperishable, through the living and enduring word
> of God. For,
>
> > "All people are like grass,
> >   and all their glory is like the flowers of the field;
> > the grass withers and the flowers fall,
> >   but the word of the Lord endures forever."
>
> And this is the word that was preached to you. (1 Pet 1:22–25)

Our lives are fleeting. We wither and fade like flowers and grass. But what we preach is the word of the Lord, a word that stands forever.

It regenerates sinners, granting them new birth into God's permanent family, from which those born into it can never be excluded.

As preachers, most of us want to speak to life in the present. We don't want to feel like museum pieces, fossils or relics of a bygone day (though, sadly, I have met some who actually do prefer this and wear it as a badge of honour). This desire to speak to our contemporaries is right and natural and normal. After all, the people who lived in the past are gone and the people to come aren't here yet!

Yet trying to be relevant to our contemporaries can become a trap if it leads us to abandon or twist God's word. This happens with astonishing frequency. Preachers de-emphasize the cross, fudge the nature of the Bible, stretch the boundaries of salvation, or shrink God's capacity to know everything. The point to remember and rejoice in is that we don't have to make those changes to be relevant, precisely because the word is eternal. It is perennial. It speaks to every generation precisely because it does not change. Nor do God and the human predicament.

The durability of the word, rooted in God's eternality, means that we don't have to look for a new message for our day. So what is it that we may change in comparison to past generations of preachers? We may change the entry point for the gospel because the needs people currently feel do change, and we may use these perceived needs to get to the unchanging needs common to all people of all times. We may change the format of our sermons, their length, the way we illustrate biblical truths, the way we call for response, the time or day we preach. We may change visual and auditory aids, what we wear, how we comb our hair.

These changes are permissible; what is not permissible is to change what God says in the Scripture. For instance, when God says he hates divorce (Mal 2:16), we are not at liberty to adjust his attitude to fit current practice. When God says he loves righteousness, as he does in Psalm 33:5, we have no warrant to portray that love as no more than a mild preference. When Romans 3:9–20 builds a scriptural case for the universality of sin, we mustn't explain that away to excuse the sins of any era, group or individual. Moreover, the balance and tone of Scripture as a whole must shape our preaching plans.

Remembering our gardening role in God's field is liberating. We are planters. Yes, there are weeds to be pulled and watering to be done, but the imperishable seed is alive, and in good soil it germinates and bears fruit. Our job is to plant good seed and trust that it will take root and bear fruit.

Thanks, Lord, for the good seed of the word. Help me to sow it abundantly and expect an abundant harvest. Amen.

Day 70

Philip found Nathanael and told him, "We have found the one Moses wrote about in the Law, and about whom the prophets also wrote – Jesus of Nazareth, the son of Joseph." (John 1:45)

The Bible Is God's Testimony to Christ

Jesus instructed his disciples concerning how every part of Scripture points to himself. He links this fundamental truth about the Bible to their preaching:

> He said to them, "This is what I told you while I was still with you: Everything must be fulfilled that is written about me in the Law of Moses, the Prophets and the Psalms."
>
> Then he opened their minds so they could understand the Scriptures. He told them, "This is what is written: The Messiah will suffer and rise from the dead on the third day, and repentance for the forgiveness of sins will be preached in his name to all nations, beginning at Jerusalem. You are witnesses of these things. I am going to send you what my Father has promised; but stay in the city until you have been clothed with power from on high." (Luke 24:44–49)

The Lord's post-resurrection seminar did not present new material; he had often intimated that everything about him in the Bible had to be fulfilled. But like all biblical teaching, this could be understood only by those whose minds were supernaturally opened. This matters because preaching is bearing witness from the Scriptures to Christ's death and resurrection and offering forgiveness in Jesus' name. We speak on his behalf, and the offer of forgiveness is conditional upon repentance, which God himself grants (Acts 5:31; 2 Tim 2:25). The message is universal and is therefore to be taken to the ends of the world. Yet this should not be attempted without the power of the Holy Spirit, who was initially to be poured out in Jerusalem in keeping with God's promise. The Holy Spirit came as predicted, and the word has testified to Jesus ever since, whenever and wherever he is preached in the power of the Holy Spirit.

When we preach, we are bearing a doubly biblical testimony to the saving acts at the core of the gospel. We are recounting God's anticipatory testimony from the Hebrew Scriptures, the Old Testament, and are reaffirming the apostolic testimony of their fulfilment recorded in the New. Our task as preachers is to put the Old and New Testaments on the witness stand and let them speak of Christ.

The Bible speaks of many things that are important and true, but we must not let any of them eclipse its central message, the good news of the gospel. Nor must we allow any of them to upstage its central offer of repentance and forgiveness. While not all biblical texts point us to Jesus in the same way, all of them, in some way or another, do testify to Christ. We are reminded of this when John records that John the Baptist testified to Jesus, as did the Saviour's own works, but that the Father also testified:

> And *the Father who sent me has himself testified concerning me.* You have never heard his voice nor seen his form, nor does his word dwell in you, for you do not believe the one he sent. You study the Scriptures diligently because you think that in them you possess eternal life. *These are the very Scriptures that testify about me*, yet you refuse to come to me to have life. (John 5:37–40)

In preaching, we let the Father tell us what he thinks of his Son. We don't have to guess what he thinks, but we do have to discern it and look for it in order to be able to proclaim it. Preaching that focuses on the immediate needs of parishioners can too easily neglect what God wants to say in favour of something we want to say.

Lord Jesus, give me eyes to see in every passage of Scripture how the inspired writers pointed to you. Help me not to write you into texts intended only to show me my sin, but let me not miss the point of those that prepare the way of the Lord. Amen.

Our Response to God's Word

Day 71

The apostles said to the Lord, "Increase our faith!" (Luke 17:5)

We Believe and Speak

The verse that for me summarizes how we who preach should apply all these biblical descriptions and images comes from Paul's testimony about his preaching:

> It is written: "I believed; therefore I have spoken." Since we have that same spirit of faith, we also believe and therefore speak, because we know that the one who raised the Lord Jesus from the dead will also raise us with Jesus and present us with you to himself. All this is for your benefit, so that the grace that is reaching more and more people may cause thanksgiving to overflow to the glory of God. (2 Cor 4:13–15)

Paul uses the Septuagint translation of Psalm 116:10 to underscore the connection between believing and speaking. The NIV translation of this verse reads: "I trusted in the Lord when I said, 'I am greatly afflicted.'" Like the psalmist, Paul knew affliction. Like the psalmist, he spoke. The psalmist spoke to God, to himself, and to his human listeners. Paul, believing in the resurrection of Christ and all those in him, speaks *for* God, carrying the treasure of the gospel message in his clay jar of a body so that his weakness might display God's power for God's glory. Had Paul not believed, he would not have spoken.

When we who preach fail to believe all that the prophets and apostles write about Scripture, we are less likely to speak in the name of Christ, because to do so seems such a feeble weapon, such an anaemic response to the great challenges of the world. Of course we are to be doers of the word and not only hearers, but our particular role in the body of Christ is to be speakers of that word. When doubts about its potency reduce our expectations of what it can achieve, we will end up devoting our best efforts to things other than preaching.

The good news is that we can repent of unbelief. Most of us can echo the words of the sad father in Mark 9:24, "I do believe; help me overcome my unbelief." We can be "helped" out of unbelief. What matters is not so much the quantity or quality of our faith but the object of our faith. We are not called to exercise great faith. Even tiny faith, as small as a grain of mustard seed, in a worthy object is sufficient. Scripture is God's word, and we can trust it to do what God has claimed for it.

Some may despise Billy Graham's famous decision to trust the Bible as God's word. Yet such a decision is not necessarily anti-intellectual. Trust in God's word opens the door to the hard work of studying and obeying it. Failure to trust it puts us on the prowl for some other means to build the church.

Since faith is not static, we need to assess our trust in God's word relatively often. But the question remains, assuming that you and I take God at his word about his word, what will characterize our relationship to his word? Trust is foundational. But we will also love and respect it, submit to it, approach it with humility, and learn, serve and guard it. Each response arises from our relationship with God. I am not advocating idolatry of the word but glory to God. Exalting God entails thinking highly of his word.

Before reading further, take some time to join me in asking God to repair any unbelief that is hampering our ministry of the word. Then, as you work through the meditations that follow, prayerfully evaluate your response to his word.

Gracious Lord, I confess that I do believe the truth about your word and trust you to speak truth though it and use it to sanctify me and those to whom I preach. I must also confess that sometimes my trust is weak. There are even times when my trust is misplaced. I succumb to the temptation to trust my efforts, my gifts, my intellectual abilities or even my track record of faithfulness in the pulpit. Help me, I pray, to trust only you and to express that faith by growing confidence that you will use your word and my preaching of it, despite the weakness of my preaching because your strength is made perfect in my weakness. Amen.

Day 72

Oh, how I love your law! I meditate on it all day long. (Ps 119:97)

We Love God's Word

Because we love God, we love his word. Love for God's word is a theme of many verses in Psalm 119 (47, 48, 97, 113, 119, 127, 159, 163, 165, 167). But what will this love look like in practice? Because we love God's word, we delight in it (v. 47). We long for it and meditate upon it (vv. 49, 97). We let it inform and strengthen our antipathies:

> I hate double-minded people,
> > but I love your law. (119:113)

> Because I love your commands
> > more than gold, more than pure gold,
> and because I consider all your precepts right,
> > I hate every wrong path. (119:127–128)

Love for God's law is not merely the basis of our action; it is also our response to God's righteous verdict upon the wicked:

> You reject all who stray from your decrees,
> > for their delusions come to nothing.
> All the wicked of the earth you discard like dross;
> > therefore I love your statutes. (119:118–119)

Because we love God's word, we obey it:

> I obey your statutes,
> > for I love them greatly.
> I obey your precepts and your statutes,
> > for all my ways are known to you. (119:167–168)

My hope is not that you will come to the place where you can claim to love God's word, but that others will see that you do because they see how it shapes your attitudes, affections and behaviour. We should not need to parade our love for Scripture; it should be visible. I can give a personal example of what this means: One Sunday morning in worship I read the prologue to John's gospel before expounding it. After the service, a beaming parishioner reported that during the reading he suddenly realized, "Pastor Greg really loves this word!"

How do we cultivate love for God's word? We *prove* it. As we trust God to act in accordance with his word, and when he does, not only does our faith in it grow, but our love for it grows. Pastors are in the wonderful position of seeing the word of God at work in many lives. As you see the word working, your love for it grows.

Father it is not easy for me to express love, not even to those I love the most. Forgive me for withholding this altogether appropriate response, to them and to you. I love you and I want that love to engender love for your word the way I love letters and notes from my wife. May it be increasingly the case that I love your word. Amen.

Day 73

The lion has roared – who will not fear? The Sovereign LORD has spoken – who can but prophesy? (Amos 3:8)

We Respect God's Word

Because we respect God, we respect his word. Love and respect are related but not identical. When the priests in Malachi's day failed to bring proper sacrifices, they treated God's table with contempt, and God took that personally. If fathers and governors deserve honour, how much more does the living God? If God's altar deserved respect because it was connected with his name, then surely his word deserves respect too.

"A son honours his father, and a slave his master. If I am a father, where is the honour due me? If I am a master, where is the respect due me?" says the Lord Almighty.
"It is you priests who show contempt for my name.
"But you ask, 'How have we shown contempt for your name?'" (Mal 1:6)

Respect for Scripture means respecting its human origins and history as well as its divine inspiration. If we fail to respect the fact that each text was written by a historical person within a cultural context and was written for some specific purpose, we will treat the passage as if these things don't matter. In extreme cases, this leads some people to exalt an English translation as if it were directly inspired by God.

Inspiration elevates the text we have; it does not give us licence to treat it superficially or magically. We must respect God's wisdom in deciding to give the text as it is, and treat the product of that wisdom with respect. Thus we must seek to understand what each human author meant by the words he used, the syntax, grammar and genre that governed how he put those words together, the setting of his first hearers, and how other parts of the canon shed light on the text being considered. We may also want to review how this verse has been interpreted by the church across history.

Until we gain a good idea of what a biblical author was saying to his first hearers, we cannot discern what God wants to say through those words to our listeners. Here is why: If we approach a text of Scripture without seeking to discover its original meaning, the text will become merely something that prompts or triggers our own thinking. We may then impose our thoughts on the text, and the result is impository preaching, not expository preaching. If our minds are filled with Scripture, these thoughts may be relatively good, even true. But the goal of preaching is not for us to tell the congregation what comes to our minds when we read Scripture. The goal is for all of us, preachers and listeners alike, to hear what God is saying to us through what he said.

If I appear to be listening to someone but am actually thinking about what I am going to say when he or she finishes speaking, I am not really listening. The same is true of Bible study. As preachers, we must discipline ourselves to be quick to listen and slow to speak. We must respectfully wait to hear what God has said and then prayerfully discern how that word relates to us. This means that preachers must study the words of the Bible and the contexts in which they were originally spoken. If we constantly take what the Bible says out of context, we cannot expect to grasp its message as a whole. That limitation, in turn, impairs our ability to grasp the message of its parts.

Lord, remind me to treat my physical Bible well as an expression for what it is – your very word. Help me to hold your holy word in highest esteem that those who watch me might learn to do the same. Amen.

Day 74

I will bow down towards your holy temple and will praise your
name for your unfailing love and your faithfulness, for you have so
exalted your solemn decree that it surpasses your fame. (Ps 138:2)

We Submit to God's Word

Psalm 81 calls Israel to worship God who delivered his people from bondage
in Egypt. On the basis of that track record, Asaph invites his contemporaries
to trust God and to open their mouths wide to be filled with his bountiful
provision. But just as God had a track record with them, so they, unfortunately,
had a record with him. His record was bountiful salvation; theirs was failure
to listen and obey, that is, failure to submit to him and follow him. (Note the
poetic parallelism in italics).

> Sing for joy to God our strength;
>> shout aloud to the God of Jacob!
> Begin the music, strike the timbrel,
>> play the melodious harp and lyre.
> Sound the ram's horn at the New Moon,
>> and when the moon is full, on the day of our festival;
> this is a decree for Israel,
>> an ordinance of the God of Jacob.
> When God went out against Egypt,
>> he established it as a statute for Joseph.
> I heard an unknown voice say:
> "I removed the burden from their shoulders;
>> their hands were set free from the basket.
> In your distress you called and I rescued you,
>> I answered you out of a thundercloud;
>> I tested you at the waters of Meribah.
> Hear me, my people, and I will warn you –
>> if you would only listen to me, Israel!
> You shall have no foreign god among you;
>> you shall not worship any god other than me.
> I am the LORD your God,
>> who brought you up out of Egypt.

Open wide your mouth and I will fill it.
"But *my people would not listen to me*;
Israel would not submit to me.
So I gave them over to their stubborn hearts
to follow their own devices.
"*If my people would only listen to me,*
if Israel would only follow my ways,
how quickly I would subdue their enemies
and turn my hand against their foes!
Those who hate the LORD would cringe before him,
and their punishment would last forever.
But you would be fed with the finest of wheat;
with honey from the rock I would satisfy you."

The positive, gracious, patient promise of vindication and satisfaction in the final verses still stands. When we listen to God's word and do what he asks, we reveal that we submit to him.

Submission to God's word means listening to it and obeying it. Instead of trying to wriggle out from under its authority, instead of resisting its claims to my allegiance and obedience, I surrender to it – not out of frustrated resignation but as a conquered rebel happily laying down my weapons before the power of my liberator. I submit with the assurance that to be Jesus' disciple is to give up the tyranny of my old master, sin, for the Saviour's easy yoke. As long as we fight against Scripture we miss much of its benefit. Submitting is somewhat like enduring a chiropractic adjustment with every muscle tense and resistant to changing our painful condition. When we relax, Scripture, like a skilful chiropractor, works to put us back where we were designed to be.

Submission to God's word is to be so total and complete that it can be described as letting the word of Christ dwell in us richly (Col 3:16), reflecting the Lord Jesus' description of the word dwelling in us in John 15:7. Mutual admonitions within the church will be the overflow when the word is richly at home in every part of our lives.

Lord Jesus, thank you for your easy yoke. Grant me the grace to put my neck beneath it and wear it happily so that my burden might be light. Amen.

Day 75

Humble yourselves, therefore, under God's mighty hand, that he
may lift you up in due time. (1 Pet 5:6)

We Humble Ourselves before God's Word

Humility is our proper posture before God; therefore, we humble ourselves
before God's word. Isaiah 66:1–2 captures the connection well:

This is what the LORD says:

> "Heaven is my throne,
>   and the earth is my footstool.
> Where is the house you will build for me?
>   Where will my resting place be?
> Has not my hand made all these things,
>   and so they came into being?"
>   declares the LORD.
> "These are the ones I look on with favour:
>   those who are humble and contrite in spirit,
>   and who tremble at my word."

"Trembling" at God's word goes well beyond loving, respecting and
submitting to it. It means taking seriously the one who stands behind it, the
one who delights to bless but also intends to be obeyed, the one who is not to
be trifled with. Humility is the reflexive posture of people who hear the word of
God as what it is. We do not adopt this posture after mature consideration; we
humble ourselves instinctively because of its innate authority as God's word.

When Ezra heard that the leaders and officials led the way in unfaithful
intermarriages (Ezra 9), he was appalled and showed his anguished humility
and self-abasement by tearing his clothes (tunic and cloak) and by pulling
out his hair from his head and beard. Then, verse 4 says, "*everyone who
trembled at the words of the God of Israel* gathered around me because of
this unfaithfulness of the exiles. And I sat there appalled until the evening
sacrifice." We may safely assume that the people trembled at God's word
because Ezra did. What followed was truly leadership from the knees.
Ezra's heartfelt confession sparked more confession, and ultimately sin was
dealt with.

Listeners to our sermons will always sense whether our attitude to them is humble. But far more basic than our humility toward them is our humility toward God. If this humility is genuine, it will manifest itself as humility toward God's word. I encourage you to pray regularly that your frequent handling of Scripture does not leave you callous to its awesome authority. If we do not tremble at God's word, our listeners will sense that and take his word less seriously than they should.

Lord, as I handle your word every day protect me from treating it callously or neglecting its authority over me. Thank you for examples of preachers who studied your word on their knees just to remind themselves of the right posture toward you and your word. Please remind me too. Amen.

Day 76

> For Ezra had devoted himself to the study and observance of the
> Law of the LORD, and to teaching its decrees and laws in Israel.
> (Ezra 7:10)

We Learn God's Word

I have focused on the right attitude to Scripture because the wrong attitude can too easily lead to a routine, formulaic handling of the text. But even the best attitudes towards the Bible do not excuse us from applying our minds to the hard work of learning its contents.

We will never master Scripture; indeed we want to be mastered by it. But because we know God and want to grow in our knowledge of him, we need to learn his word. This is the duty of all God's people, as Moses instructed the Israelites:

> Assemble the people – men, women and children, and the foreigners residing in your towns – so they can listen and learn to fear the LORD your God and follow carefully all the words of this law. (Deut 31:12)

Understanding not only follows learning; it precedes learning:

> Your hands made me and formed me;

> give me understanding to learn your commands. (Ps
> 119:73)

Recognize also that learning is the special duty of ministers of the word:

> Do your best to present yourself to God as one approved, a
> worker who does not need to be ashamed and who correctly
> handles the word of truth. (2 Tim 2:15)

These words speak of eager, disciplined labour by one who knows that he is accountable to God. Preachers entrusted with the gospel, who speak on behalf of God himself, must recognize that sloppy handling, lazy studying or incorrectly applying the Bible will leave them ashamed in the presence of the Master who entrusted the word to them.

Correct ways of handling the word of truth exist, ways that do not cloud or distort the word's truth but state it plainly (2 Cor 4:2). However, knowing and applying these ways takes effort – and we who preach must put in that effort. Yet the fact that it is hard work should not make Bible study a drudgery. One of the great blessings of serving as a preaching pastor is being able to dedicate several hours each week to studying the Bible. Thank God for this privilege and make the most of it. Every time you give yourself wholeheartedly to hear what God is saying in the text, you increase the fund of knowledge that you can draw on to help you understand other texts. Expound books from throughout the canon so that you can see how all the parts contribute to the drama of redemption, and then help your listeners place each text in its proper setting.

Your labour to know the Bible will be even more fruitful if you also know yourself! Learn how you learn! Are you a visual learner? Draw diagrams. Are you a tactile or motor learner? Write out the text. Take notes. Are you an auditory learner? Read passages aloud. Do you need repetition? Read again and again and again. Do you learn by speaking? Discuss Scripture during mealtimes and with study partners. Remember, too, that we tend to learn in different ways at different times in our lives. Memorize while you are young! You will be very glad you did.

My most helpful learning technique is interrogation. By asking the right questions about the text, I discover truths that I would not typically notice.

Learning the Bible is not the same thing as feeding upon it, but unless you work hard at learning the whole book you will remain a "snacker," picking up a morsel here or there instead of genuinely feasting on its riches.

Remember, systematic theologies and Bible dictionaries and encyclopaedias can help greatly in reviewing biblical ideas, but they do not substitute for a growing grasp of the whole Bible itself.

Thank you Father for freeing me to study your word. Thank you for giving me a mind that can understand its meaning. As I study it, help me to learn it not for my sake alone although I certainly need to feed on it, but for the benefit of my listeners. Amen.

Day 77

This, then, is how you ought to regard us: as servants of Christ and as those entrusted with the mysteries God has revealed. Now it is required that those who have been given a trust must prove faithful. (1 Cor 4:1–2)

We Serve God's Word

When one group within the Jerusalem church felt neglected in the daily distribution of food, the apostles asked the church to appoint seven wise, Spirit-filled men to wait on tables. They did this to protect what they referred to as the ministry of the word:

In those days when the number of disciples was increasing, the Hellenistic Jews among them complained against the Hebraic Jews because their widows were being overlooked in the daily distribution of food. So the Twelve gathered all the disciples together and said, "It would not be right for us to neglect the ministry of the word of God in order to wait on tables. Brothers and sisters, choose seven men from among you who are known to be full of the Spirit and wisdom. We will turn this responsibility over to them and will give our attention to prayer and the ministry of the word."

This proposal pleased the whole group. They chose Stephen, a man full of faith and of the Holy Spirit; also Philip, Procorus, Nicanor, Timon, Parmenas, and Nicolas from Antioch, a convert to Judaism. They presented these men to the apostles, who prayed and laid their hands on them.

So the word of God spread. The number of disciples in Jerusalem increased rapidly, and a large number of priests became obedient to the faith. (Acts 6:1–7)

The widows felt neglected in the ministry of alms, that is, in the distribution of food. The apostles were unwilling to neglect the ministry of the word. Both are ministries and both are important, but those called to minister the word must make sure that nothing keeps them from doing so and from the prayer that is its natural counterpart.

When this division of labour was put in place, the word of God grew and the number of disciples greatly increased. Even some unlikely Jewish religious leaders became obedient to the faith. Later, the Apostle Paul could describe himself (Rom 1:1) as a servant of Christ Jesus whose call was to be an apostle and as having been set apart for the gospel of God. He served God by preaching the gospel:

God, whom I serve in my spirit in preaching the gospel of his Son, is my witness how constantly I remember you. (Rom 1:9)

Paul considered himself a servant of the gospel:

I became a servant of this gospel by the gift of God's grace given me through the working of his power. (Eph 3:7)

Peter captures the connection between serving God, serving God's people and serving the word in 1 Peter 4:10–11. Whatever one's gift, whether it is speaking or serving, we should be good stewards of God's grace in its various forms. The ESV translates these verses well:

As each has received a gift, use it to serve one another, as good stewards of God's varied grace: whoever speaks, as one who speaks oracles of God; whoever serves, as one who serves by the strength that God supplies – in order that in everything God may be glorified through Jesus Christ. To him belong glory and dominion forever and ever. Amen.

Service to God is described here as service to our fellow Christians. We serve each other by serving the word of God in the strength of God for the glory of God.

What does it mean in practice to be a minister of the word, a servant of the word? It does not mean to serve the word as if the word has a need we are addressing, a lack that we must overcome, a deficiency for which we have to compensate. No, we serve the word by daily distributing it to the hungry souls within our charge. We do more than preach. As stewards, we set the word before the people as often and in as many ways as necessary to help them feed upon it and grow.

Thank you Lord for the calling upon my life to serve the word to hungry and needy souls. May I be found faithful. Amen.

Day 78

> That is why I am suffering as I am. Yet this is no cause for shame,
> because I know whom I have believed, and am convinced that
> he is able to guard what I have entrusted to him until that day.
> (2 Tim 1:12)

We Guard God's Word

Another way we serve the word is by guarding it. This is not to say that the word is defenceless or vulnerable. In fact, it is living, powerful and eternal. So our responsibility is really to guard it by giving it the place it deserves in the church and in the hearts of those we serve. Guarding was at the heart of Timothy's calling:

> Timothy, guard what has been entrusted to your care. Turn away
> from godless chatter and the opposing ideas of what is falsely
> called knowledge. (1 Tim 6:20)

> Guard the good deposit that was entrusted to you – guard it with
> the help of the Holy Spirit who lives in us. (2 Tim 1:14)

Part of being stewards of what we have received is entrusting it to others who will pass it on to others who can faithfully teach it (2 Tim 2:2). Its ultimate safety is in God's hands, but guarding the word is nevertheless our responsibility.

As you complete this part of the meditations, take some time to evaluate your relationship to the Bible. Review what it wants to be and do for you and how you respond to it. The outcome described in Acts 6:7 suggests the following questions:

- Is the word of God growing in you and around you?
- Do you love it more than you did last year?

- Do you respect it?
- Are you humbly submitting to it, learning it, serving it, guarding it?

Lord, thank you that I can trust you to guard me and all I have entrusted to you, and in that way enable me to guard the gospel you have entrusted to me. Amen.

Part Three

Our Relationship with Our Listeners

Of the three intertwined relationships preachers must attend to, the relationship with their listeners is the most complicated. This complication arises because there are so many variables.

There are no variables when it comes to God. He does not change like shifting shadows (Jas 1:17), and since Scripture is rooted in God's character, the Bible does not change either:

> God is not human, that he should lie,
>> not a human being, that he should change his mind.
> Does he speak and then not act?
>> Does he promise and not fulfil? (Num 23:19)

The writer to the Hebrews argues concerning God's promises and purposes:

> When God made his promise to Abraham, since there was no one greater for him to swear by, he swore by himself, saying, "I will surely bless you and give you many descendants." And so after waiting patiently, Abraham received what was promised.
>
> People swear by someone greater than themselves, and the oath confirms what is said and puts an end to all argument. Because God wanted to make the unchanging nature of his purpose very clear to the heirs of what was promised, he confirmed it with an oath. God did this so that, by two unchangeable things in which it is impossible for God to lie, we who have fled to take hold of the hope set before us may be greatly encouraged. We have this

hope as an anchor for the soul, firm and secure. It enters the
inner sanctuary behind the curtain, where our forerunner, Jesus,
has entered on our behalf. He has become a high priest forever,
in the order of Melchizedek. (Heb 6:13–20)

Our relationships with God and his word are dynamic, but we are not
trying to relate to a moving target. God's relationship to his word and his
word's relationship to him are fixed and immutable. Furthermore, our
relationships with God and his word are asymmetrical: God and his word
initiate, dominate and ultimately sustain their relationships with us.

When we relate to our listeners, the number of variables increases
immediately and the relationships are more nearly symmetrical. We and our
hearers have some fundamental similarities. God made us all in his image and
each of us has some sort of relationship to him, whether actual and vibrant,
potential, lapsed or active rebellion. Moreover, God loves us all – we who
preach and those to whom we speak – even when unbelieving listeners do
not acknowledge God or his love. Likewise, both we and our listeners have a
relationship with Scripture. Our listeners may know the Bible better than we
do and obey it more readily. Or, they may have never heard of it, much less
read or heard it expounded. Most of our listeners will be somewhere between
these two poles. There are also many other characteristics that we may or may
not share with our listeners.

In this part of the book we will meditate on how we get to know our
listeners, what links us to them, what we can expect from our listeners, and
what we owe them.

How We Get to Know Our Listeners

For we do not write you anything you cannot read or understand.
(2 Cor 1:13a)

We Must Know Our Listeners

This crucial responsibility of getting to know our listeners so we can speak in ways they understand involves at least four undertakings: (1) grasping biblical anthropology that describes universal human characteristics; (2) putting ourselves in their place; (3) discerning and critically listening to the reports and insights of others; and (4) learning from the listeners themselves. All of these practices shaped Paul's ministry of the word. For instance, he describes why he uses an analogy when communicating with his listeners:

> I am using an example from everyday life because of your human limitations. Just as you used to offer yourselves as slaves to impurity and to ever-increasing wickedness, so now offer yourselves as slaves to righteousness leading to holiness. (Rom 6:19)

Paul's identification with his listeners for the sake of the gospel was an intentional strategy:

> Though I am free and belong to no one, I have made myself a slave to everyone, to win as many as possible. To the Jews I became like a Jew, to win the Jews. To those under the law I became like one under the law (though I myself am not under the law), so as to win those under the law. To those not having the law I became like one not having the law (though I am not free from God's law but am under Christ's law), so as to win those not having the law. To the weak I became weak, to win the weak. I have become

all things to all people so that by all possible means I might save some. I do all this for the sake of the gospel, that I may share in its blessings. (1 Cor 9:19–23)

We owe it to our listeners to really study them, to read, think, discuss and seek the best information available, accepting only what conforms to the truth of Scripture.

For instance, when Paul became aware of areas of ignorance among the Corinthians, he addressed them directly:

For I do not want you to be ignorant of the fact, brothers and sisters, that our ancestors were all under the cloud and that they all passed through the sea. (1 Cor 10:1)

Now about the gifts of the Spirit, brothers and sisters, I do not want you to be uninformed. (1 Cor 12:1)

Come back to your senses as you ought, and stop sinning; for there are some who are ignorant of God – I say this to your shame. (1 Cor 15:34)

Lord, open my eyes and ears to understand those to whom you call me to preach. Protect me from faulty assumptions about them or invalid generalizations or gullible acceptance of untrue reports. Help me to be willing to grow in my knowledge and love of my listeners. Amen.

Day 80

If any of you lacks wisdom, you should ask God, who gives generously to all without finding fault, and it will be given to you. But when you ask, you must believe and not doubt, because the one who doubts is like a wave of the sea, blown and tossed by the wind. That person should not expect to receive anything from the Lord. Such a person is double-minded and unstable in all they do. (Jas 1:5–8)

We Get to Know Our Listeners by Praying

God invites us to ask him for wisdom and we are foolish to decline his gracious offer. Prayer is foundational to every part of preaching. We constantly ask the living God for wisdom as we select which book we should expound next, divide that book into preachable texts, discover the thrust of each unit of thought, and consider how each passage addresses our listeners. To discern the claim our preaching portion has upon our listeners, we simply must know as much about them as we can. We can observe some things. We will hear reports of some things. We can learn about the culture that influences our listeners, but we can't begin to know all God knows about them. He is the God who knows everyone's heart (Acts 1:24) , and so we pray, "Lord, what do you want to say from this text to the people you know will be at worship that day?" When we do this, even if God does not disclose details about the people to us, he can guide us to shape our sermons so that they speak to our listeners. Most of us who pray like this before we preach have had listeners ask us how we knew they were facing the very issue the passage addressed. When this happens to me, I confess that I did *not* know they were facing that issue, but God did and in answer to prayer he led me to see that truth in the text and speak it on his behalf.

Moreover, faithful pastors are always in prayer meetings with their parishioners. If we can resist the temptation to dominate these, we will learn about our parishioners as we hear them pray. They will hear our hearts when we pray, much as Paul intentionally recorded his ongoing prayers for his beloved Christian friends in the churches to which he wrote.

Of course the most important thing about praying and preaching is not that it helps us get to know our listeners, but that God hears our prayers and answers them. He does abundantly more than we can ask or think.

Gracious Lord, remind me to talk to you about my listeners and for them before I talk to them about and for you. Amen.

Day 81

Then I heard the voice of the LORD saying, "Whom shall I send? And who will go for us?" And I said, "Here am I. Send me!"
He said, "Go and tell this people: 'Be ever hearing, but never understanding; be ever seeing, but never perceiving.' Make the

heart of this people calloused; make their ears dull and close
their eyes. Otherwise they might see with their eyes, hear with
their ears, understand with their hearts, and turn and be healed."
(Isa 6:8–10)

We Get to Know Our Listeners by Knowing God's Word

When the Lord commissioned Isaiah to speak on his behalf, he told him to
expect hard-heartedness and spiritual blindness. Indeed, God warned Isaiah
that his preaching would actually produce this judicial blindness. When God's
people hear his word and turn from it, they lose the capacity to receive it as
passages like 2 Corinthians 3:15, John 3:16–21 and Psalm 81:11–12 affirm.
The Lord reinforced this message to Isaiah later in Isaiah 30:8–11:

> Go now, write it on a tablet for them,
>   inscribe it on a scroll,
> that for the days to come
>   it may be an everlasting witness.
> For these are rebellious people, deceitful children,
>   children unwilling to listen to the LORD's instruction.
> They say to the seers,
>   "See no more visions!"
> and to the prophets,
>   "Give us no more visions of what is right!
> Tell us pleasant things,
>   prophesy illusions.
> Leave this way,
>   get off this path,
> and stop confronting us
>   with the Holy One of Israel!"

But not all the Bible has to say about our listeners is this discouraging.
The Bible is simply realistic about human nature. It likens all of us to lost
sheep (Isa 53:6); but it also describes the Bereans as more noble than those
in Thessalonica (Acts 17:11). The key skill to develop is the ability to read the
Bible anthropologically as well as theologically. That is, we let it tell us not
only about God and his plan and ways but also about ourselves and our ways.
It is important to distinguish between the universals such as the fact that we
are all made in the image of God (Jas 3:9), and affirmations that do not apply
to all such as when Paul called the Galatians foolish and bewitched (Gal 3:1).

As you read the Bible, look for insights about human nature. James 1:22–25 reminds us how the Bible works:

> Do not merely listen to the word, and so deceive yourselves. Do what it says. Anyone who listens to the word but does not do what it says is like someone who looks at his face in a mirror and, after looking at himself, goes away and immediately forgets what he looks like. But whoever looks intently into the perfect law that gives freedom, and continues in it – not forgetting what they have heard, but doing it – they will be blessed in what they do.

Lord, thank you that your word is a mirror. Help me see my true self in it. Help me also see my listeners as they are so that I can speak to them. Amen.

Day 82

While Paul was waiting for them in Athens, he was greatly distressed to see that the city was full of idols. So he reasoned in the synagogue with both Jews and God-fearing Greeks, as well as in the marketplace day by day with those who happened to be there. A group of Epicurean and Stoic philosophers began to debate with him. Some of them asked, "What is this babbler trying to say?" Others remarked, "He seems to be advocating foreign gods." They said this because Paul was preaching the good news about Jesus and the resurrection. Then they took him and brought him to a meeting of the Areopagus, where they said to him, "May we know what this new teaching is that you are presenting? You are bringing some strange ideas to our ears, and we would like to know what they mean." (All the Athenians and the foreigners who lived there spent their time doing nothing but talking about and listening to the latest ideas.)

Paul then stood up in the meeting of the Areopagus and said: "People of Athens! I see that in every way you are very religious. For as I walked around and looked carefully at your objects of worship, I even found an altar with this inscription: TO AN UNKNOWN GOD. So you are ignorant of the very thing you

worship – and this is what I am going to proclaim to you." (Acts
17:16–23)

We Get to Know Our Listeners by Direct Observation

Acts 17 famously describes how Paul observed the rampant idolatry in Athens
and then tailored his sermon to address that sin, beginning with an artefact
both he and his hearers could see. Every preacher needs to move beyond
mere seeing to observing. We need to grasp the significance of what is right
in front of us. This will not happen unless we put ourselves in a position to
see our parishioners where they live, work, study, and play. If we only observe
them at church, we won't get a clear or complete picture of the lives they lead.
Make every effort to visit people where they live and in their work places,
and ask the Lord to help you make significant observations concerning what
they do and say and how they relate to others. Sometimes what we see will
be obvious as when Moses saw the golden calf (Deut 9:13–16). On other
occasions, careful observation will reveal underlying emotions as when
Nehemiah saw fear.

> After I looked things over, I stood up and said to the nobles,
> the officials and the rest of the people, "Don't be afraid of them.
> Remember the Lord, who is great and awesome, and fight for
> your families, your sons and your daughters, your wives and
> your homes." (Neh 4:14)

Nehemiah is a model of letting his observations shape his ministry. He
not only spoke against the various sins he saw but forcefully acted to reinforce
his words. Nehemiah 13 chronicles his vigorous response to the abuses he
saw. Many of the rebukes we read in the prophets arose from first-hand
observation, coupled with a word from the Lord.

Often careful thought enables us to see trends and make valid
generalizations. This was Solomon's experience.

> All this I saw, as I applied my mind to everything done under the
> sun. There is a time when a man lords it over others to his own
> hurt. (Eccl 8:9)

Lord, give me eyes to see people as you do and to discern how your word
speaks to their circumstances, needs, and desires. Amen.

Day 83

Korah son of Izhar, the son of Kohath, the son of Levi, and certain
Reubenites – Dathan and Abiram, sons of Eliab, and On son of
Peleth – became insolent and rose up against Moses. With them
were 250 Israelite men, well-known community leaders who had
been appointed members of the council. They came as a group to
oppose Moses and Aaron and said to them, "You have gone too
far! The whole community is holy, every one of them, and the
LORD is with them. Why then do you set yourselves above the
LORD's assembly?"

When Moses heard this, he fell facedown. Then he said to Korah
and all his followers: "In the morning the LORD will show who
belongs to him and who is holy, and he will have that person come
near him. The man he chooses he will cause to come near him.
You, Korah, and all your followers are to do this: Take censers and
tomorrow put burning coals and incense in them before the LORD.
The man the LORD chooses will be the one who is holy. You Levites
have gone too far!" (Num 16:1–7)

We Get to Know Our Listeners by Listening to Them

When the council members accused Moses of setting himself above the
whole assembly, it was almost impossible for him *not* to listen to them! Moses
was able to tailor his response precisely to what they said. In that regard,
Moses had it easy. For us, we may be tempted to neglect what people say and
disregard it as a primary way of knowing them. The Lord Jesus made it plain
that "the mouth speaks what the heart is full of" (Matt 12:34) so we should
listen carefully if we want to know what is in our listeners' hearts. Words
will reveal fears, prejudices, longings and joys. It will not always happen, but
more times than we expect, if we listen to our listeners, they will tell us their
spiritual struggles. Jonah 1:7–10 bears remarkable testimony to this fact:

Then the sailors said to each other, "Come, let us cast lots to find
out who is responsible for this calamity." They cast lots and the
lot fell on Jonah. So they asked him, "Tell us, who is responsible
for making all this trouble for us? What kind of work do you do?

Where do you come from? What is your country? From what
people are you?"

He answered, "I am a Hebrew and I worship the LORD, the
God of heaven, who made the sea and the dry land."

This terrified them and they asked, "What have you done?"
(They knew he was running away from the LORD, *because he had
already told them so.*) [emphasis added]

*Father, thank you for being the God who hears. Make me like you. Help me to
listen and to learn. Amen.*

Day 84

My brothers and sisters, some from Chloe's household have
informed me that there are quarrels among you. What I mean is
this: One of you says, "I follow Paul"; another, "I follow Apollos";
another, "I follow Cephas"; still another, "I follow Christ."
(1 Cor 1:11–12)

We Get to Know Our Listeners by Listening Discerningly to Eyewitness Reports

When Chloe's people gave specifics of problems at Corinth, Paul listened and
spoke into their situation appropriately. He could not have addressed this
problem had he not paid attention to the report he received. This is not an
isolated example. The letters to the Thessalonians are shaped by Timothy's
report of how things were going in Thessalonica. That report prompted not
only praise to God for what he was evidently doing (1 Thess 1), but also led
Paul to defend his ministry (1 Thess 2) and to address both doctrinal and
behavioural deficiencies (the balance of these letters).

Of course, not all reports are true. Remember Nehemiah 6:5–8:

Then, the fifth time, Sanballat sent his aide to me with the
same message, and in his hand was an unsealed letter in which
was written:

"It is reported among the nations – and Geshem says it
is true – that you and the Jews are plotting to revolt, and
therefore you are building the wall. Moreover, according

to these reports you are about to become their king and have even appointed prophets to make this proclamation about you in Jerusalem: 'There is a king in Judah!' Now this report will get back to the king; so come, let us meet together."

I sent him this reply: "Nothing like what you are saying is happening; you are just making it up out of your head."

So, ask the Lord to give you discernment, confirm what you hear, and do not assume anything. But when you have the unshakeable facts, let the light of God's word shine into every part of everyone's life.

Lord, please give me wisdom to discern what is going on in the church and in individual lives that I may speak a word in season every time I preach. Amen.

Day 85

Brothers and sisters, think of what you were when you were called. Not many of you were wise by human standards; not many were influential; not many were of noble birth. But God chose the foolish things of the world to shame the wise; God chose the weak things of the world to shame the strong. God chose the lowly things of this world and the despised things – and the things that are not – to nullify the things that are, so that no one may boast before him. (1 Cor 1:26–29)

We Get to Know Our Listeners by Knowing Their History

Or do you not know that wrongdoers will not inherit the kingdom of God? Do not be deceived: Neither the sexually immoral nor idolaters nor adulterers nor men who have sex with men nor thieves nor the greedy nor drunkards nor slanderers nor swindlers will inherit the kingdom of God. And that is what some of you were. But you were washed, you were sanctified, you were justified in the name of the Lord Jesus Christ and by the Spirit of our God. (1 Cor 6:9–11)

The Apostle Paul had first-hand knowledge of the Corinthian church as well as reports of their current state of affairs. He was wise enough to take into account not only where they stood but also where they had been, both individually but also collectively as a church. This sort of knowledge is indispensable to the preacher. On the one hand, it helps us be more compassionate to people who are really coming from behind. People who have more to overcome, or who struggle with learning disabilities or chronic pain or dysfunctional upbringings cannot be expected to respond to Scripture in precisely the same ways as those who do not face these challenges and difficulties. On the other hand, like Paul, we must not hesitate to hold people accountable to biblical demands. When we know where they have been, we can urge them to the obedience of faith on the basis of what God has already done in and for them in Jesus. It is only a slight exaggeration to say that everything in the Old Testament story after the Exodus is predicated upon that event in Israel's history and it supplies the leverage the prophets used to urge their listeners to repent. No preacher will regret spending time with people to learn as much as possible of their stories.

Thank you Father for redeeming me. Thank you for persevering with me when, having put my hand to the plough, I have been tempted to turn back. Thank you for your gracious work in the lives of those to whom I preach. Make me willing to learn of your grace to them already that I may better equip them to continue to walk with you. Amen.

Day 86

> When Jesus came to the region of Caesarea Philippi, he asked his disciples, "Who do people say the Son of Man is?" (Matt 16:13)

We Get to Know Our Listeners by Asking Questions

> While the Pharisees were gathered together, Jesus asked them, "What do you think about the Messiah? Whose son is he?"
> "The son of David," they replied.
> He said to them, "How is it then that David, speaking by the Spirit, calls him 'Lord'? For he says,

"'The Lord said to my Lord:
　"Sit at my right hand
　until I put your enemies
　　under your feet."'

　　If then David calls him 'Lord,' how can he be his son?" (Matt
　22:41–45)

Jesus was masterful at asking questions. He used them to help people see the truth and where they stood in relation to it. We too should employ questions when we preach and should do so for the same reasons Jesus did. But what Jesus models also applies to how we get to know our listeners.

For many years my wife and I hosted a Bible study for those considering joining our church. It met in our home every Wednesday night and we studied the passage that I was scheduled to expound the following Sunday morning. I led this inductive study for which I carefully crafted questions of the passage which I then lobbed out into the group and which I scrupulously avoided answering. How people responded to these questions helped me understand how they related to the Bible. Some of them knew how to handle the Bible very well. Others did not. Just listening to their answers helped me tailor my upcoming sermon to counter common misconceptions I heard voiced in the Bible study.

But when I say that we learn about our listeners by asking questions, I am not limiting the realms in which I can learn to Bible knowledge or spiritual needs. Skilful conversationalists who genuinely care about other people have learned how to ask questions that help their conversation partners talk about themselves. This is a skill well worth developing. (Of course, no preacher should divulge anything in a sermon that is someone else's private concern. If you are in doubt about whether an item falls into that category, don't even think about including it in a sermon. If you do quote someone from the congregation, two things are absolutely required. First, secure their permission, and second, tell the congregation in the sermon that you have done so.)

Obviously, asking good questions is a skill that is not limited to those questions directed toward our listeners. Good research of any kind necessitates asking good questions of other sources of knowledge too, and that includes Scripture.

Lord, please give me the wisdom to ask good questions and the humility to use what I learn for the good of your people and the glory of your Name. Amen.

Day 87

"For in him we live and move and have our being." As some of
your own poets have said, "We are his offspring." (Acts 17:28)

One of Crete's own prophets has said it: "Cretans are always liars,
evil brutes, lazy gluttons." (Titus 1:12)

We Get to Know Our Listeners by Reading Widely and Discerningly

When Paul told Titus how to shepherd the flock in Crete, his diagnosis of
Cretan character was reinforced by literary evidence that Paul did not accept
uncritically. He affirmed what was true. Notice that in the same breath Paul
rejects ideas from other writings:

One of Crete's own prophets has said it: "Cretans are always liars,
evil brutes, lazy gluttons." This saying is true. Therefore rebuke
them sharply, so that they will be sound in the faith and will pay
no attention to Jewish myths or to the merely human commands
of those who reject the truth. (Titus 1:12–14)

We serve our listeners by learning about everything. God through Christ
is creator of the universe and Lord of all that exists. As the Dutch statesman
Abraham Kuyper famously remarked, "In the total expanse of human life
there is not a single square inch of which the Christ, who alone is sovereign,
does not declare, 'That is mine!'" That fact alone should make us interested in
the Lord's handiwork.

Learning extensively requires developing our faculties of observation and
budgeting time to read, because no matter how widely travelled we may be,
we cannot see everything with our own eyes. Nor can our eyes see everything
even in what we do see; we need the expert eyes and ears of others to interpret
reality for us. That is why good literature and well-practised science are of
great value.

I encourage you to learn to see the world in all its majesty and distortion
from an eschatological perspective. Recall Romans 8:18–25:

I consider that our present sufferings are not worth comparing
with the glory that will be revealed in us. For creation waits in
eager expectation for the children of God to be revealed. For the
creation was subjected to frustration, not by its own choice, but

by the will of the one who subjected it, in hope that the creation itself will be liberated from its bondage to decay and brought into the freedom and glory of the children of God.

We know that the whole creation has been groaning as in the pains of childbirth right up to the present time. Not only so, but we ourselves, who have the firstfruits of the Spirit, groan inwardly as we wait eagerly for our adoption to sonship, the redemption of our bodies. For in this hope we were saved. But hope that is seen is no hope at all. Who hopes for what they already have? But if we hope for what we do not yet have, we wait for it patiently.

Everything is a visual aid of what God is doing in salvation history, a reminder of God's ultimate plan in the world. Broad and extensive knowledge helps us keep this big picture in mind and become better at helping our listeners see the world as God sees it.

Learning is a true service to our listeners because the world offers many faulty interpretive grids through which to view life. When we preach, we offer a radically different interpretation of the same facts. But our perspective – even if truly biblical – is not likely to be accepted if we are ill-informed about the "facts" around us, that is, the facts of science, literature, and current events. When we are aware of the world our listeners live in, we are in a position to help them put their observations in the framework God supplies.

Our study of current trends must never be at the expense of knowing the Bible and the world in which its human authors lived. But given that caution, the more we know, the better we can serve our hearers.

Lord, thank you for this your world. Despite its wholesale rebellion, it remains yours by virtue of creation. Come quickly to assert your rule over it for the glory of your Name. Amen.

Day 88

After they had gone a long time without food, Paul stood up before them and said: "Men, you should have taken my advice not to sail from Crete; then you would have spared yourselves this damage and loss. But now I urge you to keep up your courage, because not one of you will be lost; only the ship will be destroyed. Last night

an angel of the God to whom I belong and whom I serve stood
beside me and said, 'Do not be afraid, Paul. You must stand trial
before Caesar; and God has graciously given you the lives of all
who sail with you.' So keep up your courage, men, for I have faith
in God that it will happen just as he told me." (Acts 27:21–25)

Sometimes, Perhaps, We Get to Know Our Listeners by a Gift of Knowledge

I list this means of knowing our listeners last because in no sense is this one
under our control. We can always count on God to be faithful, but we cannot
count on him to grant us special revelations. He has not promised to do this.
On the other hand, God does sometimes reveal things to his servants when
it is for the good of the body of Christ and enhances his own glory to do so.
Although some Bible teachers dispute that God still gives such gifts, I find no
compelling reason to believe that 1 Corinthians 12:7–11 is no longer operative:

> Now to each one the manifestation of the Spirit is given for the
> common good. To one there is given through the Spirit a message
> of wisdom, to another a message of knowledge by means of the
> same Spirit, to another faith by the same Spirit, to another gifts
> of healing by that one Spirit, to another miraculous powers, to
> another prophecy, to another distinguishing between spirits,
> to another speaking in different kinds of tongues, and to still
> another the interpretation of tongues. All these are the work of
> one and the same Spirit, and he distributes them to each one, just
> as he determines.

What is this "message of knowledge"? I cannot say for sure. Whatever it
is, it will certainly not contradict what stands written in Scripture, nor is it
on a par with Scripture as if it could supplement it in any normative sense.
For these reasons, this knowledge is not something a preacher would preach.
Indeed, the knowledge I am speaking of here must be tested and could well
be rejected (1 Thess 5:21). The most I am comfortable saying is that preachers
sometimes develop convictions about what God is doing or will do that
open their eyes to things the Scriptures genuinely teach – things they would
probably not have seen, had the Lord not granted them insight in a way that
goes beyond other means of knowing. If you think you have this gift, use it
sparingly and very carefully! As you ask the Lord to show you what book
of the Bible to expound next, do not be surprised if you become convinced

of a certain book and that it proves to be appropriate in ways you could not have known or planned. As you study its individual preaching portions, don't be surprised if some parts seem to be almost highlighted and that these parts when clearly and faithfully opened to your listeners speak directly to their situations.

Lord, thank you for all the gifts you give. Thank you for those times you have helped me see something I would have completely missed had it not been for your gracious intervention because you love the church and you want her to grow into the fullness of the measure of the stature of Christ. Amen.

Commonalities and Differences

> So in Christ Jesus you are all children of God through faith, for all of you who were baptized into Christ have clothed yourselves with Christ. There is neither Jew nor Gentile, neither slave nor free, nor is there male and female, for you are all one in Christ Jesus. If you belong to Christ, then you are Abraham's seed, and heirs according to the promise. (Gal 3:26–29)

Believers' Equal Status in Christ

Assuming that we who preach are regenerate, the greatest thing we have in common with believing listeners is our status in Christ. We have "everything we need for a godly life" (2 Pet 1:3), including (among much else) justification, the forgiveness of sins, eternal life, citizenship in heaven, the indwelling presence of the Holy Spirit to illuminate Scripture, brothers and sisters in the body of Christ who have received gifts to edify us, and the hope of glory. Because of our adoption as God's children, we have the same Father; we are family, no matter where on earth we live. So we relate to older men as fathers, younger men as brothers, younger women as sisters and older women as mothers (1 Tim 5:1–2). This familial relationship has ethical implications, and it also has a direct impact on how we speak:

> Do not rebuke an older man harshly, but exhort him as if he were your father. (1 Tim 5:1a)

Speaking the truth at all times, including from the pulpit, follows logically from our shared membership in Christ's body:

> Therefore each of you must put off falsehood and speak truthfully to your neighbour, *for we are all members of one body*. (Eph 4:25)

We can expect certain things of our fellow believers because the word of God is already at work in them (1 Thess 2:13) and they have already been taught by Christ (Eph 4:20–24). Thus we can assume they know certain truths:

For *you know* the grace of our Lord Jesus Christ, that though he was rich, yet for your sake he became poor, so that you through his poverty might become rich. (2 Cor 8:9)

I am writing to you, fathers,
    because *you know* him who is from the beginning.
I am writing to you, young men,
    because you have overcome the evil one.
I write to you, dear children,
    because *you know* the Father. (1 John 2:13–14a)

But *you know* that he appeared so that he might take away our sins. And in him is no sin. (1 John 3:5)

Anyone who hates a brother or sister is a murderer, and *you know* that no murderer has eternal life residing in him. (1 John 3:15)

Father, please protect me from the temptation to think of myself more highly than I ought simply because you have called and gifted me to preach your word. Remind me often, I pray, of the profound equality I share with all my listeners that I may serve them humbly as I ought. Amen.

Day 90

Therefore, remember that formerly you who are Gentiles by birth and called "uncircumcised" by those who call themselves "the circumcision" (which is done in the body by human hands) – remember that at that time you were separate from Christ, excluded from citizenship in Israel and foreigners to the covenants of the promise, without hope and without God in the world. But now in Christ Jesus you who once were far away have been brought near by the blood of Christ.

For he himself is our peace, who has made the two groups one and has destroyed the barrier, the dividing wall of hostility, by setting aside in his flesh the law with its commands and regulations. His purpose was to create in himself one new humanity out of the two, thus making peace, and in one body to reconcile both of them to

God through the cross, by which he put to death their hostility. He came and preached peace to you who were far away and peace to those who were near. For through him we both have access to the Father by one Spirit. (Eph 2:11–18)

Believers' Radical Equality

We should not presume that the basic scriptural truths are at the forefront of the minds of believing listeners. Like us, they need reminders. Peter had to exercise this ministry of reminding as he expresses in 2 Peter in different ways:

> Dear friends, this is now my second letter to you. I have written both of them as reminders to stimulate you to wholesome thinking. I want you to recall the words spoken in the past by the holy prophets and the command given by our Lord and Saviour through your apostles. (3:1–2)

> But do not forget this one thing, dear friends: With the Lord a day is like a thousand years, and a thousand years are like a day. (3:8)

> Bear in mind that our Lord's patience means salvation, just as our dear brother Paul also wrote you with the wisdom that God gave him. He writes the same way in all his letters, speaking in them of these matters. His letters contain some things that are hard to understand, which ignorant and unstable people distort, as they do the other Scriptures, to their own destruction.
>
> Therefore, dear friends, since you have been forewarned, be on your guard so that you may not be carried away by the error of the lawless and fall from your secure position. (3:15–17)

The fact that we are all forgiven sinners is the great equalizer in the body of Christ. Who we are in Christ eclipses other differences, no matter how real or enduring:

> So in Christ Jesus you are all children of God through faith, for all of you who were baptized into Christ have clothed yourselves with Christ. There is neither Jew nor Gentile, neither slave nor free, nor is there male and female, for you are all one in Christ Jesus. If you belong to Christ, then you are Abraham's seed, and heirs according to the promise. (Gal 3:26–29)

It is true that we who teach have authority to the extent that we teach and live faithfully (1 Thess 4:2; 1 Tim 4:12; Titus 2:15). But this authority is no excuse for lording it over others or being overbearing. Paul, in his defence of his apostleship, was eager to make plain that authority and gentle humility can go together:

> Examine yourselves to see whether you are in the faith; test yourselves. Do you not realize that Christ Jesus is in you – unless, of course, you fail the test? And I trust that you will discover that we have not failed the test. Now we pray to God that you will not do anything wrong – not so that people will see that we have stood the test but so that you will do what is right even though we may seem to have failed. For we cannot do anything against the truth, but only for the truth. We are glad whenever we are weak but you are strong; and our prayer is that you may be fully restored. This is why I write these things when I am absent, that when I come I may not have to be harsh in my use of authority – the authority the Lord gave me for building you up, not for tearing you down. (2 Cor 13:5–10)

Lord of glory, thank you for including me, a Gentile, in your family. Thank you that I am now one with fellow believers from every tribe and language and people and nation. Amen.

Day 91

> Examine yourselves to see whether you are in the faith; test yourselves. Do you not realize that Christ Jesus is in you – unless, of course, you fail the test? And I trust that you will discover that we have not failed the test. (2 Cor 13:5–6)

Spiritual Life

Because preaching includes evangelizing, on many occasions some listeners will *not* have rebirth in common with those who preach to them. Because the light has not turned on for these listeners (2 Cor 4:6), they are dead in their trespasses and sins (Eph 2:1) and blind (2 Cor 4:4). Unlike the believer, they can't understand the things of God as Paul says in 1 Corinthians 2:9–16:

However, as it is written:

> "What no eye has seen,
>   what no ear has heard,
> and what no human mind has conceived" –
>   the things God has prepared for those who love
>   him –

these are the things God has revealed to us by his Spirit.

The Spirit searches all things, even the deep things of God. For who knows a person's thoughts except their own spirit within them? In the same way no one knows the thoughts of God except the Spirit of God. What we have received is not the spirit of the world, but the Spirit who is from God, so that we may understand what God has freely given us. This is what we speak, not in words taught us by human wisdom but in words taught by the Spirit, explaining spiritual realities with Spirit-taught words. The person without the Spirit does not accept the things that come from the Spirit of God but considers them foolishness, and cannot understand them because they are discerned only through the Spirit. The person with the Spirit makes judgments about all things, but such a person is not subject to merely human judgments, for,

> "Who has known the mind of the Lord
>   so as to instruct him?"

But we have the mind of Christ.

We should not despair that the unbeliever cannot understand, but should rely on the Holy Spirit, to use the word we speak to impart life. Our awareness of spiritual blindness, death and enslavement should in fact spur us on to preach with a sense of urgency as well as humility, compassion, understanding and hope. Remember Paul's wise words to the Corinthians:

> Or do you not know that wrongdoers will not inherit the kingdom of God? Do not be deceived: Neither the sexually immoral nor idolaters nor adulterers nor men who have sex with men nor thieves nor the greedy nor drunkards nor slanderers nor swindlers will inherit the kingdom of God. *And that is what some of you were. But you were washed, you were sanctified, you*

were justified in the name of the Lord Jesus Christ and by the Spirit of our God. (1 Cor 6:9–11)

Father, thank you for the wonderful privilege of proclaiming the gospel to unbelievers. When I do so, help me to be faithful and attend my preaching with the power of the Holy Spirit so that blind eyes will be opened and hearers will become obedient to you and your word. Amen.

Day 92

Though I am free and belong to no one, I have made myself a slave to everyone, to win as many as possible. To the Jews I became like a Jew, to win the Jews. To those under the law I became like one under the law (though I myself am not under the law), so as to win those under the law. To those not having the law I became like one not having the law (though I am not free from God's law but am under Christ's law), so as to win those not having the law. To the weak I became weak, to win the weak. I have become all things to all people so that by all possible means I might save some. I do all this for the sake of the gospel, that I may share in its blessings. (1 Cor 9:19–23)

Different Cultures

The word "culture" derives from a Latin word meaning "to grow," and in the form "cultivate" it is used of growing plants and of growing minds. Someone we describe as "cultured" has good manners and a wide knowledge of the arts, literature, and philosophy. But here I am using "culture" with quite a different meaning, and one that has great importance for us who preach in an increasingly globalized environment. Lesslie Newbigin writes:

> I have been speaking about "our culture" and I must now try to say what I mean by this phrase. A convenient dictionary definition is as follows: "The sum total of ways of living built up by a human community and transmitted from one generation to another." Culture thus includes the whole life of human beings in so far as it is a shared life. It includes the science, art,

technology, politics, jurisprudence and religion of a group of people. Fundamental to any culture is language which embodies the way in which a people grasps and copes with experience, sharing it with one another within the group. So long as one lives one's life within one culture, one is hardly aware of the way in which language provides the framework in which experience is placed, the spectacles through which one "sees."[1]

Therefore, even those of us who have never been accused of being cultured are steeped in a culture (perhaps more than one). Even people from similar cultures still have some (sometimes large) cultural distance between them. For example, I have spent most of my life in the United States, but my wife was born to British parents and spent most of her first eighteen years in East Africa. Both of us had to learn to recognize and adapt to the cultural differences between us.

Preachers need to recognize that we all bring a culture to any relationship that is not identical to the one others bring. This is not a new challenge. Writing in the fourth century AD, Augustine used the concept of culture to explain why even devout interpreters of Scripture may take a command as figurative rather than literal:

> But as men are prone to estimate sins, not by reference to their inherent sinfulness, but rather by reference to their own customs, it frequently happens that a man will think nothing blameable except what the men of his own country and time are accustomed to condemn, and nothing worthy of praise or approval except what is sanctioned by the custom of his companions; and thus it comes to pass that if Scripture either enjoins what is opposed to the customs of the hearers or condemns what is not so opposed, and if at the same time the authority of the word has a hold upon their minds, they think that the expression is figurative.[2]

In recent decades, biblical scholars, theologians and missionaries have given this cultural problem a lot of thought.[3] At the risk of oversimplifying a

---

1. Paul Weston, ed., *Lesslie Newbigin: Missionary Theologian: A Reader* (Grand Rapids, MI: Eerdmans, 2006), 189.

2. St. Augustine, *On Christian Doctrine*, Book III: 15.

3. I have been especially helped by D. A. Carson, "Church and Mission: Contextualization and Third Horizons," in *The Church in the Bible and the World,* ed. D. A. Carson (Grand Rapids, MI: Baker, 1987); and Matthew A. Cook, "Unchanging 'Truth' in Contextual Exegesis,"

complicated subject, we who preach need to remember that we stand between the text of Scripture and our listeners, mediating it to them by restating its message in words they can understand, submit to and, by faith, obey. The text, though not bound by culture, was produced within one. That is the *first culture*. We read Scripture from a *second* cultural perspective, that is, from within our own culture, which is separated from that of the writers of the Bible by time and distance. Our listeners represent a *third* culture that may be similar to ours or very different from ours. Indeed, it is likely that whenever and wherever we preach, some of our listeners will be from cultures that are different from our own and perhaps from those of other listeners present.

We need to prayerfully seek to recognize our own cultural blind spots that will keep us from seeing what is actually in the biblical text. And because we love our listeners, we will use words, expressions, and images that make sense in their culture when we preach. We will try to put ourselves in their shoes as we spell out the implications of what the Bible says. We won't, for instance, discuss the implications of a text for a technological society if we are speaking to a rural congregation with little education.

Lord, because my own culture has shaped the way I think and what I value, I often wonder if I am about as alert to my own culture as a fish is to water. And the more contact I have with people from other places, the more painfully aware I become of how little I understand them. I can only guess that some things I think I have said plainly to them were not plain at all. Help me to express my love for my listeners by studying their worlds and learning how they think. Amen.

Day 93

When the time came for her to give birth, there were twin boys in her womb. The first to come out was red, and his whole body was like a hairy garment; so they named him Esau. After this, his brother came out, with his hand grasping Esau's heel; so he was named Jacob. Isaac was sixty years old when Rebekah gave birth to them. The boys grew up, and Esau became a skilful hunter, a

Evangelical Review of Theology 31, no. 3 (2007): 196–206.

man of the open country, while Jacob was content to stay at home among the tents. Isaac, who had a taste for wild game, loved Esau, but Rebekah loved Jacob. (Gen 25:24–28)

Different Styles

In addition to the cultural differences that shape whole communities, there are also individual differences between people. It may be worth mentioning a few of them, because although they are obvious, preachers easily neglect them. My list here is not comprehensive; there are doubtless many other points you could add to it.

Our congregations consist of some people who are highly educated and others who are not, even though the intelligence of the less educated may be similar (or higher). Moreover, people have different kinds of intelligence, and different thinking styles. Some are straight-line thinkers for whom logic is paramount; others think in images and associations. Many people think visually, but not everyone does. Some have an impressive attention span; others do not. Some thrive on details; others want pictures painted with the broadest of brush strokes. Some are men; others women. The range of ages means that people have different preoccupations related to their various stages of life.

Many people come with expectations derived from their denominational history and the size and style of the church in which they were brought up. I sometimes have my preaching students complete the sentence, "I don't feel the pastor has really preached until . . ." The way they complete that sentence is usually shaped by their experience (not biblical directives), which in turn is rooted in cultural (or subcultural) expectations.

Our task as preachers is not to preach the way our listeners prefer (2 Tim 4:3–4). Nevertheless, if some relatively minor adaptation will gain a hearing for the message, it is worth making. Augustine, deeply influenced by the teachers of rhetoric of antiquity, said that our three tasks as Christian teachers are to teach, to please and to move. Each of these, he says, calls for a different style. I chafe against the task of pleasing because I resist doing anything to make a name for myself as a preacher, and pleasing sounds too much like being a "people-pleaser" (Gal 1:10; 1 Thess 2:4). But if pleasing means using a speaking style that minimizes my listeners' resistance and increases my credibility, I may be wise to use it as a way of becoming all things to all people in service of the gospel, so long as the message of the text is not distorted. After all, Paul accommodated not merely cultural distinctives but individual deficiencies as well:

> "To the weak I became weak, to win the weak. I have become all things to all people so that by all possible means I might save some." (1 Cor 9:22)

Lord Jesus, thank you for coming into our world and speaking a human language understood by those to whom you spoke. Thank you for saying only what the Father commanded you to say. Help me to do both. Amen.

Handling Differences

The Samaritan woman said to [Jesus], "You are a Jew and I am a
Samaritan woman. How can you ask me for a drink?" (For Jews do
not associate with Samaritans.) (John 4:9)

Be Culturally Sensitive

Our three tasks as preachers are exegesis, interpretation and communication.
In practice these tasks are difficult to separate because we bring our cultural
perspective to the undertaking.

Exegesis requires that we try to get inside the culture of the writer and the
original hearers to discover what the words meant to them. It requires careful
study of the text. From there, we move on to interpretation – discerning the
meaning of the text. To minimize distortion of this meaning by unwittingly
imposing our own meaning on the text, we must be alert to our own cultural
biases and misconceptions and invite the Holy Spirit to let the whole of
Scripture correct them so that we can see what our text in its canonical
context really means. Third, we must communicate that meaning to our
listeners in ways that take into account their culture or cultures, including
their language, thought forms and life experience. However, just as Scripture
taught, rebuked, corrected and trained its first listeners, we must let it do
the same to us, whatever our culture, and for our listeners, whatever their
cultural biases.

All three relationships – with God, with Scripture, and with our listeners –
come into play when we consider culture. Our relationship with Scripture
requires a growing grasp of the cultures in which it originated so that we don't
misread it out of ignorance. Our relationship with our listeners necessitates
knowing their cultures as well as our own. We need wisdom gained through
our relationship with God to hear his word correctly so that we preach it
faithfully, neither misunderstanding it nor distorting it because of our own
cultural blindness, nor corrupting it to pander to the cultures of our listeners.

The last problem seems to me to be the greatest challenge for many preachers today. It is painfully easy to go beyond cultural sensitivity, which serves listeners by learning how they think, learn and grow, to cultural servitude, which subjects Scripture to the perceived needs of the listeners instead of letting it challenge their fallen ways. One way to embrace the former (sensitivity) without succumbing to the latter (servitude) is simply to get to know as much about your listeners as possible. Learn from them as well as about them. Let them tell you their stories. Study the history of your region, its mobility patterns, its family structures, its folklore and its values.

Studying your preaching text with others in a small group will help you discover what may initially strike your hearers. It may also reveal some of your own biases. None of us should think of ourselves as being acultural (without a culture) or supracultural (beyond the influence of culture). Not even the Bible is acultural. It is, however, supracultural, transcending all cultures. Its whole message speaks to every culture, including the ones from which we come and the ones into which we speak.

Relating rightly to our listeners necessitates living humbly and prayerfully with the difficult task of fairly articulating the meaning of the text in its context without distilling its message to something that says more about our cultural biases than about Scripture's content and intent.

Lord, guard me from selling out to the audience and telling them only what I know they want me to say, or from offering a message I claim is from you but which is incomprehensible or irrelevant to them. Amen.

Day 95

As soon as it was night, the believers sent Paul and Silas away to Berea. On arriving there, they went to the Jewish synagogue. Now the Berean Jews were of more noble character than those in Thessalonica, for they received the message with great eagerness and examined the Scriptures every day to see if what Paul said was true. (Acts 17:10–11)

Avoid Assumptions

Probably as a consequence of the fall, we as preachers tend to assume that our listeners think like we do. Thinking of a close friendship or of your marriage should quickly remind you that this is not the case! Such relationships are a blessing not merely because we learn from and about the other person but also because in so doing we learn something about ourselves. Until this happens, we are like those who are deaf to their own accent and oblivious of the fact that they may even have an accent. This was my position when I first moved to Britain from the United States. I knew that the British had accents, but I didn't! They quickly disabused me of this perception.

Both speaker and listeners bring their differences to oral communication. What is true of language is true of culture in general. Until we awaken to this fact, we are as unaware of our own culture as a fish is of water.

The opposite temptation to assuming that our listeners think just like ourselves is to assume that they are very different and to over-emphasize these differences. True, there are differences between old and young, rural and urban, "modern" thinkers and "post-modern" thinkers, but they all have much more in common than they have differences.

If your ministry of the word is exclusively to one group, what you learn about that group can be allowed to influence the shape of your message and your style of delivery more than if you speak to a group containing representatives from different generations. However, the best approach is to test each suggestion about listeners by Scripture and hold fast to that which is good. For instance, young postmodernists are said to favour authenticity more than logic. But surely authenticity is a biblical value that every preacher should embody in any setting, no matter who is listening. If you doubt that, reread the first seven chapters of 2 Corinthians! Paul was no phony; he was genuine to the core, and because of this he could challenge those who criticized his ministry. The same dynamic is at work in 1 Thessalonians 1–2.

Lord, when I observe my listeners and assess their common strengths and weaknesses, help me to exercise Spirit-given discernment so that I am not guilty of making false generalizations that blind me to their true needs and capacities to receive your word. Amen.

Day 96

> "I am not insane, most excellent Festus," Paul replied. "What I am saying is true and reasonable." (Acts 26:25)

Use Suitable Logic

One of the most instructive examples of sensitivity to our listeners comes from Paul's defence before Festus and Agrippa (Acts 26). Paul had been arrested and had courageously grasped the opportunity to speak to the mob (Acts 21:33–22:21). Their reaction to his testimony was unambiguous:

> The crowd listened to Paul until he said this. Then they raised their voices and shouted, "Rid the earth of him! He's not fit to live!" (Acts 22:22)

When Paul was about to be beaten, he strategically mentioned his Roman citizenship, a fact that would lead to his being sent to Rome (23:11). On the way, a stormy confrontation with the Sanhedrin (22:30–23:10), a providential escape from a plot to kill him (23:12–22) and a heavily-armed escort brought Paul to Caesarea (23:23–35). There the Jews brought charges against Paul that he answered. However, Felix, the well-informed governor, deferred any decision on the case. He did, however, often speak to Paul during the remaining two years of his tenure. Paul knew that Felix was ruthless, greedy and lustful, so he made sure that his talks with him included the biblical topics of "righteousness, self-control and the judgment to come" (24:25).

When Festus succeeded Felix, Paul was still in prison. But within two weeks of taking up his new position, Festus had Paul and the Jews brought before him. Once again, Paul used a valid legal manoeuvre to avoid the Jews' demand that he be sent on a dangerous trip to Jerusalem. He appealed to Caesar, and Festus granted his request.

A few days later, King Agrippa arrived with Bernice his sister (25:13) and Festus discussed Paul's case with him. When Agrippa expressed a desire to hear Paul speak, Festus arranged a hearing for the next day, a meeting that had all the trappings of an audience with the king, attended by people from the highest levels of society (25:23).

Festus made it plain that he especially wanted the king's comments before sending the prisoner on to Rome (25:26):

> But I have nothing definite to write to His Majesty about him. Therefore I have brought him before all of you, and especially before you, King Agrippa, so that as a result of this investigation I may have something to write.

Paul's words in this situation reveal how conscious he is of his audience and of the constraints imposed by this being a trial. He knows why he is there, and he knows that Agrippa is aware of things Jewish (26:3) and of the climactic events in the life of Jesus (26:26):

> The king is familiar with these things, and I can speak freely to him. I am convinced that none of this has escaped his notice, because it was not done in a corner.

Thus Paul can freely speak of what the Jews would know about his life, including his training and his zeal as a Pharisee and persecutor of the church (26:4–11). He also knows that the heart of his message – that the risen Jesus met him on the Damascus Road and commissioned him as a servant and witness – rested on two pillars that his primary hearers would agree with: (1) God raises the dead (26:8), and (2) the prophets and Moses said that the Christ would suffer and rise and would proclaim light to his own people and to the Gentiles (26:23).

Paul could have framed his defence differently, but he probably selected his approach because his target listener, Agrippa, agreed with his starting point (26:27):

> King Agrippa, do you believe the prophets? I know you do.

This statement puts Agrippa in an awkward position. If he admits to believing the prophets, he will have trouble ruling out either that God can raise the dead or that the prophets predicted the death and resurrection of the Messiah. The fact that Agrippa may not like Paul's use of logic does not lessen its force.

Paul dismisses Festus' objection that his great learning has driven him mad. He not only asserts his sanity and the truth and reasonableness of his defence, but he also, significantly, reminds Festus that he is speaking primarily to Agrippa, who agrees with Paul's premise (26:25–26).

Here, Paul deftly employs logic, but he begins with a premise with which his listener would agree. His method is surely a model for us. Audience awareness and sensitivity used in service to gospel proclamation are always appropriate.

Thank you gracious Lord for designing your world in ways that make sense to those who have the mind of Christ. Grant me wisdom to speak for you in such a way that those who hear will have to acknowledge that what I say is both internally consistent and externally verifiable. Amen.

The Response of Our Listeners

Then Jesus said, "Whoever has ears to hear, let them hear."
(Mark 4:9)

They Will Listen and Pray

Every preacher's three foundational relationships – with God, Scripture and listeners – are reciprocal and overlapping and involve a response. What response can we expect from our listeners?

We must begin by facing the fact that almost nothing is guaranteed; we cannot control their side of the relationship. Therefore, instead of speaking of what is normal, since no norm exists, let us consider first the ideal, what we hope and pray will happen, and then, secondly, the weakest, least desirable possibility.

It would be wonderful if all our listeners could embrace and affirm Cornelius' words spoken of those who gathered at his home to hear Peter's message:

So I sent for you immediately, and it was good of you to come.
Now we are all here in the presence of God to listen to everything
the Lord has commanded you to tell us. (Acts 10:33)

Notice the warm personal welcome, the apparent absence of any uninterested attendees ("we are all here . . . to listen"), the affirmation of God's presence, the commitment to hear not just some part of the sermon but everything Peter has to say. Cornelius, speaking for all the assembled listeners, expected Peter's message to be authoritative (commanded by the Lord) and personalized ("to tell us"). What a joy to speak to listeners who come with such humble, eager, submissive, expectant attentiveness!

Peter was just warming to his subject when the Holy Spirit interrupted him:

> While Peter was still speaking these words, the Holy Spirit came
> on all who heard the message. (Acts 10:44)

These hearers not only benefited from God's grace but also became object lessons for their Jewish brothers. God had clearly prepared both preacher and hearers for this encounter.

Ideally, our listeners will pray for us. Paul repeatedly asked the recipients of his letters to pray for his preaching ministry:

> Pray also for me, that whenever I speak, words may be given me
> so that I will fearlessly make known the mystery of the gospel.
> (Eph 6:19)

> Devote yourselves to prayer, being watchful and thankful. And
> pray for us, too, that God may open a door for our message, so
> that we may proclaim the mystery of Christ, for which I am in
> chains. Pray that I may proclaim it clearly, as I should. (Col 4:2–4)

> I urge you, brothers and sisters, by our Lord Jesus Christ and by
> the love of the Spirit, to join me in my struggle by praying to God
> for me. Pray that I may be kept safe from the unbelievers in Judea
> and that the contribution I take to Jerusalem may be favourably
> received by the Lord's people there, so that I may come to you
> with joy, by God's will, and in your company be refreshed. (Rom
> 15:30–32)

When our listeners pray for us, even when they do not directly benefit from the immediate answers, everyone benefits. We need boldness, clarity, open doors and rapport with the people we serve. God can abundantly meet these needs and delights to do so in answer to prayer.

Lord, without you I can do nothing. Remind me often that because you want to speak through me to your people when I preach, it only makes sense for me to ask you what you want me to say to them. Please prompt me to pray, not merely when I am stuck, but at all times as I prepare to preach. Graciously raise up an army of prayer partners who will actively invite you to speak through me to them and others. Amen.

Day 98

The large crowd listened to him with delight. (Mark 12:37b)

They Will Eagerly Learn

Ideally, our listeners will be eager students of the word of God and will give us their undivided attention. They will be like those characters in the Bible who were steeped in the Scriptures and able to see God's hand in their own day: Daniel knew what to expect and pray for (Dan 9:2); Simeon waited for the consolation of Israel (Luke 2:25); Anna and others looked forward to the redemption of Israel (Luke 2:38); and the Bereans heard Paul preach in their synagogue, received his word and tested its truthfulness by the Scriptures (Acts 17:11–12):

> Now the Berean Jews were of more noble character than those in Thessalonica, for they received the message with great eagerness and examined the Scriptures every day to see if what Paul said was true. As a result, many of them believed, as did also a number of prominent Greek women and many Greek men.

Crowds who wanted to hear the word of God were common in the early days of Jesus' ministry too (Mark 12:37; Luke 5:1), but many of them ultimately rejected him. He told them,

> You study the Scriptures diligently because you think that in them you have eternal life. These are the very Scriptures that testify about me, yet you refuse to come to me to have life. (John 5:39–40)

Paul predicted a similar situation in 2 Timothy 3:5–9, warning of people who had a form of godliness and were always learning yet were never able to acknowledge the truth. As far as faith was concerned, they were rejected. So there is no guarantee that our listeners will readily receive our word.

These cautions notwithstanding, a biblically literate congregation is a wonderful friend to the faithful preacher. When we know that some of our listeners are like Apollos, "learned . . . with a thorough knowledge of the Scriptures" (Acts 18:24), we will be stretched to stretch them, and we will probably handle the word more carefully when we realize that they are testing our sermons by Scripture. You may feel threatened by such people; it is far better to rejoice in their presence.

I once pastored a newly planted church with perhaps one hundred and forty attendees, of whom about a dozen had seminary training. The fact that one of them taught classical languages at a local university helped me to resist any temptation to overstate conclusions based on the original Greek, given my limited grasp of the Greek New Testament! On another occasion, someone with very little formal education asked me about my exposition of a text that revealed his understanding of the biblical storyline was much better than mine. That awareness sent me back to my knees and to my study.

Gracious Father, I praise you for eager students of your word whose appetite for it remains ravenous, who are thrilled to be fed and are grateful for every morsel. Raise up more of these people and make them examples to others, not merely as hearers of the word, but doers of it as well. Amen.

Day 99

And now, brothers and sisters, we want you to know about the grace that God has given the Macedonian churches. In the midst of a very severe trial, their overflowing joy and their extreme poverty welled up in rich generosity. For I testify that they gave as much as they were able, and even beyond their ability. Entirely on their own, they urgently pleaded with us for the privilege of sharing in this service to the Lord's people. And they exceeded our expectations: They gave themselves first of all to the Lord, and then by the will of God also to us. (2 Cor 8:1–5)

They Will Give

Ideally, the listeners in the local church you serve or the sending church that supports your evangelistic ministry will underwrite your ministry financially. This support is expected of churches, as the following texts make plain:

The hardworking farmer should be the first to receive a share of the crops. (2 Tim 2:6)

Dear friend, you are faithful in what you are doing for the brothers and sisters, even though they are strangers to you. They have told the church about your love. Please send them on their way in a manner that honours God. It was for the sake of the Name that they went out, receiving no help from the pagans. We ought therefore to show hospitality to such people so that we may work together for the truth. (3 John 5–8)

Nevertheless, the one who receives instruction in the word should share all good things with their instructor. (Gal 6:6)

Am I not free? Am I not an apostle? Have I not seen Jesus our Lord? Are you not the result of my work in the Lord? Even though I may not be an apostle to others, surely I am to you! For you are the seal of my apostleship in the Lord.

This is my defence to those who sit in judgment on me. Don't we have the right to food and drink? Don't we have the right to take a believing wife along with us, as do the other apostles and the Lord's brothers and Cephas? Or is it only I and Barnabas who lack the right to not work for a living?

Who serves as a soldier at his own expense? Who plants a vineyard and does not eat of its grapes? Who tends a flock and does not drink of the milk? Do I say this merely on human authority? Doesn't the Law say the same thing? For it is written in the law of Moses: "Do not muzzle an ox while it is treading out the grain." Is it about oxen that God is concerned? Surely he says this for us, doesn't he? Yes, this was written for us, because whoever ploughs and threshes should be able to do so in the hope of sharing in the harvest. If we have sown spiritual seed among you, is it too much if we reap a material harvest from you? If others have this right of support from you, shouldn't we have it all the more?

But we did not use this right. On the contrary, we put up with anything rather than hinder the gospel of Christ.

Don't you know that those who serve in the temple get their food from the temple, and that those who serve at the altar share in what is offered on the altar? In the same way, the Lord has commanded that those who preach the gospel should receive their living from the gospel. (1 Cor 9:1–14)

But what if you are not receiving financial support? Do not be discouraged. You are in good company! Even the Apostle Paul sometimes had to support himself by making tents. He models the type of attitude we should have in his letter to the Philippians, which is a sort of thank-you note for their support. In this letter, Paul reveals his trust in God and a gracious spirit towards those who lacked either the opportunity or the ability to support him:

> I rejoiced greatly in the Lord that at last you renewed your concern for me. Indeed, you were concerned, but had no opportunity to show it. I am not saying this because I am in need, for I have learned to be content whatever the circumstances. I know what it is to be in need, and I know what it is to have plenty. I have learned the secret of being content in any and every situation, whether well fed or hungry, whether living in plenty or want. I can do all this through him who gives me strength. (Phil 4:10–13)

Father, please grant me gratitude for the generosity of those who support me in ministry and contentment with my station in life. Make me a cheerful giver because you gave your inexpressible gift of Jesus to me. Amen.

Day 100

> And this is my prayer: that your love may abound more and more in knowledge and depth of insight, so that you may be able to discern what is best and may be pure and blameless for the day of Christ, filled with the fruit of righteousness that comes through Jesus Christ – to the glory and praise of God. (Phil 1:9–11)

They Will Love and Grow

Ideally, our listeners will give us candid feedback. Priscilla and Aquila modelled this when they dealt with Apollos:

> Meanwhile a Jew named Apollos, a native of Alexandria, came to Ephesus. He was a learned man, with a thorough knowledge of the Scriptures. He had been instructed in the way of the Lord, and he spoke with great fervour and taught about Jesus accurately, though he knew only the baptism of John. He began to speak boldly in the synagogue. When Priscilla and Aquila heard him, they invited him to their home and explained to him the way of God more adequately. (Acts 18:24–26)

The godly couple corrected him privately, in their home. It seems they saw Apollos' impressive gifts and gently helped him to teach more adequately what was already accurate. Affirmation became the context of coaching and education.

Ideally, our listeners will receive the word humbly with evident eagerness and zeal to do what it calls for. The day of Pentecost was a textbook case of the response we hope and pray for:

> "Therefore let all Israel be assured of this: God has made this Jesus, whom you crucified, both Lord and Messiah."
>
> When the people heard this, they were cut to the heart and said to Peter and the other apostles, "Brothers, what shall we do?"
>
> Peter replied, "Repent and be baptized, every one of you, in the name of Jesus Christ for the forgiveness of your sins. And you will receive the gift of the Holy Spirit. The promise is for you and your children and for all who are far off – for all whom the Lord our God will call."
>
> With many other words he warned them; and he pleaded with them, "Save yourselves from this corrupt generation." Those who accepted his message were baptized, and about three thousand were added to their number that day. (Acts 2:36–41)

To take another example, the Thessalonians, turning from idols to the true God in response to the gospel, imitated Paul, Silas and Timothy and the sending churches in Judea by becoming Christ-like, and so became models to younger churches (1 Thess 1–2). Ideally, our listeners will love and respect us because of the office we hold and the diligence with which we fulfil it:

> Now we ask you, brothers and sisters, to acknowledge those who work hard among you, who care for you in the Lord and who admonish you. Hold them in the highest regard in love because of their work. Live in peace with each other. (1 Thess 5:12–13)

Paul experienced that love from many and acknowledged it:

> Greet those who love us in the faith. Grace be with you all. (Titus 3:15b)

The ideal response makes our work a joy, as the writer to the Hebrews knew:

> Have confidence in your leaders and submit to their authority, because they keep watch over you as those who must give an

account. Do this so that their work will be a joy, not a burden, for
that would be of no benefit to you. (Heb 13:17)

And this is my prayer: that your love may abound more and more in
knowledge and depth of insight, so that you may be able to discern what is best
and may be pure and blameless for the day of Christ, filled with the fruit of
righteousness that comes through Jesus Christ – to the glory and praise of God.

Day 101

The Jews who were there gathered around him, saying, "How
long will you keep us in suspense? If you are the Messiah, tell us
plainly." Jesus answered, "I did tell you, but you do not believe. The
works I do in my Father's name testify about me, but you do not
believe because you are not my sheep. My sheep listen to my voice;
I know them, and they follow me." (John 10:24–27)

Some Will Reject Your Teaching

Fortunately, the Bible is wonderfully realistic. When it describes drunkenness
at the Lord's Table, incest within the church and squabbling about one ethnic
group being neglected in the distribution of food, it tells us that sanctification
is a process that remains incomplete. We should not be surprised when
reactions to God's word fall short of the ideal. Thus in the interest of candour,
I remind you of a few of the ways people have reacted to the preaching of
God's word. Your listeners may do the same.

Some Pharisees sneered at Jesus (Luke 16:14). The sophisticated Athenians
derided Paul's preaching (Acts 17:32–34). On the day of Pentecost, observers
made fun of those who praised God in other tongues (Acts 2:13). However,
their reaction was nothing compared to the "Rid the earth of him! He's not fit
to live!" (Acts 22:22) that the Jews shouted after hearing Paul preach that the
Lord would send him to the Gentiles!

More often, we can expect people to respond with apathy or inaction
despite their curiosity, as Herod did in his highly ambiguous relationships
with John the Baptist and the Lord Jesus, despite his role in their deaths.

For Herod himself had given orders to have John arrested, and he had him bound and put in prison. He did this because of Herodias, his brother Philip's wife, whom he had married. For John had been saying to Herod, "It is not lawful for you to have your brother's wife." So Herodias nursed a grudge against John and wanted to kill him. But she was not able to, because Herod feared John and protected him, knowing him to be a righteous and holy man. When Herod heard John, he was greatly puzzled; yet he liked to listen to him. (Mark 6:17–20)

When Herod saw Jesus, he was greatly pleased, because for a long time he had been wanting to see him. From what he had heard about him, he hoped to see him perform a sign of some sort. He plied him with many questions, but Jesus gave him no answer. The chief priests and the teachers of the law were standing there, vehemently accusing him. Then Herod and his soldiers ridiculed and mocked him. Dressing him in an elegant robe, they sent him back to Pilate. (Luke 23:8–11)

Jesus makes it plain that people who speak for him should expect to be treated as he was:

Remember what I told you: "A servant is not greater than his master." If they persecuted me, they will persecute you also. If they obeyed my teaching, they will obey yours also. (John 15:20)

The less-than-ideal response to most of our ministries will be more mundane. It will be characterized by distraction; lack of hunger for God's word; limited financial support, even when willingness exists (see Phil 4:10–19); and slowness to put their hands to the plough.

How should we respond in such situations? Sometimes it is right to shake the dust from our feet and move on, as Paul does in Acts 18:6 and as Jesus anticipates in his instructions to the Twelve:

And if any place will not welcome you or listen to you, leave that place and shake the dust off your feet as a testimony against them. (Mark 6:11)

More often, God calls us to persevere, to endure hardship as a good soldier of Jesus (2 Tim 2:3). We cannot directly control how our listeners respond to our preaching, but we can increase the likelihood that they will respond positively, and to this we now turn.

Lord Jesus, thank you for sending your servants as the Father sent you and for warning us to expect the sort of reception you received. Forgive me for sometimes thinking that I deserve something better than you. Amen.

What We Owe Our Listeners

Day 102

This, then, is how you ought to regard us: as servants of Christ and as those entrusted with the mysteries God has revealed. Now it is required that those who have been given a trust must prove faithful. I care very little if I am judged by you or by any human court; indeed, I do not even judge myself. My conscience is clear, but that does not make me innocent. It is the Lord who judges me. Therefore judge nothing before the appointed time; wait until the Lord comes. He will bring to light what is hidden in darkness and will expose the motives of the heart. At that time each will receive their praise from God. (1 Cor 4:1–5)

Faithfulness

Our aim is to let God speak from his word, not to elevate the audience at the expense of Scripture. Yet it is tempting to accommodate the message to gain listeners rather than to adapt ourselves to gain a hearing. At a minimum, though, we owe our listeners faithfulness, prayer, love, authenticity, humility, respect and service.

Paul felt, and rightly so, that he was "obligated" (Rom 1:14) to preach the gospel that had been entrusted to him, and he did:

> Now, brothers and sisters, I want to remind you of the gospel I preached to you, which you received and on which you have taken your stand. By this gospel you are saved, if you hold firmly to the word I preached to you. Otherwise, you have believed in vain.
>
> For what I received I passed on to you as of first importance: that Christ died for our sins according to the Scriptures, that he was buried, that he was raised on the third day according to

the Scriptures, and that he appeared to Cephas, and then to the Twelve. (1 Cor 15:1–5)

Paul did not invent his message; he received it and faithfully passed it on. He was not like the prophets in Jeremiah's day who succumbed to the temptation to "prophesy the delusions of their own minds," tell their dreams, or steal material from one another (Jer 23:25–32). The Lord's response was to remind them of his requirement for his messengers: "let the one who has my word speak it faithfully" (Jer 23:28b).

All the apostles understood why the duty to "obey God rather than human beings" (Acts 5:29) supersedes all others. The reason is that such a stance helps others see us as they should, "as servants of Christ and as those entrusted with the mysteries God has revealed" (1 Cor 4:1–2).

But faithfulness involves more, though never less, than conveying the received content of the gospel accurately. Paul says it also involves a genuine effort not to distort the message, not to resort to deception to make it more attractive, and not to draw attention to ourselves:

> Rather, we have renounced secret and shameful ways; we do not use deception, nor do we distort the word of God. On the contrary, by setting forth the truth plainly we commend ourselves to everyone's conscience in the sight of God. And even if our gospel is veiled, it is veiled to those who are perishing. The god of this age has blinded the minds of unbelievers, so that they cannot see the light of the gospel that displays the glory of Christ, who is the image of God. For what we preach is not ourselves, but Jesus Christ as Lord, and ourselves as your servants for Jesus' sake. (2 Cor 4:2–5)

Notice how realistic Paul is. He does not blame himself for the failure of some to hear God's word. To them the gospel is veiled. They are blind. The light has not dawned.

Faithfulness also includes faithfulness of tone. Our tone in delivery should match that of the text. For example, Paul requested prayer for an outspoken, fearless boldness that fitted his message (Eph 6:19–20).

Faithfulness includes spiritual faithfulness. That is, our preaching should always address the actual individual and corporate deficiencies in our listeners as Scripture describes them. Hebrews models this by addressing the first listeners' temptation to retreat into Judaism.

We must also be faithful to theology and the author's original intent. Never interpret Scripture in a way that contradicts other scriptural texts, and never violate the author's intention. When you build upon a text by extending its application, do so only in ways that are congruent with the text. Paul describes this when he warned those in Corinth:

> By the grace God has given me, I laid a foundation as a wise builder, and someone else is building on it. But each one should build with care. (1 Cor 3:10)

Nothing will compensate for your failure to handle the word of God faithfully. Indeed, to be a skilful and impressive speaker of lies or half-truths is counterproductive. Our job is to set forth the truth plainly, working hard to use terms and thought forms that are plain to our audience.

Father, if I fail at everything else as a preacher, help me to succeed at this. Enable me to be faithful. Amen.

Day 103

> For this reason, since the day we heard about you, we have not stopped praying for you. We continually ask God to fill you with the knowledge of his will through all the wisdom and understanding that the Spirit gives, so that you may live a life worthy of the Lord and please him in every way: bearing fruit in every good work, growing in the knowledge of God, being strengthened with all power according to his glorious might so that you may have great endurance and patience, and giving joyful thanks to the Father, who has qualified you to share in the inheritance of his holy people in the kingdom of light. For he has rescued us from the dominion of darkness and brought us into the kingdom of the Son he loves, in whom we have redemption, the forgiveness of sins. (Col 1:9–14)

Prayer

We hope our listeners will pray for us. Whether they do or not, we have a duty to pray for them. Once again the Apostle Paul models this. He prayed for believers continually, usually beginning with thanksgiving.

> We ought always to thank God for you, brothers and sisters, and rightly so, because your faith is growing more and more, and the love all of you have for one another is increasing. (2 Thess 1:3)

His prayers may have included more mundane concerns, but the prayers reported in his letters are dominated by loftier matters. For many years, my custom was to pray Philippians 1:9–11 aloud at the beginning of each sermon, placing emphasis on the "my":

> And this is *my* prayer: that your love may abound more and more in knowledge and depth of insight, so that you may be able to discern what is best and may be pure and blameless for the day of Christ, filled with the fruit of righteousness that comes through Jesus Christ – to the glory and praise of God.

Think of this as a prayer for success in preaching. We ask God to work in our hearers in such a way that they gain not only knowledge but also insight and ethical discernment. We ask that these will yield abundant righteousness and growing love. We ask that all these virtues and graces will be seen as coming through Jesus Christ, that he will enable them to stand before him on the last day, and that they will all reflect glory and praise to God, both now and then. That is praying theologically!

The responsibility for success in preaching does not rest entirely with the listeners. James's invitation (and its accompanying promise) is for all Christians, but who needs to heed it more than us preachers?

> If any of you lacks wisdom, you should ask God, who gives generously to all without finding fault, and it will be given to you. (Jas 1:5)

To preach without praying is like trying to sail a boat on a completely calm day. You may launch the boat and hoist the sails, but you won't go anywhere. It is striking that when the apostles clarified their two foundational responsibilities and delegated the others, they mentioned prayer first and the ministry of the word second:

So the Twelve gathered all the disciples together and said, "It would not be right for us to neglect the ministry of the word of God in order to wait on tables. Brothers and sisters, choose seven men from among you who are known to be full of the Spirit and wisdom. We will turn this responsibility over to them and will give our attention to prayer and the ministry of the word." (Acts 6:2–4)

So, Lord, I ask you now, that in addition to granting me faithfulness, you would enable me to preach your word with great boldness, exceptional clarity, joy and perseverance. Amen.

Day 104

For I wrote you out of great distress and anguish of heart and with many tears, not to grieve you but to let you know the depth of my love for you. (2 Cor 2:4)

Love

In a way, all the debts we owe our listeners flow from love, but I discuss love separately because it is so important and so easily neglected.

Let no debt remain outstanding, except the continuing debt to love one another, for whoever loves others has fulfilled the law. The commandments, "You shall not commit adultery," "You shall not murder," "You shall not steal," "You shall not covet," and whatever other command there may be, are summed up in this one command: "Love your neighbour as yourself." Love does no harm to a neighbour. Therefore love is the fulfilment of the law. (Rom 13:8–10)

Paul practised what he preached. He knew that love comes with a gentle spirit as opposed to a whip (1 Cor 4:21), he knew the value of expressing his love in words (1 Cor 16:24; 2 Cor 2:4), and he did not hesitate to call upon God as his witness (2 Cor 11:11). Second Corinthians is full of indicators of how sacrificial Paul's love was. For instance, he was eager to do nothing to wound any listener's conscience (4:2; 5:11). Or, to put the same idea positively, love moved him to live in such a way that the church could take pride in him (5:12). He was willing to spend everything he had for them, including himself (12:15). Paul's catalogue of sufferings gives evidence that his motive was not only service to God but also love for the churches:

> We put no stumbling block in anyone's path, so that our ministry will not be discredited. Rather, as servants of God we commend ourselves in every way: in great endurance; in troubles, hardships and distresses; in beatings, imprisonments and riots; in hard work, sleepless nights and hunger; in purity, understanding, patience and kindness; in the Holy Spirit and in sincere love; in truthful speech and in the power of God; with weapons of righteousness in the right hand and in the left; through glory and dishonour, bad report and good report; genuine, yet regarded as impostors; known, yet regarded as unknown; dying, and yet we live on; beaten, and yet not killed; sorrowful, yet always rejoicing; poor, yet making many rich; having nothing, and yet possessing everything.
>
> We have spoken freely to you, Corinthians, and opened wide our hearts to you. We are not withholding our affection from you, but you are withholding yours from us. As a fair exchange – I speak as to my children – open wide your hearts also. (2 Cor 6:3–13)

Paul's Christ-like willingness to be despised and deprived as long as others were built up is striking. His is a cross-shaped ministry, where dying with Christ is the secret to experiencing his resurrection power, as can be seen also in 2 Corinthians 4:7–18 and here in 13:4–10:

> For to be sure, he was crucified in weakness, yet he lives by God's power. Likewise, we are weak in him, yet by God's power we will live with him in our dealing with you.
>
> Examine yourselves to see whether you are in the faith; test yourselves. Do you not realize that Christ Jesus is in you – unless, of course, you fail the test? And I trust that you will discover that we have not failed the test. Now we pray to God that you will not do anything wrong – not so that people will see that we have stood the test but so that you will do what is right even though we may seem to have failed. For we cannot do anything against the truth, but only for the truth. We are glad whenever we are

weak but you are strong; and our prayer is that you may be fully restored. This is why I write these things when I am absent, that when I come I may not have to be harsh in my use of authority – the authority the Lord gave me for building you up, not for tearing you down.

Willingness to be considered a failure is a commodity in short supply among preachers. Yet it is the way of the cross and, therefore, ultimately the way of true power. Perhaps surprisingly, it is also the way of joy.

Father, I truly want to be like Jesus, but I don't always really want to be like Jesus the crucified. Enable me by your Spirit to be conformed to his death that I may experience his resurrection life. Amen.

Day 105

> For I am the least of the apostles and do not even deserve to be
> called an apostle, because I persecuted the church of God. But
> by the grace of God I am what I am, and his grace to me was not
> without effect. No, I worked harder than all of them – yet not
> I, but the grace of God that was with me. Whether, then, it is I
> or they, this is what we preach, and this is what you believed.
> (1 Cor 15:9–11)

Authenticity

Listeners yearn for authenticity. They will sense if a preacher is insincere or is peddling God's word for profit (2 Cor 2:17). Peddlers use the gospel message to enrich or otherwise benefit themselves, but sincere preachers imitate Christ, who looked not to his own interests but to those of others (Phil 2:5–11). Paul also contrasts sincerity with selfish ambition (Phil 1:17) and currying human favour (Col 3:22).

There is no quick fix for phoniness for it often has deep roots in pride. We want people to think highly of us and so we cultivate a false image. This hypocrisy – living a lie – reveals a profound misunderstanding of our qualifications to preach. We have a credible message because we are forgiven sinners, not because we do not need forgiveness (1 Tim 1:15). Our lives display the abundance of God's grace, not our impressiveness (1 Cor 15:10–11). Our identity is not rooted in how good we are but in how gracious God is.

Preachers who grasp that God already knows them completely are free to be real before others. Instead of labouring to *look* holy, they can actually *pursue* holiness. This pursuit is crucial for preaching because whether we like it or not, people will imitate us. True, Scripture invites (1 Cor 11:1), urges (1 Cor 4:16) and commands (Phil 3:17; Heb 6:12; 13:7) imitation of leaders. But more to the point, it just happens (1 Thess 1:4–6; 2:13–14). The Thessalonians became imitators of Paul's team and the churches that sent them. Why? Because the gospel came to them with power as the word of God and went to work in them (1 Thess 1:4–6; 2:13–14).

Remembering that the word of God is not rendered impotent by our weakness should encourage us who preach. Indeed, as Paul says, "we have this treasure in jars of clay to show that this all-surpassing power is from God and not from us" (2 Cor 4:7). Even when the preacher is shackled, the word of God is not:

> Remember Jesus Christ, raised from the dead, descended from David. This is my gospel, for which I am suffering even to the point of being chained like a criminal. But God's word is not chained. (2 Tim 2:8–9)

Even when other preachers have dubious motives, we, like Paul, can rejoice when Christ is preached:

> It is true that some preach Christ out of envy and rivalry, but others out of goodwill. The latter do so out of love, knowing that I am put here for the defence of the gospel. The former preach Christ out of selfish ambition, not sincerely, supposing that they can stir up trouble for me while I am in chains. But what does it matter? The important thing is that in every way, whether from false motives or true, Christ is preached. And because of this I rejoice. (Phil 1:15–18a)

Nevertheless, we owe our listeners authenticity. This sincerity is possible for the forgiven who hope in Christ. Instead of being hypocritical liars with seared consciences (1 Tim 4:2), we must "set an example for the believers in speech, in conduct, in love, in faith and in purity" (1 Tim 4:12). Wholehearted perseverance in both life and doctrine is the way to save our hearers (1 Tim 4:12–16).

Lord, I confess that I am strongly tempted to project an image of myself that is better than the reality. Grant me a deep awareness that in Christ I am accepted by you and that you know everything. Help me to live by your grace and in your sight this day. Amen.

Day 106

To the elders among you, I appeal as a fellow elder and a witness of Christ's sufferings who also will share in the glory to be revealed: Be shepherds of God's flock that is under your care, watching over them – not because you must, but because you are willing, as God wants you to be; not pursuing dishonest gain, but eager to serve; not lording it over those entrusted to you, but being examples to the flock. And when the Chief Shepherd appears, you will receive the crown of glory that will never fade away. In the same way, you who are younger, submit yourselves to your elders. All of you, clothe yourselves with humility towards one another, because, "God opposes the proud but shows favour to the humble." Humble yourselves, therefore, under God's mighty hand, that he may lift you up in due time. (1 Pet 5:1–6)

Humility

Authenticity and humility are first cousins. Authenticity means making sure the image and the reality match. Humility means admitting to yourself and others what that reality is. I address humility separately here because one of the besetting sins of the preacher is pride, the polar opposite of humility. As always, the Lord Jesus is our supreme example (Phil 2:5–11). Matthew makes the point vividly with Jesus' words:

Come to me, all you who are weary and burdened, and I will give you rest. Take my yoke upon you and learn from me, for *I am gentle and humble in heart*, and you will find rest for your souls. For my yoke is easy and my burden is light. (Matt 11:28–30)

Humility and gentleness go together, for the humble preacher identifies with people who are "slow to believe" (Luke 24:25) and slow to learn (Heb 5:11). Often, we feel conflicted about this because we are encouraged to pursue knowledge (Prov 10:14; 13:16; 14:18; 18:15; 23:12), but we realize that "knowledge puffs up while love builds up" (1 Cor 8:1).

Pride and ambition also go together. We can easily think we know something when we don't. Paul diagnosed this problem among the false teachers in Ephesus:

> They want to be teachers of the law, but they do not know what they are talking about or what they so confidently affirm. (1 Tim 1:7)

While aspiring to the noble task of being an overseer is not wrong (1 Tim 3:1), ambition for position is not always God-given. It is far better to reaffirm that we are living sacrifices (Rom 12:1) and lowly servants entrusted with the gospel (1 Cor 4:1–5).

Sometimes listeners misunderstand our role, as they did that of Paul and Barnabas in Lystra (Acts 14:11–18) and that of Peter when he went to preach in Cornelius' house:

> As Peter entered the house, Cornelius met him and fell at his feet in reverence. But Peter made him get up. "Stand up," he said, "I am only a man myself." (Acts 10:25–26)

Herod's experience should warn us of the danger of being slow to acknowledge our lowly position!

> On the appointed day Herod, wearing his royal robes, sat on his throne and delivered a public address to the people. They shouted, "This is the voice of a god, not of a man." Immediately, because Herod did not give praise to God, an angel of the Lord struck him down, and he was eaten by worms and died. (Acts 12:21–23)

Our Master is free to deploy us where he will and give us the status he thinks best. Praying this prayer attributed to the Puritan Richard Alleine and used by John Wesley has helped our family in this effort to see ourselves as we should. Make it your prayer today, as I do.

"I am no longer my own, but Thine. Put me to what Thou wilt, rank me with whom Thou wilt; put me to doing, put me to suffering; let me be employed for Thee or laid aside for Thee, exalted for Thee or brought low for Thee; let me be full, let me be empty; let me have all things, let me have nothing; I freely and

heartily yield all things to Thy pleasure and disposal."[1]

Day 107

> Be devoted to one another in love. Honour one another above
> yourselves. (Rom 12:10)

Respect

Genuine respect for our listeners is indispensable. They will notice if we talk down to them or exalt ourselves over them. Even if they don't notice, God who shows no partiality will (Mal 2:9; Jas 2:1–4). How then do we show respect to our listeners? We do so in many ways, a few of which we will consider here and in the next few meditations.

We show respect to our listeners by acknowledging their identity and status, identifying with them where we can. Each preacher in Acts goes out of his way to address his listeners respectfully and even generously in ways that emphasize solidarity without lumping disparate groups together. For example, Peter addresses his listeners as "Fellow Jews and all of you who live in Jerusalem" (2:14); Stephen addresses his accusers as "Brothers and fathers" (7:2). Paul urges the Jews and proselytes to Judaism in Antioch to "continue in the grace of God" (13:43) and acknowledges that his Athenian listeners are very religious (17:22). Later speeches and defences follow this same pattern of respectfully acknowledging the distinct status of listeners and, when possible, affirming common ground. This respectful tone of address is not unique to Christian preachers, but it is the norm for them.

We also show respect to our listeners by communicating our plans to them, following Paul's example:

> After I go through Macedonia, I will come to you – for I will be going through Macedonia. Perhaps I will stay with you for a while, or even spend the winter, so that you can help me on my journey, wherever I go. For I do not want to see you now and make only a passing visit; I hope to spend some time with you, if the Lord permits. But I will stay on at Ephesus until Pentecost,

---

1. J. I. Packer, *Knowing and Doing the Will of God* (Ann Arbor, MI: Servant, 2000), 262.

because a great door for effective work has opened to me, and there are many who oppose me. (1 Cor 16:5–9)

You may think this passage has absolutely nothing to do with preaching; Paul is just alerting them to an upcoming visit. Of course, when his plans changed he had seven chapters worth of explaining to do (2 Cor 1–7)! But it is worth stressing that how we treat listeners before and after we preach significantly influences whether or not they can receive the word of God from our lips.

One practical way to show respect for our listeners is by communicating our preaching plan to them well ahead of time. Sadly, some preachers practise a quasi-mystical approach to selecting a preaching text and leave it to the last minute. Some listeners consider this a badge of deep spirituality. They even consider it better if the preacher introduces the sermon by announcing that the previously selected text was discarded a few minutes prior to the service when the Lord intervened with fresh direction.

Certainly, every preacher should maintain humble flexibility up to and through the preaching event, but prayerfully planning and communicating God's leading well ahead of time frees team members who equally must wait upon the Lord for direction to seek his face concerning liturgical elements, such as songs and readings. Their task is much easier when they know the preaching text well ahead of time. When coordinated, all the elements of the worship service can reinforce and complement each other.

Lord, protect me from thinking too highly of myself and so failing to treat others with the respect they deserve. Amen.

Day 108

In the presence of God and of Christ Jesus, who will judge the living and the dead, and in view of his appearing and his kingdom, I give you this charge: Preach the word; be prepared in season and out of season; correct, rebuke and encourage – with great patience and careful instruction. For the time will come when people will not put up with sound doctrine. Instead, to suit their own desires, they will gather around them a great number of teachers to say what their itching ears want to hear. (2 Tim 4:1–3)

Patience and Forbearance

Patience also communicates respect. That is why Paul instructs Timothy to preach the word "with great patience" or, more literally, "with all patience" (2 Tim 4:2). When I am impatient in conversation, it communicates that what I want to say is of more value than what you want to say. Impatience in preaching adds the insulting implication that the message presented is so clear and compelling that any intelligent person would only need to hear it once! But Scripture itself reveals that repetition is necessary. The Bible contains many texts that address the same truths, and we hear them repeatedly in various forms and from many people before they sink in. Preaching is far more than just conveying ideas; it is releasing the word to go to work in the hearts of our listeners. We don't expect the truth to hit its target the first time or every time, or to get through to every heart immediately.

Forbearance is another way to show respect. Romans 15:1–4 describes forbearance in the context of building up others with scriptural teaching:

> We who are strong ought to bear with the failings of the weak and not to please ourselves. Each of us should please our neighbours for their good, to build them up. For even Christ did not please himself but, as it is written: "The insults of those who insult you have fallen on me." For everything that was written in the past was written to teach us, so that through the endurance taught in the Scriptures and the encouragement they provide we might have hope.

Of course, it is possible to "put up with others" with a peevish attitude of annoyance at their weaknesses. But Jesus' example pushes us beyond this to Christ-like endurance and hope. Scripture ("everything that was written in the past") enabled Christ to endure; it will enable us to endure, and it will have the same hope-giving ministry with our listeners. The very message we proclaim enables us to treat weak people to whom we proclaim it with the same forbearance that God showed us in Christ. When the Bible ministers *to* us, it ministers *through* us.

If you find it difficult to respect your listeners because you consider them weak, the reason may be that you have not fully grasped your own weakness. Hebrews 5:2 states that every high priest is subject to weakness so that he can "deal gently with those who are ignorant and are going astray." That is the pattern for us, too, and one of the reasons Paul boasted in his weakness in which God's power was made perfect.

Lord, too often I wish I could trade my weaknesses for another preacher's strengths. Remind me that you could have made me like that person but for your own good reasons chose not to do so. Thank you that your strength can be made perfect in my weakness. Help me not use this as an excuse to be lazy or undisciplined, but as a comfort when I have poured out my soul on the altar of the faith of others and it feels to me like something less than an acceptable sacrifice. Amen.

Day 109

> At one time we too were foolish, disobedient, deceived and
> enslaved by all kinds of passions and pleasures. We lived in malice
> and envy, being hated and hating one another. But when the
> kindness and love of God our Saviour appeared, he saved us, not
> because of righteous things we had done, but because of his mercy.
> (Titus 3:3–5a)

Kindness, Manifested in Listening

We show respect to our hearers by listening to them. The best preaching is always dialogical. James's counsel to be quick to hear and slow to speak (1:19) applies to all interpersonal relationships, including that between preachers and congregants. As we have seen, several New Testament letters to believers in certain cities or regions were written because the writer heard news from that place. Listening to listeners is not only a good way to know and understand them. When we listen to our hearers they are far more likely to listen to us, because they sense that we are speaking with them, not merely to them, or worse, at them.

Another way we show respect is by being kind to all our listeners. Paul's instructions to the young Timothy make this specific:

> And the Lord's servant must not be quarrelsome but must be
> kind to everyone, able to teach, not resentful. Opponents must be
> gently instructed, in the hope that God will grant them repentance
> leading them to a knowledge of the truth. (2 Tim 2:24–25)

It is striking that Paul's instruction to Timothy links kindness of intention with gentleness of demeanour and repentance on the part of the opponent.

We owe our listeners kindness. You may encounter opponents among those you preach to every week, but gentleness is one way we show kindness even to them.

Faith is manifested by the hope that God will grant them repentance that will enable them to accept the truth. It might seem unrealistic to think that the unrepentant can receive the biblical message. But God uses his word to work repentance. For example, Jonah's simple warning of judgment, offered in belated obedience to God, turned the Ninevites from their evil ways (Jonah 3:1–10). And no king was as bad as Ahab when it came to doing evil in the eyes of the Lord, but when he heard the word of the Lord from Elijah and humbled himself, God saw his humility and delayed the predicted disaster (1 Kgs 21). Take heart.

Lord, thank you for your kindness to me in the gospel and in giving me all things in Jesus. When I feel critical towards my listeners – especially when it is little, insignificant things that irritate me – remind me of your kindness and help me to show it to others on your behalf. Amen.

Day 110

This, then, is how you ought to regard us: as servants of Christ and as those entrusted with the mysteries God has revealed. (1 Cor 4:1)

Willingness to Serve

"The only thing that counts is faith expressing itself through love" (Gal 5:6a) and love shows itself in service (5:13). Service is the opposite of greedily lording it over our hearers:

Be shepherds of God's flock that is under your care, watching over them – not because you must, but because you are willing, as God wants you to be; not pursuing dishonest gain, but *eager to serve*; not lording it over those entrusted to you, but being examples to the flock. (1 Pet 5:2–3)

We can demonstrate that we put the interests of our listeners before our own by serving them in specific ways. One of the most basic ways we serve them is by speaking their language. Notice the impact Paul's willingness to do this had on a very hostile audience:

Paul answered, "I am a Jew, from Tarsus in Cilicia, a citizen of no ordinary city. Please let me speak to the people."

Having received the commander's permission, Paul stood on the steps and motioned to the crowd. When they were all silent, he said to them in Aramaic:

"Brothers and fathers, listen now to my defence."

When they heard him speak to them in Aramaic, they became very quiet. (Acts 21:39–22:2a)

Some young preachers (and not a few greying ones) yield to the temptation to use slang, crude expressions or popular verbal and grammatical atrocities in an attempt to identify with their listeners. Identification is good, but not at the expense of loving service. We don't serve our listeners by cheapening our discourse. We are ambassadors of the King of kings. Our language should reflect his commission. Notice how intentional Paul is with regard to setting an example, setting aside his rights so that his listeners would not be misled by his behaviour. Literally, he made himself a model for his listeners to imitate:

In the name of the Lord Jesus Christ, we command you, brothers and sisters, to keep away from every believer who is idle and disruptive and does not live according to the teaching you received from us. For you yourselves know how *you ought to follow our example*. We were not idle when we were with you, nor did we eat anyone's food without paying for it. On the contrary, we worked night and day, labouring and toiling so that we would not be a burden to any of you. *We did this, not because we do not have the right to such help, but in order to offer ourselves as a model for you to imitate*. For even when we were with you, we gave you this rule: "Anyone who is unwilling to work shall not eat." (2 Thess 3:6–10)

Your example applies to everything, including your speech.

Lord Jesus, I confess that sometimes I serve those to whom I preach without really being willing to define myself as their servant. I like to be in control. So, once again, I submit myself to you, that you may teach me to be eager to serve because I have given up my rights to you. Amen.

Day 111

But if I say, "I will not mention his word or speak anymore in
his name," his word is in my heart like a fire, a fire shut up in my
bones. I am weary of holding it in; indeed, I cannot. (Jer 20:9)

Passion and Sacrifice

We serve our listeners by being both passionate and logical. The apostles
consistently reasoned and argued for the faith, but they did not do so in a
dispassionate, detached way. They delivered messages of truth on fire. Their
lives and especially their willingness to suffer for the gospel validated what
they said. So did the fact that their *manner* matched their *matter*, as the
Puritans used to say about the delivery and content of sermons. Take the
example of Saul (Paul) in Jerusalem shortly after his conversion:

> But Barnabas took him and brought him to the apostles. He told
> them how Saul on his journey had seen the Lord and that the
> Lord had spoken to him, and how in Damascus he had preached
> fearlessly in the name of Jesus. So Saul stayed with them and
> moved about freely in Jerusalem, speaking boldly in the name
> of the Lord. He talked and debated with the Hellenistic Jews, but
> they tried to kill him. When the believers learned of this, they
> took him down to Caesarea and sent him off to Tarsus.
>
> Then the church throughout Judea, Galilee and Samaria
> enjoyed a time of peace and was strengthened. Living in the fear
> of the Lord and encouraged by the Holy Spirit, it increased in
> numbers. (Acts 9:27–31)

Twice we read that Paul preached boldly in the name of Jesus. His
passionate presentation matched the content of his gospel message. But
his message was part of a larger conversation with the Hellenistic Jews, a
conversation characterized by discussion, argument and debate. Enduring
persecution underscored Paul's commitment to the message (2 Tim 3:12).
The church, fuelled by such preaching and conversations, manifested spiritual
reality that mirrored what they saw in the gospel preachers. Passion without
truth is worse than nothing; but truth without passion falls short of conveying
the message accurately.

We also serve our listeners by removing barriers to their accepting our preaching as a word from God. Clearly, Paul practised what he preached (Rom 14:13). He made up his mind to put no stumbling block in anyone's way; he would rather "put up with anything rather than hinder the gospel of Christ" (1 Cor 9:12).

What barriers should we be alert to? Paul was willing to forego secondary practices, including cultural distinctions regarding diet and ritual celebrations. Whether we like it or not, when people stumble because of unimportant things, servanthood requires that we give up those things. For instance, our clothing should not attract attention because it looks too expensive, flashy or immodest, nor should we neglect our appearance. People may also find it a barrier if our speech is cluttered with um's and ah's, or if we have other nervous habits such as constantly clearing our throats. Furthermore, people won't hear God's voice if they can't hear ours. Practising projecting your voice, breathing from the diaphragm and carefully enunciating words is a way of serving your listeners.

Lord, when it comes down to it, preaching is hard work, especially when the fire in my bones has gone out. Draw me to yourself again and kindle the flame that I may joyfully give myself to the hard yet joyful work of speaking for you. Amen.

Day 112

> And pray for us, too, that God may open a door for our message,
> so that we may proclaim the mystery of Christ, for which I am in
> chains. Pray that I may proclaim it clearly, as I should. (Col 4:3–4)

Clarity

We serve our listeners when we labour to make our message clear. In earlier days in some churches, preachers had the most minute and detailed divisions and subdivisions in their sermons and made all sorts of subtle side comments. They often cited authorities like the church fathers. Their messages were unlikely to have been clear even to most highly-motivated listeners. But clarity is a non-negotiable necessity as Paul's request indicates:

Pray that I may proclaim it clearly, *as I should.* (Col 4:4, emphasis added)

Paul's unwavering standard was that *nothing* should fall short of this criterion:

For we do not write you anything you cannot read or understand. (2 Cor 1:13a)

How do we achieve clarity in our sermons? The answer is not complicated. At the most basic level, we use the best simple words that convey our meaning. We arrange those words in short sentences with as few dependent clauses as possible. We put the sentences in paragraphs that develop a single idea. We use sufficient repetition and paraphrasing to make sure people stay with us. Oral discourse needs this much more than written discourse.

We illustrate everything so that those who think in images and those who think in concepts will both be served. Writing out our sermons helps us edit them for clarity. But clarity is also accomplished by organizing the whole sermon in a way that is easy to follow. Because we want our sermons to be biblical, we discern the main idea from the text we are expounding and ask what that truth, insight or claim has to do with our listeners. The answer should be expressed as a single, simple sentence. Then each major part of the sermon should develop that claim in some obvious way.

We serve our listeners best when our sermons are clear.

Father, thank you for making your word clear. May every message I preach reflect that clarity, that not one of my words might fall to the ground. Amen.

Day 113

Follow my example, as I follow the example of Christ. (1 Cor 11:1)

I am writing this not to shame you but to warn you as my dear children. Even if you had ten thousand guardians in Christ, you do not have many fathers, for in Christ Jesus I became your father through the gospel. Therefore I urge you to imitate me. For this reason I have sent to you Timothy, my son whom I love, who is faithful in the Lord. He will remind you of my way of life in Christ

Jesus, which agrees with what I teach everywhere in every church.
(1 Cor 4:14–17)

Model Obedience

Supremely, we serve our hearers when we help them understand what it means to listen to the word. That is, we really serve our listeners when we help them respond with obedience.

On one occasion the prophet Jeremiah was told to go and buy a new linen belt, probably a colourful and attractive sash worn around the waist. Jeremiah bought it and wore it. Even before it was washed, he was instructed to hide it in a crack in the rocks. Later he returned to find the belt he had hidden there. The belt was completely ruined and utterly worthless. This was a visual aid to draw attention to God's coming judgment on Judah. Notice how God describes Judah's disobedience:

> "These wicked people, who *refuse to listen to my words*, who follow the stubbornness of their hearts and go after other gods to serve and worship them, will be like this belt – completely useless! For as a belt is bound around the waist, so I bound all the people of Israel and all the people of Judah to me," declares the LORD, "to be my people for my renown and praise and honour. But *they have not listened*." (Jer 13:10–11, emphasis added)

By saying, "they have not listened" God means that they have not *obeyed*. So God's appeal to them through Jeremiah is to "listen and give heed" (NASB) or "Hear and pay attention, do not be arrogant, for the LORD has spoken" (Jer 13:15).

The proper response to the word of God is humility, which leads to obedience. We serve our listeners when we handle the word reverently, submit to it ourselves, and expect no less of them (2 Thess 3:14).

Paul boasted of his weaknesses as we noted in 2 Corinthians, but he also gloried in the obedience that his preaching in the power of the Holy Spirit accomplished:

> I myself am convinced, my brothers and sisters, that you yourselves are full of goodness, filled with knowledge and competent to instruct one another. Yet I have written you quite boldly on some points to remind you of them again, because of the grace God gave me to be a minister of Christ Jesus to the

Gentiles. He gave me the priestly duty of proclaiming the gospel of God, so that the Gentiles might become an offering acceptable to God, sanctified by the Holy Spirit.

Therefore I glory in Christ Jesus in my service to God. I will not venture to speak of anything except what Christ has accomplished through me in leading the Gentiles to obey God by what I have said and done – by the power of signs and wonders, through the power of the Spirit of God. So from Jerusalem all the way around to Illyricum, I have fully proclaimed the gospel of Christ. It has always been my ambition to preach the gospel where Christ was not known, so that I would not be building on someone else's foundation. (Rom 15:14–20)

When the gospel is fully preached by word and deed, by God's grace and in the power of the Holy Spirit, Christ accomplishes something through us! Our listeners obey God, which in the context of the letter to the Romans means they believe the gospel. They also become acceptable sacrifices to God, sanctified by the same Holy Spirit who gave them new life. Sanctification always entails obedience. We should not be satisfied with anything less in our preaching.

Notice that Paul did not reckon he himself did this; Christ did this work through him. The same dynamic is recorded in 2 Corinthians:

Are we beginning to commend ourselves again? Or do we need, like some people, letters of recommendation to you or from you? You yourselves are our letter, written on our hearts, known and read by everyone. You show that you are a letter from Christ, the result of our ministry, written not with ink but with the Spirit of the living God, not on tablets of stone but on tablets of human hearts. (2 Cor 3:1–3)

The transformed lives of the Corinthians were both evidence of the Spirit and the result of Paul's ministry. We serve our listeners when we help them truly hear God's voice and do what is appropriate when God speaks – obey.

Lord Jesus, every time I preach, help me to listen to what you are saying to me through the text I am expounding – not merely to hear it, but so that truly hearing it, I may also heed it. Amen.

Epilogue

It is my prayer that these meditations have opened a window to a panorama of just a few of the biblical texts that disclose the need for deepening our three key relationships. I urge you by the Holy Spirit to keep growing in your love for God, his word and his people. When these relationships are characterized by humble, submissive service, our preaching will be closer to what God intends it to be and God will be honoured.

Scripture Index

Langham Literature and its imprints are a ministry of Langham Partnership.

Langham Partnership is a global fellowship working in pursuit of the vision God entrusted to its founder John Stott –

> *to facilitate the growth of the church in maturity and Christ-likeness through raising the standards of biblical preaching and teaching.*

Our vision is to see churches in the majority world equipped for mission and growing to maturity in Christ through the ministry of pastors and leaders who believe, teach and live by the Word of God.

Our mission is to strengthen the ministry of the Word of God through:
- nurturing national movements for biblical preaching
- fostering the creation and distribution of evangelical literature
- enhancing evangelical theological education

especially in countries where churches are under-resourced.

Our ministry

Langham Preaching partners with national leaders to nurture indigenous biblical preaching movements for pastors and lay preachers all around the world. With the support of a team of trainers from many countries, a multi-level programme of seminars provides practical training, and is followed by a programme for training local facilitators. Local preachers' groups and national and regional networks ensure continuity and ongoing development, seeking to build vigorous movements committed to Bible exposition.

Langham Literature provides majority world preachers, scholars and seminary libraries with evangelical books and electronic resources through publishing and distribution, grants and discounts. The programme also fosters the creation of indigenous evangelical books in many languages, through writer's grants, strengthening local evangelical publishing houses, and investment in major regional literature projects, such as one volume Bible commentaries like *The Africa Bible Commentary* and *The South Asia Bible Commentary*.

Langham Scholars provides financial support for evangelical doctoral students from the majority world so that, when they return home, they may train pastors and other Christian leaders with sound, biblical and theological teaching. This programme equips those who equip others. Langham Scholars also works in partnership with majority world seminaries in strengthening evangelical theological education. A growing number of Langham Scholars study in high quality doctoral programmes in the majority world itself. As well as teaching the next generation of pastors, graduated Langham Scholars exercise significant influence through their writing and leadership.

To learn more about Langham Partnership and the work we do visit **langham.org**